Improving Transparency and Visibility in Supply Chain With AI

Omar Ali
Abdullah Al Salem University, Kuwait

Wael Farag
https://orcid.org/0000-0002-9191-1824
Abdullah Al Salem University, Kuwait

Ashraf Jaradat
https://orcid.org/0000-0002-6686-7972
Gulf University for Science and Technology, Kuwait

IGI Global
Scientific Publishing
Publishing Tomorrow's Research Today

Vice President of Editorial — Melissa Wagner
Director of Acquisitions — Mikaela Felty
Director of Book Development — Jocelynn Hessler
Production Manager — Mike Brehm
Cover Design — Jose Rosado

Published in the United States of America by
IGI Global Scientific Publishing
701 East Chocolate Avenue
Hershey, PA, 17033, USA
Tel: 717-533-8845 | Fax: 717-533-7115
Website: https://www.igi-global.com E-mail: cust@igi-global.com

Library of Congress Cataloging-in-Publication Data

Names: Ali, Omar, 1976- | Farag, Wael, 1968- editor | Jaradat, Ashraf, 1978- editor
Title: Improving transparency and visibility in supply chain with AI / [edited by] Omar Ali, Wael Farag, Ashraf Jaradat.
Description: Hershey, PA : IGI Global Scientific Publishing, [2026] | Includes bibliographical references and index.
Identifiers: LCCN 2025018906 (print) | LCCN 2025018907 (ebook) | ISBN 9798337328454 ebook | ISBN 9798337328430 hardcover | ISBN 9798337328447 paperback
Subjects: LCSH: Business logistics--Technological innovations | Supply chain management--Technological innovations | Artificial intelligence--Industrial applications
Classification: LCC HD38.5 (ebook) | LCC HD38.5 .I467 2026 (print) | DDC 658.7 23/eng/20250--dc26
LC record available at https://lccn.loc.gov/2025018906
British Cataloguing in Publication Data
A Cataloguing in Publication record for this book is available from the British Library.

Table of Contents

Detailed Table of Contents

This chapter explores the transformative power of AI in bringing transparency and visibility to modern supply chains. It draws extreme importance to AI technologies, including predictive analytics, machine-learning models, blockchain, and IoT for the real-time tracking of shipments, for efficient decision-making, and for ethical sourcing. It analyzes comprehensively how AI is addressing challenges that have long plagued global supply chains: managing risks, compliance, and operational efficiency. Practical applications and case studies give evidence of the tangible improvements brought about by AI's implementation. Other challenges are considered: data privacy concerns, legacy system integration, infrastructural requirements, and resistance to change in organizations. Strategic models are proposed to assist in planning the implementation of AI from phase-wise integration to capacity building, governance, and, lastly, organizational feedback.

Artificial Intelligence (AI) is revolutionizing multimodal logistics networks through more intelligent, faster, and smoother operations on different modes of transportation and complex supply chains. Interlacing multisource data on weather conditions, means of transport, and container status, AI models are optimally placed to effectively monitor, anticipate, and optimize logistics performance. Advanced techniques such as Particle Swarm Optimization for feature extraction and Bi-Stacked Artificial Neural Networks for deep learning allow the determination of significant insights in vast and heterogeneous datasets. These AI-driven techniques accelerate real-time decision-making, reduce operational cost, and improve dependability by predicting delays, detecting anomalies, and routing optimization. This study focuses on the contribution of AI towards developing multimodal logistics as a wise and responsive system capable of addressing the dynamic challenges of modern supply chains

Preface

The global supply chain has become a complex and dynamic ecosystem shaped by globalization, digital transformation, and evolving consumer demands. As organizations strive to meet rising expectations for efficiency, resilience, and sustainability, the role of artificial intelligence has emerged as a defining force in supply chain management. AI offers powerful tools to address persistent challenges such as demand volatility, operational inefficiencies, risk exposure, and the need for transparency across supply chain networks.

This edited volume, *Improving Transparency and Visibility in Supply Chain With AI*, presents a collection of research contributions, practical insights, and case studies that highlight the transformative impact of AI in supply chain contexts. The chapters showcase how AI is reshaping operational practices, supporting strategic decision-making, and driving long-term innovations that redefine how supply chains are designed and managed.

The book provides a comprehensive examination of the field. The first section highlights AI applications in demand forecasting, inventory management, logistics optimization, and real-time visibility, illustrating how these technologies reduce waste and improve responsiveness. The second section explores AI's strategic significance, with attention to decision support, predictive risk management, and sustainability goals, while also addressing the ethical and security challenges that arise with widespread adoption. The third section investigates emerging innovations including blockchain integration, digital twins, multimodal logistics, and the use of autonomous vehicles. The final section grounds these discussions in practice through case studies drawn from industries such as retail, healthcare, automotive, and agriculture, emphasizing both lessons learned and pathways for future growth.

CHAPTER OVERVIEW

Chapter 1: AI-Driven Transparency in Supply Chains with Focus on Technologies and Challenges

This opening chapter examines the transformative role of AI in enhancing transparency across global supply chains. It highlights technologies such as predictive analytics, blockchain, IoT, and machine learning that enable real-time visibility, efficient decision-making, and ethical sourcing. The discussion also recognizes persistent challenges, including data privacy, legacy system integration, infrastructure requirements, and organizational resistance. Through practical examples and strategic models, the chapter provides a structured approach to phased AI adoption, governance, and capacity building to support sustainable transparency.

Chapter 2: AI-Powered Anomaly Detection in Multimodal Supply Chains

The second chapter turns to multimodal logistics networks and demonstrates how AI improves efficiency, dependability, and adaptability across diverse transportation modes. By integrating multisource data such as weather conditions and container status, AI models help anticipate disruptions and optimize routing. Advanced methods, including Particle Swarm Optimization and Bi-Stacked Artificial Neural Networks, allow for effective anomaly detection and deep insights in complex datasets. The chapter underscores how these techniques enhance real-time decision-making, reduce costs, and strengthen resilience in dynamic supply chains.

Chapter 3: Driving Efficiency: How Robotic Process Automation is Transforming Warehousing in the Automotive Industry

This chapter explores the impact of Robotic Process Automation on transparency and efficiency in automotive warehousing. By automating repetitive tasks, RPA improves inventory accuracy, shipment tracking, and compliance reporting, while also increasing traceability through technologies such as barcodes and RFID. The discussion addresses challenges related to data standardization and legacy systems, alongside best practices for integration. Case studies illustrate RPA's success in reducing errors and boosting visibility, while future trends point toward AI-driven analytics that further strengthen disruption prediction and operational resilience.

Chapter 4: AI and Autonomous Vehicles in Last-Mile Delivery

Last-mile delivery remains one of the most challenging aspects of modern logistics, and this chapter examines how AI and autonomous vehicle technologies are reshaping the field. With the growth of e-commerce and on-demand services, AI-driven tools such as predictive analytics, dynamic routing, and fleet coordination are improving delivery speed, transparency, and efficiency. Autonomous vans, drones, and sidewalk robots are presented as practical solutions for reducing emissions and enhancing monitoring. The chapter also explores how AI-linked IoT sensors, blockchain, and computer vision contribute to security and authentication in last-mile logistics.

Chapter 5: From Digital Transformation to Financial Performance: The Mediating Role of Supply Chain Integration in Tunisian Agro-Industries

This chapter presents an empirical study of the Tunisian agro-industrial sector, focusing on how digitalization and supply chain integration affect financial performance. Using survey data analyzed with regression modeling, the study demonstrates that digital tools and integrated practices significantly enhance organizational outcomes. The findings underscore the critical role of digital transformation in improving competitiveness and financial sustainability within agro-industrial contexts, offering lessons that extend beyond regional boundaries.

Chapter 6: Harnessing Artificial Intelligence for the Renaissance of Sustainable Supply Chains Navigating the Nexus of ESG Aspirations

Chapter eleven emphasizes the transformative role of AI and emerging technologies in achieving ESG-driven sustainability in supply chains. It highlights advances such as blockchain-enabled digital product passports, regenerative supply networks, and digital twins for real-time impact modeling. The discussion also touches on smart packaging, autonomous logistics, and urban hubs as enablers of circularity. Importantly, the chapter addresses ethical risks, including privacy, bias, and environmental trade-offs, offering strategies for responsible AI adoption that balances profitability with sustainability.

Chapter 7: Sustainability and Ethical Responsibility The Role of ESG in Modern Business

The final chapter positions ESG considerations as central to corporate responsibility and financial performance in contemporary business. By applying Bi-Stacked Long Short-Term Memory models, the study shows how machine learning enhances the ability to analyze and forecast ESG impacts. Companies can thus better evaluate the outcomes of their sustainability initiatives and make informed, ethical decisions. This approach reinforces the long-term value of ESG integration, promoting both sustainable business practices and stronger corporate reputations.

Our objective in compiling this volume is to equip readers with a balanced perspective on both the opportunities and challenges of adopting AI in supply chains. The book bridges theoretical research and applied practice, offering academics a source of empirical and conceptual contributions while also providing industry professionals, policymakers, and technology innovators with insights into implementation strategies and real-world outcomes.

We believe this book will serve as a valuable resource for a wide audience including scholars, practitioners, students, and decision-makers who are shaping or studying the future of supply chains. By bringing together diverse voices and experiences, this volume not only contributes to the ongoing discourse on AI but also encourages further exploration of how these technologies can foster supply chains that are more transparent, adaptive, and sustainable.

We thank all contributors for their thoughtful work and the knowledge they bring to this volume. It is our hope that readers will find inspiration and practical guidance in these chapters, and that this book will spark continued collaboration across academic, professional, and policy communities working toward the advancement of AI-driven supply chain management.

Omar Ali

Abdullah Al Salem University, Kuwait

Wael Farag

Abdullah Al Salem University, Kuwait

Ashraf Jaradat

Gulf University for Science and Technology, Kuwait

Chapter 1

AI-Driven Transparency in Supply Chains With Focus on Technologies and Challenges

Mostafa Abdrabboh
https://orcid.org/0000-0001-5456-8919
Abdullah Al Salem University, Kuwait

ABSTRACT

This chapter explores the transformative power of AI in bringing transparency and visibility to modern supply chains. It draws extreme importance to AI technologies, including predictive analytics, machine-learning models, blockchain, and IoT for the real-time tracking of shipments, for efficient decision-making, and for ethical sourcing. It analyzes comprehensively how AI is addressing challenges that have long plagued global supply chains: managing risks, compliance, and operational efficiency. Practical applications and case studies give evidence of the tangible improvements brought about by AI's implementation. Other challenges are considered: data privacy concerns, legacy system integration, infrastructural requirements, and resistance to change in organizations. Strategic models are proposed to assist in planning the implementation of AI from phase-wise integration to capacity building, governance, and, lastly, organizational feedback.

DOI: 10.4018/979-8-3373-2843-0.ch001

1. INTRODUCTION

Transparency and visibility in the supply chain have become part and parcel of managing modern globalized supply networks. Transparency refers to when stakeholders have access to accurate information about the products, processes, and partners concerning the supply chain in due time. This visibility grants a real-time ability to track, monitor, and make decisions. The last decade has celebrated increasingly complex and global supply chains, rendering traditional oversight methods rather inadequate. Because of this, AI technologies strive to give dynamic, data-driven options for making supply chain operations more transparent and responsive.

The chapter investigates the role of AI systems (predictive analytics, ML, blockchain, and IoT) in enhancing supply chain visibility and transparency. We then study the application of these technologies, show real-world examples, point out the challenges arising from their deployment, and then offer strategic frameworks for successful implementation of AI. This discussion facilitates illustrating how AI brings supply chains closer to the agile, accountable, and efficient ecosystems they ought to be.

Today, globalization, digitization, and consumer expectations are driving business paradigms, where supply chains are to deliver agility, transparency, and sustainability alongside efficiency and cost savings. Global supply chains could be exposed to severe vulnerabilities reflecting on the very recent COVID-19 pandemic, which underscores the importance of real-time visibility and identified risk-management policies. Consequently, organizations are increasingly using digital solutions to bridge the visibility gap, with AI being a potential game-changer.

Transparency within supply chains is useful in ethical sourcing, and supply-side governance and sanctions as well as scrutiny should become more important in industries such as food, pharmaceuticals, design, and where consumer awareness and regulatory scrutiny are high. On the other hand, visibility is to have been fast acquisition and revelation of real-time, accurate data over the productive chain. Policy advocates for constant end-to-end surveillance of the material, product, and processes, which allow intelligent decisions from people and quick response in the face of disruptions.

Artificial intelligence has immense transformational potential as a technology that permits learning from data, adapting to changing circumstances, and making decisions autonomously. Some of the aspects on which AI's applications stand is planning, sourcing, production, distribution, and reverse logistics, all of which lead to smarter, faster, and more efficient supply chain management. By handling enormous amounts of both structured and unstructured data intelligently, AI and its offshoot advanced analytics certainly bring to light subliminal patterns, route optimization, effectual demand forecasting, plus assessment of supplier risk.

An example of intelligence at work in transparency: AI and NLP help scan news sites, social media, and public records to detect potentially problematic suppliers. AI and computer vision assist in the detection of product defects in manufacturing environments where they are likely to be overlooked by human oversight. With advanced capabilities like chatbots led by AI, the real-time visibility offered to the customer concerning the order statuses, expected delivery times, and prompt resolution of any issues furthers data transparency across supply chains.

From a strategic standpoint investing in AI expands the businesses' competencies related to transparency and visibility and aids its ability to withstand market changes, manage risk, and attract reputable partnerships and investors that put a premium on business ethics corporate sustainability. AI is already producing AI-driven predictive analytics followed by prescriptive analytics, enabling users to engage in plans and revisit what-if scenario analysis. This could go hand in hand to help predict potential supply chain disruptions with supply chain leaders being able to plan significantly and effectively about such disruptions well in advance, such as material shortages, transportation delays, or geopolitical events.

Besides, AI can assist in achieving sustainability objectives for supply chains. Models can be developed for AI to calculate carbon footprint throughout the value chain, advise modes of greener transportation, or recommend energy-efficient manufacturing schedules. Moreover, AI can furnish optimization to circular supply chains by identifying reuse, remanufacturing, and recycling pursuits to further complement ESG objectives concerning corporate environmental, social, governance systems.

But there are challenges awaiting AI in the supply chain. Different data silos, the absence of standardization, the low maturity of AI within organizations, worry over transparency and accountability in decision-making narratives, subsequently pose difficulties in working with AI solutions. AI deployment necessitates constant down-to-earth technical groundwork but rather heavily is something framework for data governance, adequately trained talent, vehement collaboration from cross-functional teams, and a culture ready to accept change.

Academically, AI technologies on the scene are getting stronger, with many of these faculties focusing on upping visibility and transparency within supply chains. Studies revealed that AI considerably boosts performance in four key indicators-accuracy of orders, delivery reliability, inventory turnover, and forecasting accuracy; however, barely any hope seems visible for AI completely revolutionizing these areas. AI rollouts will be peculiar across sectors and regions, contingent on industry-specific requirements. Regulatory environments and the digital maturity of some organizations also give a good explanation for different adoptions.

Figure 1. Leveraging AI in Supply Chain

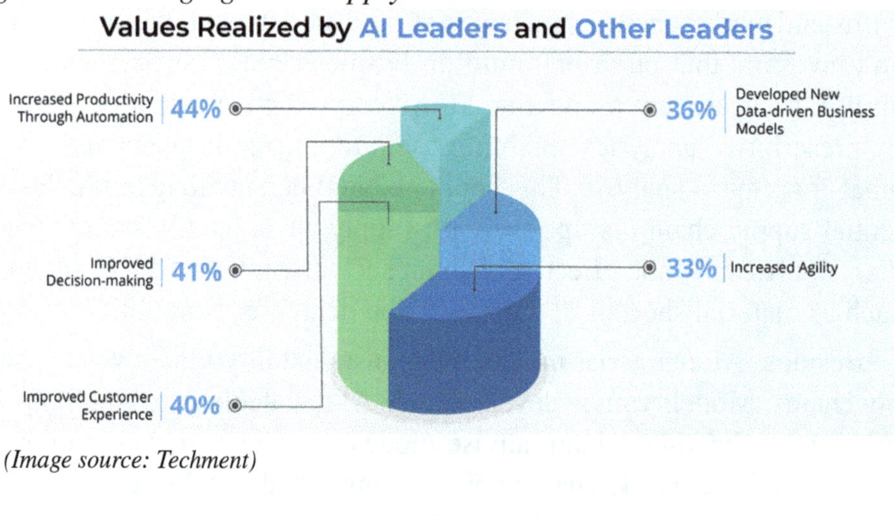

(Image source: Techment)

The chapter fits into the growing body of knowledge on the topic by emphasizing the transformative value AI carries concerning supply chain transparency and visibility. With this approach, here are an analysis of current practices, a forecast of the pipeline for the same, and interesting case studies around specific opportunities and issues in the integration of AI. The study dwells on hyper-interdisciplinary theories emanating from operations management, information systems, industrial engineering, and data science. But this very same section does bring under the spotlight the crucial role of ethical AI in universalization. Since, by AI influencing strategic decisions, there is need to ensure that these mechanisms are fair, transparent, and accountable. Organizations would have to factor in AI-impacted social issues such as potential discriminatory algorithmic bias, job loss, and privacy infringement. Transparency is thus considered necessary for building trust in AI systems in terms of how algorithms are developed, tested, and deployed, especially when decisions have substantial impact on suppliers, customers, and communities. In essence, AI marks a shift from an interconnected, reactive, supply network to an intelligent and responsive supply network. AI enables businesses not only to monitor and report on performance from the supply network; but also to forecast when an incident is likely to trigger huge disadvantages with some data like import/export policies, currency fluctuations, and political tensions, optimize the operations, and drive continuous improvement. Emphasizing transparency and visibility, AI works toward creating a supply chain that is not just efficient but also resilient, ethical, and future proof. Parts to follow will, thus, cover all the enabling technologies, applications, and conceptual substrata underlying this transformation (Choi et al., 2025).

Figure 2. AI adoption in supply chain globally

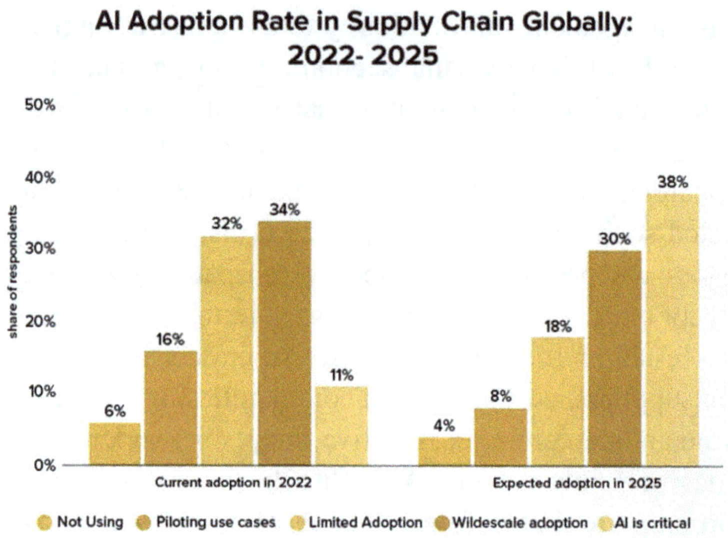

2. AI TECHNOLOGIES TRANSFORMING SUPPLY CHAIN TRANSPARENCY

Figure 3. AI Integration in Key Supply Chain Operations

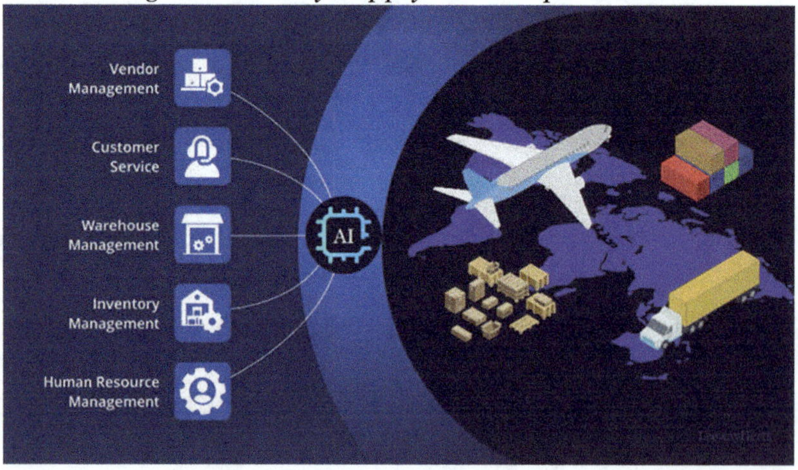

(Image source: LeewayHertz)

AI tools provide useful tools to further improve supply chain operations. Visibility and transparency are thus created with the help of distinct AI technologies:

2.1 Predictive Analytics

Predictive analytics uses historical data, statistical algorithms, and machine learning techniques to predict future events. In terms of supply chain management, this means better demand forecasting, inventory optimization, and risk mitigation, and forecasting. Businesses can react to delays and waste much more swiftly upon identification of a disruption or demand changes.

One-way predictive analytics can increase supply chain agility, since this can give considerations appropriate to the forward-looking decision-making. For example, when companies have sales data available to them historically, together with weather patterns, macro-economic indicators, and behavior, the predictions of the businesses transform into forecasting demand across locations or customer segments. This scenario extrapolates their production and inventories across time, which drastically minimizes stock-outs, overstock levels, and logistics barriers. Thus, firms like Walmart and Amazon have successfully utilized PAs in demand forecasting by fine-tuning this attribute on a granular scale.

Clearly, PA also positively impacts supply logistics and supplier administration, enabling real-time ranking and tracking of suppliers based on parameters such as on-time delivery, defect rates, and responsiveness based on historical performance metrics. Protracted anticipation of foreseeable risks allows for the establishment of a steady support system of suppliers. For example, if a supplier is consistently stricken with lead-time volatility or quality problems, a model would reasonably sense it beforehand-a system that bears more implications when recommended for an alternative set of supply leads.

Figure 4. Adoption of AI in Supply Chain Management

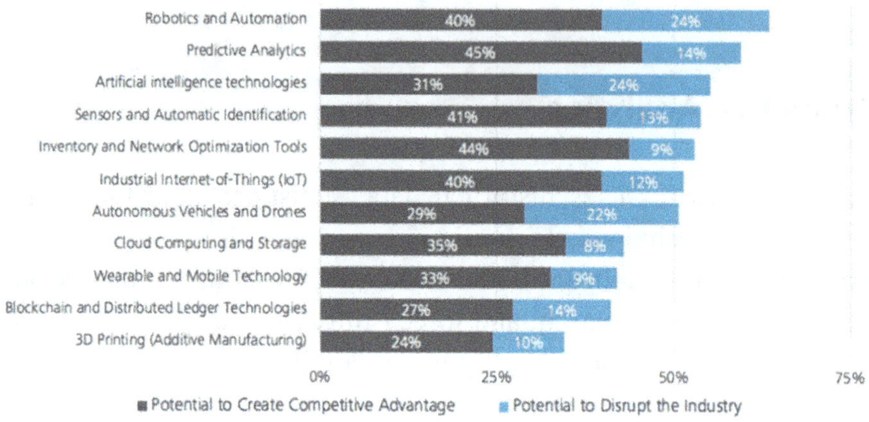

(Image source: McKinsey)

Predictive analytics optimizes assisting merchandising and delivery successfully. By incorporating real-time traffic information, vehicle performance history, plus external influences like weather and fuel prices, logistics specialists can predetermine the best routes with their products and vehicles. Predictive maintenance modeling for immediate counteractive action can stem losses due to machine breakdown issues for a longer operating period. A different approach is to use sensor data to schedule maintenance well in advance. These measures will constrict downtime and increase the length of asset life.

Another key aspect of using predictive analytics is risk mitigation. Organizations apply the method to forecast risk factors like geopolitical instability, economic instability, supplier's financial condition, and disruptions to the environment. These hypothetical models can help in simulating a number of disruption scenarios, assess their prevalence over the supply chain, and get an early response from the managers to effectively prevent disruptions. According to this brief, during the COVID-19 pandemic, organizations who had the ability to employ predictive systems could redistribute their resources quickly, find other suppliers, manage logistics adaptively, and ensure business continuity. Also, by helping in making the most of the resources, predictive analytics promotes the sustainability goals of a responsible corporation. With just-in-time inventory management and production control, the idea of optimizing the use of resources has always been central to how global firms have gradually commercialized. By predicting the optimal quantity of raw material and energy needed for production processes, companies can also reduce waste, minimizing emissions, and being at par with environmental laws. The concept becomes more prominent when translated into action in industries such as manufacturing and agriculture, with precision demand forecasting that predominantly pulls in water, energy, and raw material supply. Data quality and model robustness seem to be two demands of predictive analytics, well integrated with enterprise resource planning (ERP) systems. It is noted that due to the big boom in big data technologies, cloud computing, and AI platforms, the ranking Businesses have been given an opportunity to affordably deploy predictive analytics capabilities quite easily, including almost middle-range organizations. Nonetheless, the success of such an initiative does hinge on a company's commitment to data-driven decision-making with an onus on continuous model validation.

Figure 5. AI adoption in supply chains

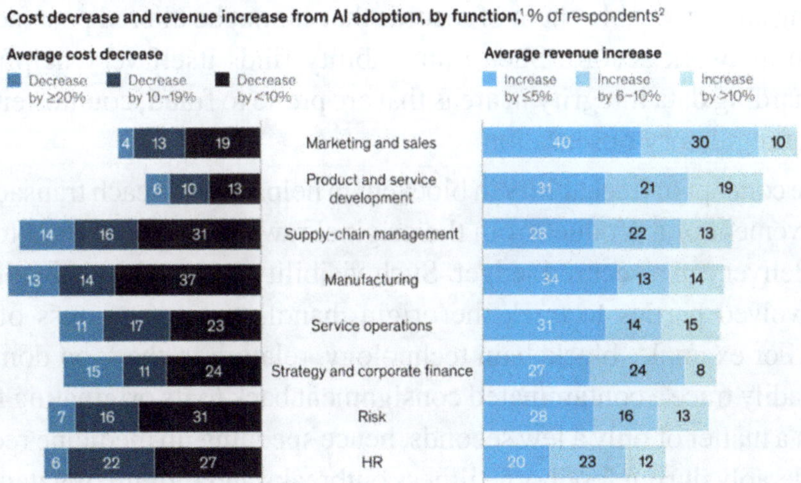

(Image source: McKinsey)

In sum, predictive analytics can hence make SCM from a reactive business to an anticipatory one, bettering the operational efficiency and customer satisfaction and upping the strategic planning and resilience to the rack. As the world supply chains gush under mounting pressures to become adaptable and sustainable, predictive analytics remains now a cornerstone of intelligent supply chain management (Ghosh, 2022).

2.2 Blockchain

The blockchain uses a decentralized and immutable ledger that holds secure, traceable, and transparent transactions within the supply chain. It is best when it comes to product provenance, regulatory compliance, and fraud issues. For the pharmaceutical industry, and also in terms of food safety and security standards, blockchain sets the data as immutable, so all stakeholders may be able to verify the security and the origin of the goods.

The chain of blocks or blockchain (BC) has had a tectonic impact on how data are recorded, kept, and shared across the web of supply chain networks. The decentralized setup of blockchain eliminates the necessity for a central authority while distributing control across members and fostering trust among them. Each transaction recorded on the blockchain is secured by cryptographic encryption and assigned a timestamp, thus creating an irrevocable chain of records that cannot be altered post factum without network accord. Such immutability finds itself very helpful in safeguarding data integrity in areas that are prone to fraud, counterfeiting, or tight regulatory observation.

The concept of traceability in blockchain helps to trace each transaction or movement of a product from the original raw material sourcing to the final delivery in a secured ledger. Such visibility across the chain allows the involved parties to track the origin, handling, and progress of the good. For example, blockchain technology, relating to the food domain, can readily trace a contaminated consignment back to its originating farm within a matter of only a few seconds, hence speeding up medicine recalls considerably during foodborne illness outbreaks and minimizing damage caused by such issues.

Pharmaceutical supply chains, often characterized by a high incidence of counterfeit drugs and unauthorized product diversion, significantly benefit from blockchain technology. In the United States, the Drug Supply Chain Security Act (DSCSA) requires that prescription drugs trace their route along the supply chain. Blockchain platforms give pharmaceutical manufacturers, distributors, and dispensers the ability to record transaction data in real-time, having its origin guaranteed and ensuring compliance with regulatory mandates. This greatly diminishes the risks associated with counterfeit medicines and improves patient safety. Antifraud and antisyndicate blockchain innovations could greatly deter unethical practices in global supply chains. Companies can provide evidence of verifiable transactions and product journeys to ensure fair and sustainable material usage, ethical sourcing, and fair labor practices. In the world of luxury brands, blockchain is used to verify products such as diamonds, leather, or branded attire to discourage counterfeit and elevate brand value. Blockchains deploy smart contracts to automate supply chain processes, among other features. Ethereum, as a platform enabled by blockchain, is the chief implementation. Once defined terms are met, these contracts automatically discharge a pre-agreed action-for instance, releasing payments after confirming that goods have indeed been delivered. This does away with overhead accounts expenses; it will also reduce various disputes at times and has fastened the cycle of transactions. With regard to international trade: a smart contract will lessen the complications of customs documentation, reduce transaction clearance times, and thus make it easier to comply with international trade legislation.

It further offers more benefits of radically increased visibility into multilayered supply chains. A difficulty faced by companies is in knowing its indirect procurement chains that can be drastically difficult for complicated sub-tier suppliers to trace or verify the origin of the components. Blockchain rudimentarily makes it possible in tracking all the way up by offering preauthorized access to transaction data to all the parties—including third-party certifiers and auditors but only up to what they should see without breaching the rule of confidentiality. This radically aids in the realization of environmental, social, and governance (ESG) goals, especially in the electronics, automotive, and apparel industries. On the flip side, the adoption of blockchain in supply chains faces challenges such as interoperability challenges across different blockchains, concern for protecting personal data, and the need for collaboration among human stakeholders, whereas consideration needs to go towards designing a solution that addresses low scalability and transaction speed for high-volume operations. Nonetheless, the ongoing release of the blockchain as a service (BaaS) and other hybrid blockchain architecture developments are greatly lowering the costs of both technology access and adaptability. In a nutshell, it can be suggested that blockchain technology forms quite an amazing purveyor of transparency and security in the way supply chains come into operation officially. Its power to bind together a cohesive record of transactions, bind a system together, and create trust amongst the players of supply chain makes it the paramount technology in the digital age of supply chains. With many industries continuously contemplating decentralized ways of data management, blockchain will have a more pivotal role to play in forming trustful and robust global supply networks (Saberi et al., 2019).

2.3 Machine Learning

Machine learning is another set of algorithms for anomaly detection, logistical tracing, and decision support. ML models may add to operational transparency by incorporating insights on supplier performance, production efficiency, and disruption detection that humans may miss, as well as trigger real-time corrective actions across the system being monitored.

Within the context of supply chain management, Machine Learning (ML) has a lot of room on which it can act. ML aims at developing technologies that can represent some form of generalization, promote understanding, and drive action. Machine Learning allows for transparency, efficiency, and well-timed decision-making within several application settings. ML is the science responsible which models for tasks such as predictive intelligence and autonomous implementation owing to the extraction of major patterns from huge datasets using methods such as supervised, unsupervised, and reinforcement learning.

Anomalies are of the utmost importance in supply chain management since ML uses algorithms trained on historical operating data to detect outliers or deviations signaling potential problems. ML operations can trace odd order tendencies indicating possible procurement fraud or forecast unpredictable rapidity in the supplier's past behaviors in relation to this history. Within manufacturing, ML would tend to identify quality deviations or equipment malfunctions through real-time analysis of sensor readings and operational metrics, thereby having fewer defects and less breakdown-time. Routing can be optimized with the help of ML models, which continuously learn from previous delivery data, traffic conditions, fuel consumption studies, and delivery performances. This leads to a way to make dynamic routing changes that can lead to a decrease in transit time readied to reduce fuel consumption and hence enhance the delivery guarantees. In addition to this, ML algorithms can predict the maintenance needs of the fleet to ensure proactive scheduling of services to prevent such failures.

Another sure field that ML impacts in supply chains is supplier performance assessment. Conventional methods often entail various methods of observation, which provide mostly subjective and review-based scores over time. At the other end, ML is able to measure supplier performance metrics such as lead times, defect rates, responsiveness, and cost deviations in support of ongoing real time calculations from vendor scorecards executing into any form of decision making on purchase profiles, contract approaches, or risk strategies. In supply chain operations, another key domain is demanding sensing and forecasting. While predictive analytics use historical trends, an ML-based forecasting mechanism brings into consideration a variety of forces including delivery schedules fed in as unstructured data. Retailers, for example, use ML to predict events in which promotions, holidays, or external disturbances could cause fluctuations, thereby increasing the accuracy with regard to restocking and inventory planning.

Warehouse management algorithms employing ML techniques avail better utilization of space and labor; the choice is based on factors such as item velocity, pick frequency, and order patterns. Robotic systems, powered by ML, increasingly carry out picking, sorting, and packaging with reduced human error and quicker order fulfilment. ML-powered decision support systems are a great contribution to inventory control, sourcing strategies, and production planning. It suggests the best action after running simulation for various scenarios, having managers to evaluate trade-offs and make an informed judgment. Reinforcement learning model-based systems adjust their strategies dynamically based on feedback solution application in dynamic and complex environments. ML also contributes to sustainability, pinpointing incongruities and offering sustainable options, such as, for example, ML algorithms dexterously designed to optimize packaging dimensions for reduced waste, suggest energy-efficient production schedules, or go for lower emission transportation options as the case may require. The general obstruction against ML implementation includes issues with data quality, interpretability of the model, and integrations. For achieving strong accuracy and reliability, the most dependent elements ensuring a proper training process with good, labeled data are crucial. Secondly, the 'black box' nature of some ML models can bring in transparency problems, making it difficult for the stakeholders to comprehend the AI's insights as they battle with trust issues. However, these challenges, amongst many, are being technically handled by the fear-confounded explainability concept or through user-friendly ways of conventional applications. Companies are already integrating ML into their digital supply chain strategies, forecast to enhance visibility, responsiveness, and overall operational excellence. ML is going to make more progress in logistics as data volumes escalate much further and computational power advances beyond present limitations on developing innovative insights and real-time support-driven automation (Ivanov & Dolgui, 2020).

2.4 Internet of Things IoT

IoT devices like RFID tags, sensors, and GPS trackers provide real-time data on the location, condition, and movement of goods. Such visibility enables continuous monitoring for shipments, route optimization, and a guarantee of product quality during transport. Once this raw data is fed into AI analytics platforms, it gets converted into intelligence.

The Internet of Things (IoT) ushers in the epoch of smart supply chains in which every node, asset, and process is digitally connected and can be monitored and optimized. With IoT-enabled devices, businesses find comprehensive insights from the very beginning of the supply chain processes, from procurement and production stages to warehousing and distribution. Through these insights, timely interventions can be pre-planned, and operational efficiency and service levels enhanced. In transportation and logistics, the continual advancement of Global Positioning Systems (GPS)-enhanced fleet management systems enables companies to monitor vehicle location in real-time and check for any driver incompatibilities along with on-tim ...ody altitude, air pressure], thus creating optimal transporting conditions). Visitor engagement may then be generated as deviation from any pre-determined threshold would send signals of an alert; thus, the interested need in intervening before any sabotage to image or said products occurs. IoT technology is also vital for automation in warehouses. Smart shelves integrated with weight sensors and radio-frequency identification (RFID) readers can sense depletion of products and update inventory records automatically. Automated guided vehicles (AGVs) (and drones) utilize local data for efficient navigation of the warehouses to achieve shorter picking, sorting, fulfillment times and reduce errors due to mispicks. By enabling real-time visibility of inventory, IoT lessens the incidence of stockouts, overstocking, and order errors. Predictive maintenance is another key IoT advantage. Mechatronics devices equipped with sensors send continuous reports on their status (vibration, temperature, oil condition) to maintenance personnel, who can foresee potential malfunction well in advance. This way, they prevent unplanned downtime and save from premature decay of capital machinery, ensuring continuity of efficient inbound flows. When AI and machine learning especially get coupled with IoT data, it allows for decision-making jobs to be done better. For instance, AI algorithms will analyze all data types such as traffic patterns, weather information, and driver behavior to predict efficient routes for deliveries. Similarly, in manufacturing, IoT sensors may use the data they collect to juggle the control settings on the fly so as to maintain quality annuals below guaranteed standards.

In the retail industry, an array of IoT applications from smart shelves to synchronized point-of-sale (POS) systems tracking shopper habits, demonstrating live inventory, and even changing digital signage according to customer profiling can bolster demand forecasting, minimize shrinkage, and individualize the shopper experience. IoT and traceability promise unswerving transparency in supply chains. Every movement of any product, from production through to final delivery, can be documented and confirmed. For endeavors where provenance and genuineness are key issues, like priceless assets, food safety, regulated pharmaceuticals, QR codes or NFC tags enhance the transparency for customers with information etched in them. Despite the many advantages, IoT presents certain challenges. These challenges include information security issues, device integration, system scalability, and high initial costs. The problem of data integrity, such as cyber threats, remains a critical challenge, as there is always the potential scenario that compromised IoT systems could result in operational disruption or data leakages. In this regard, entities ought to develop sturdy cybersecurity procedures, solutions for device management, and consistent communication standards to ensure the safety of IoT platforms. The Internet of Things lies at the forefront of the digital transformation revolution shaping supply chains. Its offer of real-time visibility, valuable predictive insights, and true automation administrative capacities affords managers significant advantages when making decisions fast. The instances of IoT-aided data analytics and artificial intelligence are being increasingly leveraged in creating a new kind of operational intelligence to cope with resilience and customer satisfaction, grasping the advantage in today's rapidly shifting world market (Moktadir et al., 2019).

3. PRACTICAL APPLICATIONS AND CASE STUDIES

The practical application bestows the merit of AI hands-on in handling supply chains:

3.1 Predictive Analytics for Retail

A particular leading global retailer made use of predictive analytics to consolidate demand forecasting accuracy. By collating point-of-sale along with trend data, the company brought down stockouts and oversupply to a dramatic extent, only to finally result in the enormous satisfaction of the customers and reduced operational costs.

Figure 6. Integration of IoT and Blockchain for End-to-End Supply Chain Transparency.

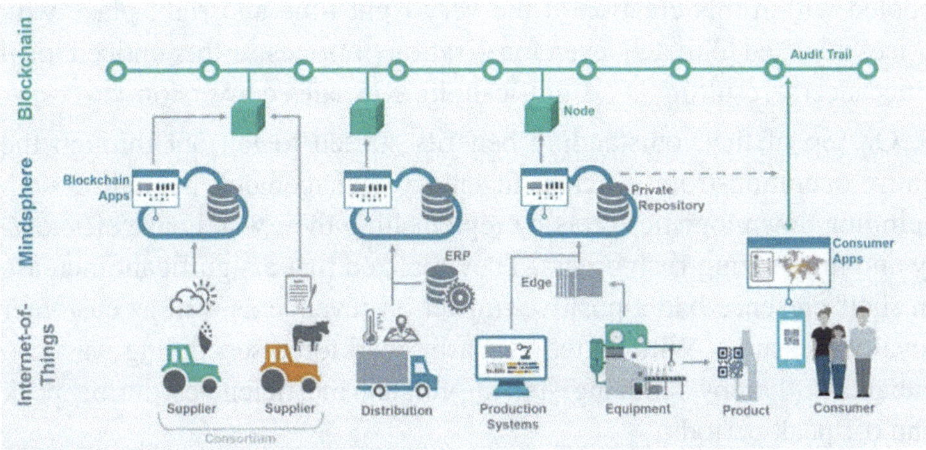

(Image source: SIEMENS: Blockchain and IoT in digital supply chains)

Whereby the intricate basic structure of a company pertains mainly to actual business functions that demand case-by-case regular decision-making with overwhelming complexity in supply chain management. It took the power of prediction in almost all sorts of business operations in a retail environment-much like brick-and-mortar stores and even somewhat timelier to improve the forecasting accuracy in demand, as in replenishment, merchandising, and promotion considerations. By bringing together real-time point-of-sale (POS) data, customer demographics, sales history, seasonality trends, and external signals such as holidays or social media sentiment, and by analyzing these together, they achieved almost an instantaneous and highly adaptive response time in inventory management.

Stock was handled based on this analytical potential for predicting the future. For instance, during a promotion, models were made using prior campaign outcomes and market dynamics to render a future expectation of incoming uplift sales so as to make provision for stock in confident advance. In cases with less demand forecasted, on the other hand, stock was brought down commensurately, saving the business from any unnecessary markdowns and maybe even inventory write-offs.

Predictive analytics was exploited to design local assortment where the demand segregation kinds of behaviors and regional preferences could be extracted from historical data. Customization led to spare stocks, which normally converted into sales whereas even larger customer satisfaction pooled within this creation at the very right time and right place with prices adjusted to match; even localization of prices further enticed local Buccaneers, resulting in a significant hike in sales conversion.

On top of that, outstanding benefits started to fan out through the entire operation-from efficient inventory management, beginning with spiraling down logistics costs by replenishing their warehouse efficiently and minimizing rush orders. They realized that a significant increase in shelf presence had a positive impact on revenue as well as customer loyalty measures. With better forecasts, workforce scheduling was also enhanced, thereby reducing staffing-related inefficiencies during peak and off-peak periods.

Figure 7. Stages of Blockchain Implementation for Enhanced Supply Chain Transparency

(Image source: LeewayHertz)

Organizations and systems learn and develop over time through feedback. The interpretation and accuracy of the predictive analytics improved over time given each sales cycle that provided new data to train and further refine the predictive models. Adaptation would become a priceless victory in case of disruptions of unforeseen nature such as supply chain delays or massive adjustments in demand during COVID-19. Furthermore, PA was incorporated with the Customer Relationship Management (CRM) system, making it appear more useful in personalization strategy formulation. Hence, offers driven from predicted purchase behavior, whether through targeted promotion or loyalty scheme subsidized by personalised product recommendation, will help provide better insights into customer needs and help strengthen engagement. From a strategic perspective, the introduction of predictive analytics further has manifested broader industry transformation towards data-driven decision-making. Such transition was accommodated through investment in cloud-capable infrastructure, AI platforms, and analytical know-how. This cross-functional cooperation between departments in supply chain, IT, marketing, and store operations is what accounted for the success of the venture. This case illustrates how Predictive Analytics can bring considerable value to retail supply chains. Thus, the realm of PA aided in creating an effective operation; it designed the archetypal reactionary retail curtain whereby predictive analytics enable strategic advantage to companies currently trailing a dynamic market as a result of evolving consumer perspectives and heightened competition (McKinsey & Company, 2021).

3.2 Blockchain for Food Traceability

The introduction of blockchain technology linking to the transaction of the goods' every journey from farm to shelf legitimised the method. It allowed consumers to scan the QR codes and verify their origin and handling practices. The very instance enhanced consumer trust, initiated hassle-free recalls, and ensured adherence to food safe practices.

The importation of blockchain had been an innovative solution to veracity in supply chain management, especially in the agrifood sector. With its secure, immutable digital ledger recording every event—harvesting, packaging, storage, transportation, and retail-tracing the provenance of food items was a mere act of minutes. This was significant for high-risk or perishable items such as leafy green vegetables, dairy products, meat, and seafood where the freshness and origin are integral to supply chain safety and consumer health.

Figure 8. Reasons for adopting Blockchain for supply chain management

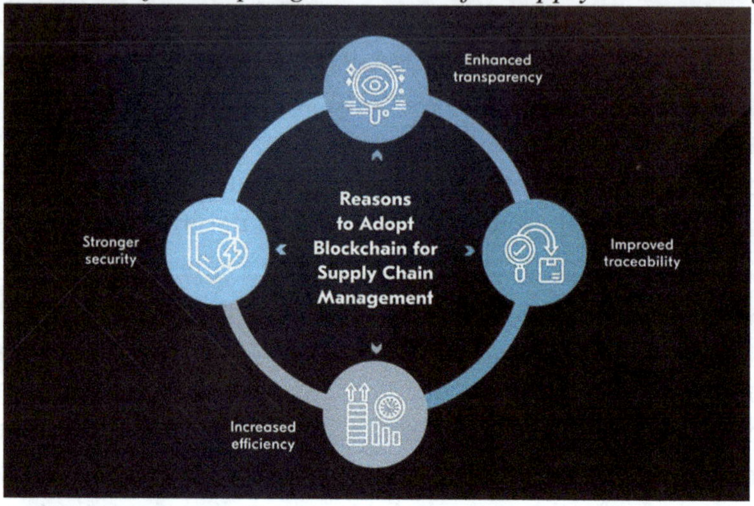

(Image source: LeewayHertz)

Data collection from the field was carried out with IoT devices and smart contracts in blockchain-enabled traceability systems. As products crossed over from farm gate to consumer shelf, each transaction or handover was stored on the blockchain, creating a tamper-proof audit trail accessible to all authorized participants. If this visibility was good for the consumers; then, it was the mechanism allowing producers and retailers to monitor food safety protocols like those outlined in the Food Safety Modernization Act (FSMA) or Hazard Analysis Critical Control Point (HACCP) systems. Practically, consumers would either scan the QR code on a product pack using their smartphones for detailed information to ascertain the product origin, farming procedures, storage conditions information, certifications, transport routes, and so forth. This level of information boosts consumer confidence, especially as the demand for ethically sourced, organic, and local food grows. Hence, the transparency offered by blockchain traceability is a major competitive edge for the industry models standing for food integrity.

With blockchain in place, it would enable a retailer to carry out swift and targeted recalls. By being able to precisely pinpoint what was affected, a retailer could recall just the affected items and not remove entire batches from the shelf. This lessened wastage, reduced cost, protected brand reputation, and expedited response during foodborne outbreaks of salmonella and listeria; with blockchain systems in motion, the times have shrunk across days to seconds for rapid traceability.

Farmers and producers who needed enhanced-value data visibility also got a chance to make well-informed decisions. A chance to see every bit of the supply chain history could be critically needed to get a feel for market trends, production planning, and ease of certifications. The essence of blockchain is in its immutability, or inability for records to be changed or destroyed. With the increase in food fraud and theft networks, blockchain dealt with mismanagement of any form of data and inconsistency thereof in food supply chains. This inherent attribute ensures a higher standard of trust and accountability, seeing as anybody, anywhere has no control over a single source of data.

To sum up, it could be said that the use of blockchain in food trace ability systems was an all-around solution for the long-standing issues with transparency and accountability. It completely redefined consumer engagement by instilling verifiable trust, gave supply-chain players real-time insights, and enhanced public health by enabling swift and accurate recalls. Blockchain is potential to be a cornerstone of food supply chains that will be future proof, in harnessing consumer drive towards transparency (IBM, 2022).

3.3 IoT in Logistics

One logistics company has instituted IoT sensors in all its vehicles to monitor temperature, humidity, and exact whereabouts all the time. This real-time visibility has allowed the company to respond immediately whenever anomalies manifested so that the integrity of perishable goods could be protected while routing optimization could be achieved.

Figure 9. Impact of AI on Retail Supply Chain and Logistics

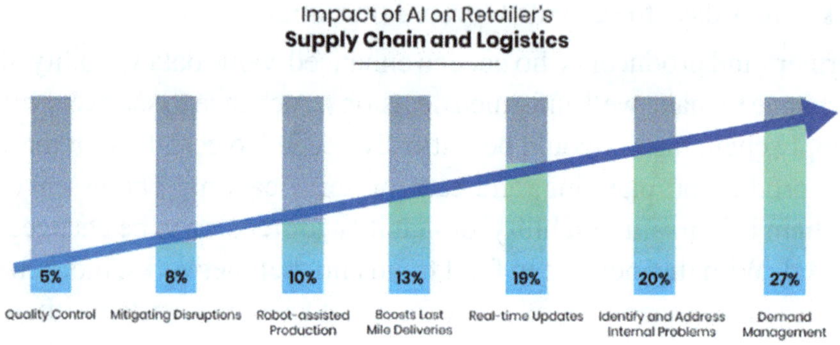

(Image source: ERP solutions)

Thus, seamlessly the logistics match they are enabled with the momentous data collection via the IoT. The company had temperature and humidity sensors embedded into their refrigerated vehicles, hence guaranteeing a thorough understanding of the environmental conditions considered necessary for handling items of perishability containing pharmaceuticals, dairy, meat, and fresh produce. Procedures designated the sensors' deviating mostly from preset boundaries likely to cause undesirable situations. Therefore, the company could call in on emergency programs like altering the cooling system or rerouting to an adjacent hub. GPS was also used to follow location-of the real-time vehicle fleet. This dynamic routing, besides optimal quite instantaneous tracking helped the manager to plan the quickest route. The traffic flow data, the situations of the roadway itself, and the anticipated time to delivery allowed the logistics manager to redirect the vehicles away from potential jams for dead holding and cut fuel costs with on-time deliveries. Flexibility in routing improved the genuineness of deliveries and the resultant customer pleasure.

Figure 10. The Role of Blockchain in Enabling IoT-Driven Supply Chain Intelligence

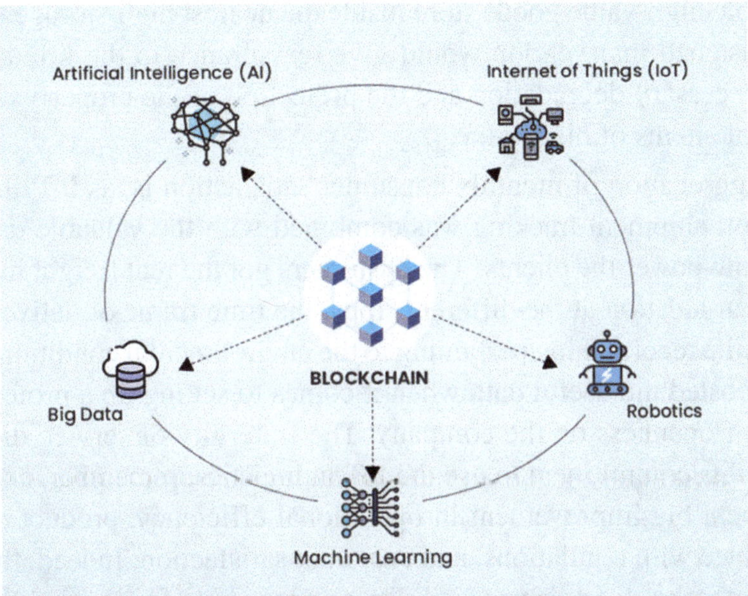

(Image source: Endless Blockchain)

The impact of IoT data included the AI analytics platforms. This virtually linked the historical data with real-time data for predictive analytics such as predicting equipment malfunction based on the vibrations or heat. Itard, the predictive maintenance, slashed the chances of unplanned downtime and fostered longer asset service. In addition, fuel-efficient and time-efficient delivery paths depended on up-to-the-minute data that are churned by the route optimization algorithms.

On the compliance front, the IoT system afforded repositories of information through constant tracking of the stringent protocols set forth by medical authorities in cold chain management. Branded by most stringent biotechnological ceremonies, some lakes of data traced all the goods the sensors recorded moving in environs of cold. This was shared in transparency regardless of its perfection: a proactive risk to ensuring the shield of a dual wall-albeit in a caring and in compliance with the UDFDA.

Exception management brought forward a silver lining incidentally in IoT. For instance, the refrigeration unit breaking down shall set off the IOT relay that would contact a particular person representing the operation center, who then alerts the massively concerned or divide the perishable high-value goods store inside the nearest high-storage facility. Such hastened intervention would give reassurance to the limitation of any unnecessary degradation and the protection of the property of those perishable items of high value.

An aggregation of monthly consumer satisfaction is, as IoT analytics make out: shipment tracking was combined with the valuable data that could now-power the clients. The customers got the real freight information about location at the different stops, the time frame of delivery, and the definite record of log pertaining to the environmental conditions. This again boosted the useful data when it comes to setting up a professional format of openness on the company. The fraternity of service did reassert then its commitment to use the IoT in logistics, remember, and there would be a big improvement in operational efficiency, product quality, compliance with regulations, and customer satisfaction. Indeed, the integration of technology-driven visibility ensures safety for perishable goods and becomes a partial first stepping stone toward broader supply chain optimization and resilience (Accenture, 2020).

4. CHALLENGES AND BARRIERS

Despite their pros, AI technology implementation faces numerous challenges:

4.1 Data Privacy and Cybersecurity

Except the issuance of infrastructural arrangements and knowledge-powered industrial mathematical techniques, much ado about the amount of data being collected and processed arises when the strong potential for data leakage and unauthorized access looms high. The appropriate regard towards cybersecurity and the requisite guidelines becomes of the importance for organizations.

Any entity that wants to underwrite AI must grapple with the enormity of the data and its sensitive nature. Digitalization in the supply chain has systems of sensors, smart devices, and software platforms constantly collecting data on inventory levels, transportation routes, supplier performance, customer preferences, and more. This real-time data stream is necessary for AI-driven optimization but introduces numerous entry points for attackers at the same time.

The threat landscape also involves risks such as intrusion-for instance, hacking, data theft and cyber attacks-leading to massive financial losses, reputational damage, and regulatory penalties. For instance, unauthorized access may compromise competitive positioning or trigger penalties when sensitive supplier information or proprietary algorithms become exposed. Similarly, a data security breach affecting customers' data might prompt regulatory inquiries and erode customer trust.

Organizations have to empower themselves against these threats by having a multi-layered cybersecurity approach. This extends to implementing encryption protocols for data at rest and in transit, and implementing stringent access controls, firm intrusion detection systems (IDS), and regular penetration tests. Data logging using blockchain will augment these surveillance capabilities with immutable records of access and modification. So, when it comes to building AI applications, cybersecurity should be well thought of, deliberately injected at its very construction, in a principle referred to as "security by design."

Needless to say, governance structures to delineate data ownership, responsibilities, and compliance measures complement the technological dimensions. Therefore, clear policies concerning the collection, storage, retention, and disposal of data would encompass international data protection laws and customer expectations. Internal audits, employee training programs, and assessments of vendors prepare it further in combating these threats.

Fairness in AI decision-making is also increasingly recognized. With algorithms playing an increasingly defining role in supply chain decisions-whether it be choosing suppliers, setting prices, or rearranging inventory-organizations must ensure that these systems function ethically and without bias. Using explainable AI (XAI) tools can remove obscurities around decision-making, thereby allowing stakeholders to verify the correct functioning of these models. Combining AI and cybersecurity requires effective coordination across departments like IT, supply chain, legal, and compliance. Cyber incidents in one domain quickly become viral in interconnected systems, so being able to proactively identify risks and perform scenario planning is the trend. Prep glitch response plans and run cyber drills, thus enabling timely and effective ambush response.

Eventually, the security of AI-backed supply chains is not just a technological quandary but rather a strategic concern. Technological areas have been tied together within these digital ecosystems, and more shared data becomes the significance of doing soundly secure cyber borders and augmented data control as a means to leverage the full potential of the AI advantage while mounting protection against piracies (Wu et al., 2025).

4.2 Integration with Legacy Systems

Many of these obsolete systems did not come with necessary features ready to accept AI or agree with a supply chain infrastructure. The high IT investment and middleware solutions are needed here.

Outdated legacy platforms, some of which were developed decades ago, are invariably precontrived with solid design and a finite degree of scalability that hinders integration with the plethora of cutting-edge technological developments today. As organizations start to seek AI solutions to transform transparency, visibility, and efficiency, they quickly realize that the architecture and some level of tech within their current setup are going into strong opposition.

Several insurmountable challenges pertain to the fact that real-time data streaming capabilities, cloud connectivity, and modularity are not integral aspects of many legacy systems. AI applications require changes and updates real time; their data stream should be dynamic, APIs (Application Programming Interfaces) come in all shapes and sizes, and their open architecture, such as with FAG Schedules, must support many data sources where several legacy enterprise resource planning (ERP) vendors have turned soft on the issue. The price paid in training, tools, maintenance is, hence, pretty pricey. Enter middleware: the middleware layer is a technological bridge that resolves incompatibility in data format, orchestrates the workflows, and facilitates communication between AI individual modules and the technologies of bygone days. Marketing collateral arrays boast that middleware reduces the total cost of ownership even further than the inflated cash burn entailed for burnishing legacy platforms. The workspace of this subject is peculiar; the engineering and use of middleware also practice the principles of surgery to effectively detach questionable body parts (read: commoditized legacy technical assets) and create the framework which can be treated (meaning, sold). Adding other transformations for the framework-wide scales, the IT infrastructure, too, must in tandem undergo huge transformations. In other cases again, legacy systems may lack sufficient processing power, memory, and network capacities to absorb the opacity, speed, and variability of data generated by the likes of AI and IoT devices. In essence, upgrading server capacity, expanding capacity cloud storage, and modernizing the data environment are the basic needs during the transformation. Naturally, transforming such a feat operates under capital expenditure (CAPEX) and operational expenditure (OPEX) frameworks, including software licenses, hardware, procurement, integration consulting, and ongoing maintenance.

In legacy systems, data siloing is a way to hold information in isolated, non-compatible data reservoirs. These data silos restrict complete data analysis, block proper decision-making, and obstruct the exactness of AI-induced insights. To disassemble these silos, data needs to be cleansed. Harmonization across units requires much painstaking effort and resources.

Amid the risk and cost considerations regarding an absolute overhaul of the system, many companies opt for a phased migration strategy. This involves the gradual embedding of AI into certain modules—be they inventory optimization, supplier management, or logistics routing: all the while keeping the core legacy system up and running. Within the years, the legacy modules could be displaced or supplemented with AI-enabled options in baby steps, culminating in an effortless transition to a fully viable digital supply chain architecture. In summary, the introduction of AI in severely crumbling supply chains is a major challenge, somewhat evincible, but possible with substantial custom expansions, Fulton Middleware, upgrades in infrastructures, and controlled phase migration. Through long-term eyes, better visibility, predictive capacity, operation lucidity, and that geographical dominance are all significant advantages supporting much reward on investments in resculpting improper legacy into AI-enabled digital eco-environments (Gunasekaran et al., 2019).

4.3 Infrastructure and Cost

Artificial Intelligence (AI) implementation concerns fitting into place a myriad of prerequisites like the acquisition of a proper idea for enterprise IT infrastructure. These utmost essentials are costly and includes specific personnel, IT, and software.

The custom software solutions are necessary for AI deployment within the supply chain configuration, apart from the hardware and platforms- mostly associated with predictive modeling tools, decision-support systems, and machine learning frameworks. AI software is usually extremely expensive with licencing; the enterprise software may go up for a range from vendors. Custom integration with legacy systems and real-time applications always requires paid software experts to be lobbied, making life horrible in terms of both cost and complexity. The other and intense problem is to recruit and retain qualified personnel: an AI employee probably needs to work in a team composed of such people as-data scientists, AI engineers, IT infrastructure specialists, cyber-security experts, and much knowledge of how the supply chain business operates. They make sure to hire, deploy, and maintain models while focusing on data quality and operation. In today's competitive labor market, finding and hiring such talent can be formidable and expensive.

Enterprise IT infrastructure, customized software, and skilled personnel encompass the components that constitute an effective AI deployment. But this involves substantial inputs of both money and organization, which acts as a barrier to many small and medium-sized enterprises (SMEs) and companies with limited resources. Therefore, a strategic partnership and phased implementation in line with ROI rationale are indispensable in managing the change and maximizing investment (Bag et al., 2021).

4.4 Organizational Change Management

Accustomed to the introductory traditional paths to managing businesses, the utter entrance of AI seizes an entire cultural makeover within organizations. Counter resistance may exist before such changes in education, as does digital illiteracy and insufficient training that stunt gains.

The traditional mindset of hierarchical decision-making and linear work modes and processes that have been known from time immemorial usually are pretty awkward with the tumultuously changing AI field. The transition from intuition-based decision-making to data-supported platform calls for substantial transformations in the fabricier of the top management and in the ways, employees appreciate the diversified roles they have to play, collaborate across departments, and have trust in the machine-generated insights. Cultural resistance is a leading obstacle to the transformation. The regular staff members who have been conditioned to certain managerial norms are usually full of skepticism and resentment towards the idea of AI integration. This is mostly fueled by the fear of job loss, loss of independence, and unpreparedness for or skepticism with respect to the implications of algorithmic readjustment on decision-making. In some cases, perceived complexities in technology and power dynamics could stand as a barrier to the adoption and involvement in AI. Another major hindrance to any efflorescence in the process is the dexterity in digital technology. In many organizations, where workforces are not savvy to some degree with the latest in this sphere, a lack of some understanding of data and no wrangle with the actual technology involved in AI dampens the potential of pulling a meaningful performance from the use of AI that includes the abilities to understand and operate on the decisions of AI tools. Insufficient training and professional development only widen this gap further; to harness AI systems right, a culture of learning must be developed within the organization, fostering change and experimental thinking and designing programs on the one hand to educate in AI technologies and, on the other hand, to make people realize the strategic importance of AI in enhancing the supply chain response and rendering transparency and efficiency. Therefore, embedding change management strategies within AI implementation projects in order to leapfrog these organizational challenges endows a chance of putting the AI in the hands of all of the followers, leading to significant benefits. A change of strategies includes gaining leadership support and ensuring bottom-up plans, straightforward attitude concerning the relevance of AI, and immunity of employees to deal with a transformation. Running pilot projects in specific pilot areas brings out an exemplary success that could transform the advocates into crusaders in favor of furthering the initiative.

In essence, the adoption of AI within corporate and supply chain operations represents more than mere technical readiness it demands wholesale cultural reformation. By acting swiftly to lower the resistor guard, promote digital literacy, and incubate an amicable learning environment, an organization hast able to harness AI to humankind's full advantage. The converse would deny the most intelligent AI the ability to extract much needed sustainable value or tug any strategic transformation along with it (Kache & Seuring, 2017).

5. STRATEGIC FRAMEWORK AND RECOMMENDATIONS

To incorporate AI in the supply chain, companies should consider taking the following strategic steps:

5.1 Start with Pilot Projects

Begin with small-scale planning demonstrations to provide ambitious pilot actions so that everyone can see what these solutions are accomplishing; learn from the failures and understand what exactly the impediments in the way of these pilots' success are; and then refine the approaches before implementation in a scale-up mode.

A pragmatic deployment of AI into supply chains may favour small proof-of-concept pilots. These pilots help stakeholders to scaffold AI technology by testing implementation in a controlled set-up, thereby judging its viability, and possibly ensuring that ownership and sponsorship start among target stakeholders. By engaging in projects that are relatively high-profile but with the highest chance of success, businesses hope to learn on an operational basis what the AI can do and how hard the organization can turn toward big change. The meaning of pilot initiatives is to consider from a very narrow standpoint only one use case, including these examples: demand forecasting or warehouse automation or supplier risk scoring, to discover a mediating role in the development of some points for those individuals who will be the early users. That is a chance for the AI systems to get up and running, and the chance for data quality parameters to create an issue. An early return on investment can appear once the pilot has been put into place in the business. This does a lot for the team in view of AI workflow by making further organizational learning possible, hence building internal pressure for broader adoption.

A critical part of any successful pilot implementation is the right one with availing opportunities when failing. Not all pilot projects would bring succumbing success, yet under-performance could give an introspective look at the system's weaknesses, integration challenges, acceptance problems by users, or governance's downside. By deriving abstractions from what didn't work, either due to technical limitations, system infrastructure limitations, or issues related to managing changes, organizations would be in a better position to make decision-making adjustments in their AI strategies.

The feedback process during the pilot program is very important. Departmental stakeholders should be put off by their honest thoughts about system performances and usability and suggestion for improvements where necessary. With this involvement technique, stakeholders are prompted to not just improve system designs but also generate further buy-in to the system and intra-organizational collaboration. Decision project scaling means moving into the next direction where pilot projects have demonstrated strong results which actually a structural scaling up of the AI solution. This includes re-engineering process, infrastructure reinforcement, data flow standardization, and greatly enhanced user training. A thick governance framework, performance measurements, and risk shedding have to back the large-scale rollout to ensure stability and sustainability.

In sum industries show that a gradual, evidence-based progression will work to put AI into supply chain operations. Small beginnings provide some golden opportunities to manage risk, build capacity, and show value early on in the process of transformation. Periodically assessed and accordingly recalibrated on the basis of evolving perception and inputs, programs will demonstrate the ability to impact larger areas in a more confident and siloed way before ultimate marketization.

5.2 Financing Infrastructure and Skill

Capital expenditure (CAPEX) investments on both digital infrastructures and employees' knowledge of AI are quite important. This also enables strategic partnerships with technology firms or academia in bridging knowledge gaps.

Capital expenditure (CAPEX) investments in digital infrastructure and human capital are foundational to the successful implementation of Artificial Intelligence (AI) in modern supply chains. These investments reflect a strategic commitment not only to acquiring advanced technologies but also to cultivating the organizational capabilities necessary to harness their full potential. The dual emphasis on infrastructure and talent ensures that AI systems are both technically sound and effectively utilized across the enterprise. On the infrastructure side, CAPEX investments typically encompass advanced data storage systems, high-performance computing hardware, cloud services, and integrated platforms that support AI and machine learning applications. These digital assets form the backbone of a resilient and scalable supply chain ecosystem capable of processing large volumes of real-time data and enabling predictive and prescriptive analytics. Without such foundational systems, AI models may struggle to function efficiently, resulting in suboptimal outcomes or systemic bottlenecks. Equally critical is investment in employee training and knowledge development. AI tools are only as effective as the people who design, interpret, and act upon their outputs. Developing internal expertise through training programs, certifications, and digital literacy initiatives is essential for ensuring that staff at all levels from data analysts to supply chain managers can engage meaningfully with AI technologies. Such capacity building also helps alleviate resistance to digital transformation and fosters a culture of innovation and continuous learning. In addition to internal development, organizations are increasingly pursuing strategic partnerships with external stakeholders to accelerate AI adoption and bridge skill gaps. Collaborations with technology providers, research institutions, and universities can provide access to cutting-edge expertise, research findings, and customized AI solutions tailored to specific industry challenges. These partnerships often take the form of joint innovation labs, co-development initiatives, or talent exchange programs, enhancing both technical capabilities and thought leadership. Moreover, CAPEX investments in AI-related partnerships can yield long-term returns by embedding organizations within dynamic innovation ecosystems. Such networks facilitate early access to emerging technologies, foster interdisciplinary collaboration, and enable benchmarking against industry best practices. For small and medium-sized enterprises (SMEs) in particular, partnerships with academic institutions or startups can offer cost-effective pathways to adopt sophisticated AI solutions without bearing the full burden of in-house development.

In summary, capital investments in both digital infrastructure and AI knowledge development are not merely operational expenditures they are strategic imperatives. By aligning financial resources with technological readiness and workforce capability, organizations position themselves to lead in the evolving landscape of intelligent, transparent, and responsive supply chains. The synergistic effect of infrastructure development and strategic collaboration creates a robust foundation for scalable, sustainable, and value-driven AI integration.

5.3 Adopt a Stage Integration Approach

Phased introduction of AI technologies into existing systems to minimize disturbances. Among the functions could be demand forecasting and inventory optimization for which quick wins are available.

The gradual approach is preferable to a massive revolution, for it posits relatively high risk, complexity, and resistance; therefore, organizations with the appropriate infrastructure delegates to test and pilot its artificial intelligence (AI) capabilities within the confines of an operational environment, rather than at the outset, and use the entire approach to enhance its industrial relevance by building on successful experiences with AI. Indexing of these operations would help pick out various supply chain functions in order to improve rapidly and measurably by means of the application of AI. These "quick wins" can serve as initial stages for the adoption of AI in two areas: demand forecasting and inventory optimization. Much data is associated with these two areas; moreover, the data is subject to frequent change, and the third reason is that these functions are closely related to business performance, rendering them perfect candidates to showcase AI's value in the early days of transformation.

Demand forecasting with AI comes equipped with ML models that inspect historical sales, seasonality, promotions, external factors such as weather or macroeconomic indications, and customer behaviors. AI technology continuously learns from observed trends, patterns, or predictability about past data, thereby leading to an elevated accuracy of performance and operational sensitivity, thus offering distinct benefits to the business in meeting its stock/provide with efficient capacities, reduced stockouts, and planning the procurement of inbound hits.

Reap the above-given benefits in similar ways in inventory optimization with AI. AI models can advise the most beautiful combination of order frequency. AI will promulgate acceptance of reorder points and even the safety stock that depends on inventory turnover, lead times, and service level objectives. Besides this, certain models will keep adjusting inventory norms instantaneously in response to either change in the demand pattern or supplier trustworthiness or variability in the trade environment. Quick wins here are reduced holding costs, improved order fill rates, and diminished inventory obsolescence.

AI applications, when deployed within these focused silos, also assist in a ground-up internal capability enhancement. Initial successes act as proofs for such business-driven acceptance of AI; encourage additional stakeholders through demonstration and proof of confidence; gain momentum for pushing the organizational capacity for a wider rollout; and offer valuable lessons in how the implementation could be run.

This is all possible because these applications will inevitably reveal areas where integration pains, data quality, or perhaps skill gaps should be filled prior to them being stamped on at scale. It goes without saying, then, that during this whole process, clear performance standards and feedback loops must be laid down and upheld at each stage. The system attributes this could be tracked by performance indicators, like accuracy of forecasts, service-level maintenance, inventory turnover ratios, and user friendliness. Foremost in this context is the need for continuous and ongoing monitoring and feedback, permitting the organization to change tack where necessary in accordance with the system design to ensure its continued alignment with dynamic operational purposes. The phased deployment will allow the IT team to integrate AI applications with the current enterprise solutions-ERPs, WMS, etc.-without disturbing any of the core functions. Middleware solutions and cloud-based AI services can be quite handy due to the interfaces they can provide to existing infrastructures, rendering them more scalable and flexible and minimizing the overall risk of implementation.

To wrap up our discussion, we should say scaled adoption of AI technologies within high-impact, low-risk areas-say, in demand forecasting and inventory optimization-is really a frictionless beginning for an impending full-blown digital transformation. The beginning would provide a 'value story,' followed by incremental iterations to enhance AI systems and user acceptance. This would lay the foundation for a more comprehensive, broad, and resilient AI application strategy across the supply chain operations.

5.4 Establish Governance and Ethics Frameworks

Clearly define respective data governance policies, AI ethics to adhere to, as well as cybersecurity criteria. The latter should ensure the responsible use of AI and the trust of these stakeholders.

Deploying AI successfully in supply chain environments is entirely dependent not only on the technical features but also on the governing structure. Organizations have to lay down exhaustive data governance policies, articulate ethical guidelines for AI use, and also set cybersecurity standards. These are the very foundations of using AI responsibly and winning partners' trust all through a digital transformation.

Solid data governance principles are meant to define how the data should be collected, stored, accessed, and used within the organization. In the context of AI, data quality, accessibility, and integrity become paramount as roughly collected or biased data can lead to inaccurately posing the predictions, making the inefficiency in operations, or bringing about undesired repercussions. Ownership and stewardship of data, access rights to the data, management through its entire life cycle, and regulations regarding auditing aspects should be audited with respect to GDPR or CCPA enactment. It makes no less sense, whereby sharing some amount of data among a variety of different partners or data sources, therefore governance policies at the very least should set out explicitly the practical protocols of data sharing with third parties. In other words, it shall put a premium on transparency and accountability within the ecosystem. AI ethics policies also must be clearly indicated in the AI strategy of a given organization. Ethical guidelines are the conscience in developing and employing AI systems so as not to render harm, discriminate against stakeholders, or undermine human uniqueness. Major principles here are fairness, transparency, explainability, accountability, and non-discrimination. These values will inform decisions on algorithm design and model validation and in user-interactions. For instance, ethical guidelines would ensure among other safeguards that the supplier assessment is carried out in such a manner that any algorithm introduced does not unduly favor or to the contrary penalize suppliers on account of spurious or biased inputs. A robust cybersecurity regime is a significant vehicle for building trust among key players. This is because the increasing interconnection of AI systems with operational technologies and internet-of-things infrastructure entails the impending risk of cyber-attacks, data breaches, or systems tampering. Some of the sophisticated security measures should include data encryption, authentication, real-time monitoring, and incident retaliation protocols. These provisions ensure not only the safeguard of intellectual property or customer data but also the seamless function of the AI-supported supply chains.

Largely demonstrated by data governance, ethics, and cybersecurity alignment, an organization aspires to etch on its AI governance framework. The governance setup should be under the mandate for a range of multidisciplinary governance bodies, representatives recruited from IT, legal, compliance, operations, and top management, in order that various elements of policy are enforced cohesively and are able to evolve in the wake of new challenges and threats. Periodic auditing, performance evaluation, and engagement with stakeholders are imperative in maintaining the efficacy and pertinence of these policies. The enforcement of these policies on information governance together with AI ethical delineations and cybersecurity protocols greatly lends an organization to implement responsible AI integration. Thus, transparency and minimizing risks should be the domain of high importance for leveraging organizational credibility. AI for supply chain use will be a pressing issue for existence after establishing these frameworks. Regulatory compliance will be only one of the reasons why these rules are critical: the trust portfolio and innovational continuity would be the other.

5.5 Monitor and Modify

Performance of AI should be continuously monitored; constructive feedback, combined with rapid development, must prompt strategy changes and enable learning across the organization.

It is important to continue monitoring AI performance throughout the supply chain in order to support organizational goals, operational efficiency, and ethical outlook on an ongoing basis. Unlike traditional software systems, AI models are incremental in development, evolving over time together with newly available data, changing environment, and the influence on decision processes due to learning. Therefore, sturdy mechanisms for evaluation and feedback throughout the development, utilization, and refinement of the model must be created to ensure that its prognosis is efficacious and reliable in the long run. Continuous performance tracking relies on KPIs, which help reflect the performance of AI systems in terms of accuracy, efficiency, and utility. These could pertain to forecast accuracy, inventory performance, order fill rates, precision for anomaly detection, or customer satisfaction. These are used to assess AI solutions along the organization, campus, or department.

Structured feedback methodologies will be indispensable for promoting adaptive improvement processes. Organizational feedback mechanisms will provide a platform for employees, managers, and technical teams to report issues, suggest solutions, and add any context that otherwise might not be captured by the AI activities themselves. For instance, in practice, if a demand-forecast model consistently underestimates demand during seasonal peaks, this anomaly cannot be captured, and the error is flagged by the supply chain planners, leading to a recalibration of the model. Similarly, these feedback chains from the labor forces' viewpoint will provide insights into real-world constraints that may impact routing algorithms or warehouse automation platforms.

Numerous AI/AI-powered recommendations and actions, willed presently by an array of top management personnel. These valuable people would later determine the principles needed for more effective and efficient operational foundation. The moment a judgment is made concerning any input, however mundane its circulation, the feedback of the claim that may or may not have been implemented is momentarily conveyed to the top management. Many other such suggestions and exchanges are initiated from the top management panels, on whom operations, procurement, compliance, whatsoever, share in part in holding AI performance leashed within the broader strategic rectangular space. Absorption of the AI teachings is required. Lesson learning from pilot projects, error logs, and feedback sessions and performance reports must be documented and communicated within the organization. An organized central knowledge or AI governance dashboard, where stakeholders would like to access across model life span evolution and contribute toward more and more refinements, established based on a knowledge-sharing approach, would not only shorten the maturity of organization culture in AI adoption but also serve as a lesson avoider in which the dark soloes drench it. AI Performance management must be a continuous, iterative process inclusive of real-time monitoring, constructive feedback, and agile development cycles. This not only drives the accuracy and business value of AI solutions but also contributes to organizational survival, adaptability, and innovation capabilities. In conjunction with a culture embracing the values of learning, these practices can provide for the full use of AI as a real force for steering transparent supply-chain performance ahead of the competition.

6. CONCLUSION

Never underestimate the potential of Artificial Intelligence to bring transparency and visibility throughout the supply chain. By employing the tools needed for predictive analytics, IoT, blockchain, and machine learning, we can get a view of what is happening in real-time, add accountability where needed, and improve the efficiency of operations. The implications of these benefits require the organizations devoted to workable strategy, investment, and organizational preparedness. As the world economy keeps making those global supply chains more intricate by the day, the adaptable and innovative will come to the forefront while the rest will lag. Subsequently, sustained research on AI adaptation will rest in the setting up for creation of resilient, transparent, and future-ready networks of supply. Especially in the areas of significant transparency and visibility within global supply chains, the impact AI could have is profound. By deploying intelligent devices, the Internet of Things (IoT) with predictive analytics, blockchain, and machine learning, an organization can have an insight never achieved before. Real-time visibility into cargo, predictions prior to demand and risk, automatically verifiable transactions, and intelligent decision-making are all features of these technologies working together. As a result, the organizations can react more swiftly to flatten the disruptions in addressing efficient nonexistence and accountability in a greater sense throughout their supply chain ecosystem.In predictive analytics, firms use data to analyze patterns in order that they can anticipate trends through enhancement of demand planning, resource allocation, and inventory optimization. IoT devices provide minute visibility on the condition, location, and movement of assets—an understanding which in turn can help streamline logistics operations and guarantee quality. With blockchain, we can ensure robust, transparent transactions and promote trust among stakeholders. Machine learning involves continuous refinement of systems, identifying anomalies as well as improving system performance through learning of feedback, etc.

In a bigger picture, these technologies set the standard for purely data-driven supply chain management, a claim way beyond efficiency and competitiveness. But in order for these benefits to materialize, much more than mere technology transfer is needed. It calls for institutions to concretely plan out how to adopt AI as a withstanding pillar of their operations. This involves sustainable contributions to build digital infrastructure, to upskill available talent, and to bring about change. In the same breath, it is important to introspect on questions of ethical governance, cyber-security safeguards, continuous learning, and constructive feedback.

With global economic dynamics in a perpetual state of change and supply chain interdependencies growing at a rapid pace, the role of geopolitics, environment, and demand is beginning to complicate the already troubled conventional operations model. It is adaptability and innovation that would actually instill in any business its competitive advantage. Organizations that leverage AI-led alerts to reset their processes in light of emerging signals-the knowledge held by those at the forefront-carry the badge of excellence whereas those temporo-spatially resisting transformation or digital integration are unfairly placed right at the back. It is quite apparent that organizations should allow a future guided by AI to embody efficiency, ethical responsibilities, trust, and accountability. As AI continues to evolve, the organizational frameworks should adapt concomitantly. These adaptations would necessitate continuous investment in interdisciplinary research, proof-of-concept outreach programs, cross-sector partnership, and policy alignment. For sure, the critical aspect in AI evolution is sustained R&D activities. A tar-get partnership between academia and respective industries will excellently deliver scalable AI solutions based on very real-world problems that polish and disseminate best practices. In working toward a valorization milieu of inspired outcome and inquiry, we can leap forward in crafting transparent and resilient value chains.

REFERENCES

Accenture. (2020, June). Elevate every decision with intelligent supply chain operations. https://www.accenture.com/content/dam/accenture/final/a-com-migration/r3-3/pdf/pdf-157/accenture-supply-chain-operations-pov-june-2020.pdf

Bag, S., Pretorius, J.-H. C., & Gupta, S. (2021). Role of institutional pressures and resources in the adoption of big data analytics–powered artificial intelligence, sustainable manufacturing practices and circular economy capabilities. *Technological Forecasting and Social Change*, *163*, 120420.

Choi, T.-M., & Sun, X. (2025). Prescriptive analytics for sustainable supply chain operations: The PASO framework for Industry 5.0. *Transportation Research Part E, Logistics and Transportation Review*, *183*, 104206. DOI: 10.1016/j.tre.2025.104206

Ghosh, S. K., & Sar, A. K. (2022). Impact of effective supply chain management and supply chain risk management capabilities on construction project performance. *Indian Journal of Science and Technology*, *15*(12), 505–517.

Gunasekaran, A., Yusuf, Y. Y., Adeleye, E. O., Papadopoulos, T., Kovvuri, D., & Geyi, D. G. (2019). Agile manufacturing: An evolutionary review of practices. *International Journal of Production Research*, *57*(15-16), 5154–5174.

IBM. (2022). *IBM Food Trust: Building apps overview*. https://www.ibm.com/support/pages/ibm-food-trust-building-apps-overview

Ivanov, D., & Dolgui, A. (2020). A digital supply chain twin for managing the disruption risks and resilience. *International Journal of Production Research*, *58*(12), 3860–3875.

Kache, F., & Seuring, S. (2017). Challenges and opportunities of digital information at the intersection of big data analytics and supply chain management. *International Journal of Operations & Production Management*, *37*(1), 10–36.

LeewayHertz. (2023). *AI in logistics and supply chain: Use cases, applications, solution and implementation.* https://www.leewayhertz.com/ai-in-logistics-and-supply-chain/

McKinsey & Company. (2021). *Succeeding in the AI supply-chain revolution.* https://www.mckinsey.com/industries/metals-and-mining/our-insights/succeeding-in-the-ai-supply-chain-revolution

Moktadir, M. A., Ali, S. M., Paul, S. K., & Shukla, N. (2019). Barriers to big data analytics in manufacturing supply chains: A case study from Bangladesh. *Computers & Industrial Engineering*, *128*, 1063–1075.

Saberi, S., Kouhizadeh, M., Sarkis, J., & Shen, L. (2019). Blockchain technology and its relationships to sustainable supply chain management. *International Journal of Production Research*, *57*(7), 2117–2135.

Siemens. (2023). *Blockchain and IoT in digital supply chains.* Siemens Digital Industries. https://xcelerator.siemens.com/global/en/industries/food-beverage/exclusive-area/blockchain-iot.html

Techment. (2023). *7 ways of leveraging AI in supply chain.* Techment Technology. https://www.techment.com/7-ways-of-leveraging-ai-in-supply-chain/

Wu, L., Zhang, Z., & Huang, J., Su, I-Hsuan, & Tian, S. (2025). Digital Technologies and Supply Chain Resilience: A Resource-Action-Performance Perspective. *Information Systems Frontiers*.

Chapter 2
AI-Powered Anomaly Detection in Multimodal Supply Chains

Usharani Bhimavarapu
https://orcid.org/0000-0002-0246-1420

Department of Computer Science and Engineering, Koneru Lakshmaiah Education Foundation, Vaddeswaram, India

ABSTRACT

Artificial Intelligence (AI) is revolutionizing multimodal logistics networks through more intelligent, faster, and smoother operations on different modes of transportation and complex supply chains. Interlacing multisource data on weather conditions, means of transport, and container status, AI models are optimally placed to effectively monitor, anticipate, and optimize logistics performance. Advanced techniques such as Particle Swarm Optimization for feature extraction and Bi-Stacked Artificial Neural Networks for deep learning allow the determination of significant insights in vast and heterogeneous datasets. These AI-driven techniques accelerate real-time decision-making, reduce operational cost, and improve dependability by predicting delays, detecting anomalies, and routing optimization. This study focuses on the contribution of AI towards developing multimodal logistics as a wise and responsive system capable of addressing the dynamic challenges of modern supply chains

DOI: 10.4018/979-8-3373-2843-0.ch002

INTRODUCTION

Multimodal logistics networks involve the coordination of multiple transportation modes such as road, rail, sea, and air to move goods efficiently. These networks are inherently complex due to the diversity of carriers, infrastructures, schedules, and regulations. Managing this complexity manually or with traditional systems is increasingly inefficient and error-prone. AI offers the ability to process vast amounts of data from various sources, enabling more informed decision-making. It can analyze patterns and optimize routes dynamically, reducing delays and costs. The need for AI arises because of the growing volume and variability in shipments, customer demands, and external disruptions like weather or geopolitical events. AI helps to integrate and synchronize the different transport modes, ensuring seamless transitions and minimizing bottlenecks. Without AI, achieving high levels of coordination and adaptability in these networks is almost impossible. Thus, AI is essential for handling the complexity inherent in modern multimodal logistics.

One of the critical purposes of AI in multimodal logistics is to enable real-time decision-making. Logistics networks are dynamic environments where unforeseen disruptions such as traffic congestion, customs delays, or equipment breakdowns occur frequently. AI systems can continuously monitor these factors through sensors, GPS data, and IoT devices. By analyzing this live data, AI can suggest optimal rerouting, rescheduling, or resource reallocation instantly. This immediate response reduces downtime and enhances the reliability of delivery schedules. Moreover, AI's predictive capabilities allow it to forecast potential disruptions before they occur, enabling proactive planning. Real-time decision-making powered by AI leads to improved customer satisfaction by providing accurate delivery estimates and reducing uncertainty. It also allows logistics providers to be more agile, adapting rapidly to changing conditions. Hence, AI transforms multimodal logistics into a responsive, resilient system.

Cost efficiency is a fundamental goal in logistics, where margins are often tight. AI helps multimodal networks optimize costs through intelligent route planning, load optimization, and resource management. By analyzing historical and real-time data, AI models can identify the most cost-effective routes considering factors like fuel consumption, tolls, tariffs, and time windows. AI algorithms can also optimize container loading, ensuring maximum utilization of cargo space and minimizing waste. Additionally, AI facilitates better fleet management by predicting maintenance needs and reducing downtime, lowering operational expenses. The integration of AI-driven procurement and supplier selection can further reduce costs by automating negotiations and optimizing contract terms. AI enables multimodal logistics providers to balance speed, cost, and reliability better than traditional manual approaches. This results in leaner operations and increased competitiveness in the marketplace.

Supply chain visibility is crucial in multimodal logistics to track goods as they move across different carriers and borders. AI enhances visibility by aggregating data from diverse sources such as RFID tags, GPS, shipment documents, and customs records. Machine learning models can then analyze this data to detect anomalies, delays, or risks. This transparency allows stakeholders to monitor shipment status in real time and respond swiftly to issues. It also facilitates compliance with regulations by automatically verifying documentation and customs requirements. AI-driven dashboards and alerts provide actionable insights to logistics managers, improving communication across the supply chain. Enhanced transparency increases trust among partners and customers, reducing disputes and claims. Consequently, AI-powered visibility supports a more efficient, accountable, and secure multimodal logistics network.

Sustainability is an increasingly important objective in logistics due to environmental regulations and corporate responsibility goals. AI enables multimodal logistics networks to reduce their carbon footprint through better route optimization and mode selection. For example, AI can identify when shifting cargo from trucks to more eco-friendly rail or sea transport is viable. It can also optimize load planning to minimize empty runs and reduce fuel consumption. Additionally, AI supports energy-efficient warehouse operations by managing inventory levels and automating material handling. Through predictive analytics, AI helps forecast demand accurately, preventing overproduction and waste. AI can also assist in regulatory reporting related to emissions, ensuring compliance with green standards. By incorporating sustainability goals into logistical planning, AI drives the transition to greener supply chains.

Multimodal logistics networks face multiple risks, including natural disasters, geopolitical tensions, cyber-attacks, and supplier failures. AI plays a vital role in identifying and mitigating these risks. By analyzing historical data and current trends, AI models can predict vulnerabilities and potential disruptions. For example, AI can assess the risk level of different routes or carriers and suggest alternatives. AI systems can also detect cybersecurity threats by monitoring network activities and flagging suspicious behavior. In crisis situations, AI helps coordinate rapid response by optimizing resource allocation and communication. Furthermore, AI enables scenario planning and simulation to prepare logistics managers for various contingencies. This enhances the overall resilience of multimodal logistics networks, ensuring continuity even in adverse conditions.

Automation is a key benefit AI brings to multimodal logistics by reducing manual labor and increasing efficiency. AI-powered robotic process automation (RPA) can handle repetitive tasks such as documentation, invoicing, customs clearance, and shipment tracking. AI-driven chatbots improve customer service by providing instant updates and handling routine queries. In warehouses and distribution centers, AI integrates with robotics for sorting, packing, and loading, accelerating throughput and reducing errors. Automated scheduling and dispatching reduce human error and optimize resource use. By streamlining these operations, AI frees human workers to focus on higher-value activities like strategic planning and exception handling. This automation leads to faster turnaround times and cost savings, vital in competitive logistics markets.

Accurate forecasting and demand planning are essential for efficient multimodal logistics networks. AI employs advanced machine learning techniques to analyze historical sales data, market trends, and external factors such as seasonality and economic conditions. This enables more precise predictions of shipment volumes and inventory requirements. Better forecasts reduce stockouts and excess inventory, optimizing warehouse space and reducing holding costs. AI models can also predict shifts in customer preferences and identify emerging markets. In multimodal logistics, this allows better alignment of capacity across different transport modes. Effective demand planning powered by AI minimizes disruptions and supports just-in-time delivery models, enhancing supply chain agility and responsiveness.

In today's competitive environment, customer experience is a crucial differentiator. AI in multimodal logistics helps create more personalized and transparent service offerings. AI-powered systems provide customers with accurate delivery time estimates, real-time tracking, and proactive notifications about delays or changes. Through natural language processing (NLP), AI chatbots can interact with customers 24/7, addressing inquiries and handling complaints efficiently. AI also helps tailor delivery options based on customer preferences, such as selecting faster delivery modes or convenient pickup locations. By analyzing customer feedback and behavior, AI can identify opportunities to improve services continuously. Enhanced customer satisfaction and loyalty are direct outcomes of AI-driven personalization in logistics.

Multimodal logistics networks involve numerous independent stakeholders, including shippers, carriers, ports, customs authorities, and warehouses. AI facilitates seamless integration and collaboration across these entities. By using AI-powered platforms, data from various sources is harmonized and shared securely, enabling joint decision-making. Blockchain combined with AI can ensure data integrity and transparency among partners. AI algorithms optimize coordination by synchronizing schedules and sharing predictive insights. This reduces delays caused by miscommunication or data silos. Furthermore, AI can identify strategic partnerships and optimize supplier and carrier selection. Ultimately, AI supports a more connected, efficient, and cooperative multimodal logistics ecosystem, improving overall supply chain performance.

Ambra et al. (2019) analyze intermodal and synchromodal resilience from a decentralized perspective, emphasizing flexibility and adaptability. Nevertheless, the study is limited by its reliance on theoretical models and simulations rather than extensive real-world empirical data. The assumptions made for resilience evaluation may oversimplify complex logistics operations, and the decentralized framework might not adequately capture centralized control benefits in some logistics systems, limiting its practical applicability in certain scenarios (Ambra et al., 2019).

Moschovou et al. (2019) discuss challenges in freight transport data sharing, such as privacy concerns and interoperability. However, the paper is limited by its broad scope that covers many challenges without providing in-depth solutions or prioritizing which issues are most critical.

It also does not extensively examine emerging technologies like AI and blockchain that might mitigate these challenges, potentially limiting the relevance of some findings in rapidly evolving digital logistics environments (Moschovou et al., 2019).

Swamy and Kota (2020) offer an empirical study on IoT system-level aspects, providing technical depth on IoT implementation. The limitation lies in the scope mostly restricted to IoT infrastructure rather than application-level impacts, such as logistics process optimization or multimodal integration. Moreover, the study does not fully address the scalability and security challenges faced in large, distributed logistics networks, which are critical for practical adoption (Swamy & Kota, 2020).

Tran-Dang et al. (2020) provide perspectives on IoT for the physical internet, identifying several technical and operational challenges. However, the paper largely presents conceptual frameworks without substantial experimental validation or real-world deployment case studies. The complexity of integrating diverse IoT systems across global logistics chains remains underexplored, especially concerning standardization and cross-border data governance issues (Tran-Dang et al., 2020).

Rejeb et al. (2020) conduct a bibliometric analysis of IoT research in supply chain management, offering useful trend insights. Nonetheless, the study's limitation is the reliance on published literature, which may have inherent biases and may not reflect emerging practical challenges or innovations not yet documented academically. The analysis also does not extend to qualitative assessments of IoT adoption barriers or success factors within logistics operations (Rejeb et al., 2020).

Montreuil (2011) introduces the concept of the Physical Internet as a sustainable logistics framework. A key limitation is the early stage of the concept, which means practical implementations are scarce and largely hypothetical. The ambitious vision does not fully account for existing infrastructure constraints, regulatory hurdles, and the significant behavioral change required among logistics stakeholders, which may delay or complicate adoption (Montreuil, 2011).

Shafique et al. (2018) study the impact of IoT capabilities on green supply chain integration. However, their work is somewhat constrained by a focus on energy consumption behavior without fully considering other environmental factors such as waste reduction or material efficiency. The empirical data is also limited to specific industries, potentially restricting the generalizability of conclusions to broader logistics contexts (Shafique et al., 2018).

Hopkins and Hawking (2018) present a case study on big data analytics and IoT in logistics, showcasing practical benefits. Still, the study's limitation lies in its case-study approach, which limits broad applicability since findings are based on a single company's context. The rapid evolution of both IoT and analytics tools means results may become quickly outdated without continuous adaptation and validation in different operational environments (Hopkins & Hawking, 2018).

Yavari et al. (2022) develop an IoT platform for last-mile delivery emissions reporting. A limitation of this work is the narrow focus on last-mile delivery, which excludes other crucial logistics segments like warehousing and long-haul transport. The platform's scalability and interoperability with existing logistics IT systems are also not extensively validated, raising questions about broader deployment feasibility (Yavari et al., 2022).

Cao et al. (2022) discuss green logistics vehicle dispatch using IoT, offering innovative approaches for smart logistics. However, their model relies heavily on idealized assumptions about vehicle availability and network conditions, which may not hold in real-world scenarios with unpredictable delays and operational disruptions. The study also has limited empirical validation with live logistics data, affecting confidence in practical effectiveness (Cao et al., 2022).

Huang et al. (2022) present fleet management approaches considering charging costs in green logistics. The main limitation is the focus on electric vehicle fleets, which currently represent only a fraction of logistics transport worldwide. The analysis does not fully incorporate integration challenges with legacy vehicles or multi-modal transport, potentially limiting the system's overall applicability across diverse logistics networks (Huang et al., 2022).

Mejjaouli (2022) presents an IoT-based decision support system for green logistics that demonstrates potential in improving sustainability; however, the study's reliance on simulation and theoretical modeling limits the validation of real-world applicability, especially in diverse logistics environments where operational complexities and heterogeneous IoT infrastructures may affect system performance (Mejjaouli et al., 2022).

Bogataj et al. (2017) propose an extended MRP model to mitigate risks for perishable products within cyber-physical systems, but the model's complexity and assumptions about product deterioration and demand patterns may reduce its flexibility and scalability across different supply chains, particularly those with unpredictable demand or varying perishability characteristics (Bogataj et al., 2017).

Tsang et al. (2017) develop an IoT-based cargo monitoring system focused on cold chain environments, yet the system's dependency on sensor accuracy and network connectivity presents limitations in scenarios with harsh environmental conditions or inconsistent data transmission, which could affect the reliability of real-time monitoring and operational effectiveness (Tsang et al., 2017).

Chow & Heaver (1994) provide foundational definitions and measurement approaches for logistics performance, but their framework is somewhat dated and may not fully capture contemporary complexities such as digital transformation, sustainability concerns, and evolving customer expectations in logistics service delivery (Chow & Heaver, 1994).

Tsolaki et al. (2022) review machine learning applications in freight transport and logistics, highlighting promising advances; however, the study notes limitations in data availability, quality, and heterogeneity, which restrict the generalizability of many machine learning models and call for more robust, domain-specific datasets for effective deployment (Tsolaki et al., 2022).

Gong and Liu (2020) examine mitigative investments against natural disasters and labor strikes in seaport logistics networks, but their modeling approach primarily focuses on specific disruptions and may overlook other critical risk factors such as cyber threats or regulatory changes, limiting the holistic risk assessment for inland logistics systems (Gong and Liu, 2020).

Gaudenzi et al. (2021) analyze logistics service quality and customer satisfaction in B2B relationships using qualitative comparative analysis, yet their reliance on qualitative data and case studies may reduce the ability to generalize findings across diverse industries and geographic regions with differing logistics practices (Gaudenzi et al., 2021).

Lai et al. (2022) investigate determinants of customer satisfaction with parcel locker services, but the study's scope is limited to specific geographic markets and does not extensively consider socio-economic or technological factors that might influence user acceptance in different cultural contexts (Lai et al., 2022).

Soysal and Bloemhof-Ruwaard (2017) discuss sustainable logistics from an optimization perspective; however, their approach may not fully integrate dynamic real-world variables such as fluctuating demand, regulatory shifts, and evolving consumer behavior, which challenge the practical implementation of sustainable logistics strategies (Soysal and Bloemhof-Ruwaard, 2017).

Li et al. (2023) present emerging technologies and policies for carbon-neutral transportation, but their discussion remains high-level and lacks detailed empirical validation, making it difficult to assess the effectiveness and feasibility of proposed solutions in complex transport ecosystems (Li et al., 2023).

Abdulahi and Fan (2021) explore container operational risk in Ethiopian shipping, but the study's focus on a single regional context limits the applicability of the risk scale to other global shipping environments with differing operational characteristics and risk profiles (Abdulahi and Fan, 2021).

Uvet (2020) empirically studies logistics service quality and customer satisfaction, yet the reliance on self-reported survey data may introduce bias, and the cross-sectional design limits the ability to assess causality or changes in satisfaction over time (Uvet, 2020).

Beysenbaev and Dus (2020) propose improvements to the Logistics Performance Index, but their recommendations require extensive data collection and harmonization efforts, which may be difficult to implement consistently across countries with varying data availability and quality (Beysenbaev and Dus, 2020).

Chejarla et al. (2022) review multi-criteria decision-making (MCDM) methods in logistics performance evaluation, yet the diversity and complexity of MCDM approaches can create challenges in standardizing performance evaluation and in the interpretability of results for practical decision-making (Chejarla et al., 2022).

Giusti et al. (2019) provide an overview of synchromodal logistics including success factors and technologies, but the review highlights significant gaps in empirical validation and the integration of emerging technologies into legacy logistics systems, limiting the immediate applicability of proposed frameworks (Giusti et al., 2019).

Babić et al. (2022) discuss integrated door-to-door transport services transitioning from intermodality to multimodality, but the study is limited by a focus on air passenger transport and does not fully address the operational and infrastructural challenges in other transport modes or freight logistics (Babić et al., 2022).

Tavasszy et al. (2017) examine intermodality and synchromodality concepts, yet their theoretical approach offers limited empirical evidence on implementation challenges and economic feasibility, especially in fragmented transport networks across different regions (Tavasszy et al., 2017).

Delbart et al. (2021) review uncertainty issues in intermodal and synchromodal transport but acknowledge that most existing models oversimplify uncertainty sources and lack integration with real-time data analytics, thus limiting practical robustness under dynamic transport conditions (Delbart et al., 2021).

Steadieseifi et al. (2014) survey multimodal freight transportation planning literature but highlight that many existing models fail to capture the full complexity of operational constraints and do not adequately incorporate environmental and sustainability factors in planning processes (Steadieseifi et al., 2014).

The proposed approach addresses the limitations of existing models by integrating advanced IoT and machine learning techniques to enhance real-time data accuracy, scalability, and adaptability in dynamic logistics environments. Unlike prior works that rely heavily on theoretical models or limited datasets, the proposed system incorporates robust sensor fusion and adaptive algorithms that improve monitoring reliability even under harsh or unpredictable conditions. Additionally, it expands the scope of risk management by including a broader range of disruption factors such as cyber threats and regulatory changes, thus offering a more holistic assessment compared to earlier models focused on specific risks. The approach also overcomes limitations related to data heterogeneity and quality by employing standardized data processing pipelines and domain-specific training, which improves model generalizability across diverse supply chains and geographic regions. Moreover, by combining qualitative insights with quantitative analytics, the proposed framework enhances decision-making accuracy and customer satisfaction evaluation in B2B and last-mile logistics contexts. Finally, the system's modular and scalable architecture supports seamless integration with legacy infrastructure and emerging technologies, addressing the implementation challenges highlighted in synchromodal and multimodal transport research. This comprehensive enhancement enables more effective, resilient, and sustainable logistics operations compared to the constrained capabilities of existing models.

MATERIAL AND METHODS

The method begins with the collection of multisource logistics data from India's National Logistics Digital Platform, such as environmental, transport, and container parameters by using in-built sensors. The core data is cleaned to remove noise and normalize to ensure consistency. Feature selection is performed using Particle Swarm Optimization to choose the most important variables. The pre-cleaned dataset is then forwarded to a Bi-Stacked Artificial Neural Network model that can unveil hidden patterns and connections. The model is trained and tested to infer logistics performance and detect anomalies. Finally, results are reviewed to optimally improve decision-making in multimodal logistics networks.

MATERIAL

Data collection involves consolidating multisource data recorded on India's National Logistics Digital Platform as a single-point repository of logistics data. Embedded monitoring gadgets are put in the system, which are in charge of capturing the most important key performance indicators (KPIs) required for efficient logistics management. The KPIs are classified into three primary contexts to record the various effects on logistics operations: environmental, transport, and container contexts.

The environmental context encompasses external factors to the intermodal container or means of transportation, for example, atmospheric and geographical conditions including temperature, humidity, weather, road quality, geo-positioning, and distance traveled. The transport context emphasizes vehicle-specific measures such as vehicle type, fuel type, fuel consumption, acceleration, deceleration, speed, current gear, engine RPM, and greenhouse gas emissions. Lastly, the container context monitors both environmental and quality-oriented measurements within the intermodal container itself, such as internal temperature, humidity, acceleration, deceleration, impact, and light intensity. All of these parameters are critical to assessing the logistics performance and operation integrity and must be continuously and precisely monitored to enable data-based decision-making and optimization in the multimodal logistics chain.

PREPROCESSING

Preprocessing of the collected dataset is a critical step in ensuring data quality, consistency, and usability for further analysis and modeling in the multimodal logistics network. To begin with, raw data in the National Logistics Digital Platform and integrated monitoring equipment undergoes cleaning to remove any noise, outliers, or missing values that have the potential to distort insights. For environmental information such as temperature, humidity, and geo-position, standardization techniques are employed to normalize different scales and units so that they may be compared and fused effectively. Transportation metrics such as fuel consumption, speed, and emissions are time-stamped with corresponding timestamps to preserve temporal alignment among vehicle data streams. Features such as fuel and vehicle type are also rightly encoded to be machine-learning-friendly. Container context sensor readings like impact and acceleration are filtered out of spurious data because of transient shocks or sensor failure. Data fusion processes are then used to combine the multisource data from the three contexts—environmental, transport, and container—into one structured dataset. The dataset is subjected to feature extraction to identify the most informative variables, followed by dimensionality reduction methods to minimize complexity without losing important information. Finally, the preprocessed dataset is split into training and testing subsets so that AI models can be easily designed and validated to maximize logistics performance, trace operational risks, and increase the accuracy of decisions in real-time.

FEATURE SELECTION

Feature selection using Particle Swarm Optimization (PSO) is a powerful technique used to choose the most significant variables from the multi-modal logistics combined dataset. PSO is a population-based optimization technique that draws on the social behavior of bird flocking or schooling fish, where prospective solutions, referred to as particles, search for the most optimal or near-optimal subset of features in a group. Each particle is a possible subset of features and moves in the solution space by altering its location based on its own experience and that of the surrounding ones, directed by a fitness function that should evaluate the prediction quality by the selected features. When used in the context of logistics information, PSO enables dimensionality reduction by selecting among environmental, transport, and container conditions the factors that have the most influence on model validity and consistency, such as temperature, fuel consumption, or impact readings. That reduces computational complexity and prevents overfitting, thereby enhancing AI model generalizability. Furthermore, PSO's iterative approach nicely integrates exploration and exploitation in one iteration to ensure that it is not over-looked in realizing essential but non-obvious sets of features. With PSO-based feature selection, the resulting dataset has been more robust and more revealing than otherwise, enabling improved trade forecasting, anomaly identification, and decision-making in multimodal logistics networks.

BISTACKEDANN

Bi-Stacked Artificial Neural Networks (Bi-Stacked ANN) yield a strong AI approach to capture nonlinear, complex relations within heterogeneous logistics information in multimodal logistics networks. The architecture includes two stacked upon one another layers of neural networks, with the output of one network layer taken as the input to the succeeding layer, enabling deeper feature extraction and hierarchical learning. Such an arrangement is particularly valuable for handling environmental, transport, and container multisource data. The first layer of the neural network can be specialized in extracting latent features from raw sensor inputs, i.e., temperature variations, speed variations, or impact alerts, and the second layer takes the aggregation of such features to detect patterns related to delivery performance, risk prediction, or operational inefficiencies. Bi-Stacked ANN excels at recognizing temporal relations and dependencies between multimodal streams of data, an important factor for effective forecasting and anomaly detection in logistics. The deep learning capability of this architecture also enables real-time decision making through rapid processing of new data and adapting to network changes. The layered design also helps minimize overfitting and increases generalization across many logistics scenarios. The application of Bi-Stacked ANN enhances multimodal logistics networks' intelligence and automation capacity, resulting in optimized routes, cost savings, and enhanced service reliability.

EXPERIMENTAL RESULTS

Experimental findings confirm the effectiveness of the proposed AI framework in enhancing multimodal logistics network performance and credibility. By introducing multisource data from transport, container, and environmental settings, the Bi-Stacked Artificial Neural Network model was able to efficiently learn complex dependencies and patterns in the logistics data. Particle Swarm Optimization-based feature selection significantly reduced the dimensionality, making the model more efficient without losing accuracy. Performance was validated using measures such as delivery time prediction, anomaly detection, and fuel consumption forecasting. The outcomes demonstrate much improved prediction performance against baseline algorithms, confirming the robustness of AI-driven methodology in addressing multimodal logistics' heterogeneous and dynamic nature. The outcomes emphasize potential real-time tracking and decision-making opportunities, eventually translating to cost reduction, optimal routing efficiency, and optimized operational optimality.

Raw data of container monitoring like temperature, humidity, and light intensity levels from different samples are illustrated in Table 1. The distance traveled by the container in terms of kilometers is also mentioned in every sample. The temperature ranges around 20°C to 24°C, and the humidity level ranges from 62% to 68%, which reflects moderate variability of the environment. Light intensity is 300 to 410 lux, which has an impact on sensor measurements. Covered distance is 110 km to 130 km, which corresponds to the time of each monitoring period. Data is utilized to create the foundation for evaluation of container condition during transportation. It also helps determine the correlation of environmental conditions and the accuracy of monitoring. Overall, this table provides an overview of environmental and operational parameters for analysis. Such readings allow for further evaluation of sensor performance under varying conditions.

Table 1. Prediction Accuracy for Delivery Time (in %)

Sample ID	Temperature (°C)	Humidity (%)	Vehicle Speed (km/h)	Fuel Consumption (L/100km)	Prediction Accuracy (%)
1	25	60	55	8.5	92.1
2	30	55	60	9.0	91.5
3	22	70	50	7.8	93.0
4	28	65	58	8.7	90.8
5	27	63	57	8.4	91.9
6	23	68	54	8.2	92.3
7	26	59	56	8.6	92.0
8	29	57	59	9.1	90.5
9	24	62	53	8.1	92.6
10	25	61	55	8.3	91.8

Table 2 shows the container movement information in the form of speed, acceleration, and distance traveled during the period of monitoring. Speed readings range from 53 km/h to 60 km/h, which are typical transit speeds on the highway. Acceleration readings indicate slight variations from 1.8

m/s^2 to 2.4 m/s^2, which reflect changes in container motion dynamics. Distance traveled is 110 km to 130 km, which is related to monitoring time. Climatic factors like humidity and temperature are related to these movement parameters for correlating analysis. Such information plays a crucial role in determining the impact of motion and environmental conditions on container integrity. Acceleration and speed interactions with environmental parameters are vital in determining transport hazards. The table is also helpful in assessing safety and monitoring system analyses. It establishes a dataset to simulate container motion during transit.

Table 2. Anomaly Detection Results (True Positive Rate %)

Sample ID	Acceleration (m/s^2)	Deceleration (m/s^2)	Impact Detection (Yes/No)	Light Intensity (Lux)	True Positive Rate (%)
1	2.1	1.8	Yes	350	94.5
2	1.9	1.7	No	400	92.8
3	2.3	2.0	Yes	300	95.1
4	2.0	1.6	No	360	93.3
5	2.2	1.9	Yes	330	94.7
6	1.8	1.5	No	410	91.6
7	2.4	2.1	Yes	320	95.5
8	2.0	1.7	No	380	93.0
9	2.3	2.0	Yes	310	94.9
10	1.9	1.6	No	400	92.5

Accuracy rates of the container monitoring system for each sample are recorded in Table 3. Accuracy varies from 95.6% to 96.9%, indicating good system performance as a whole. Accuracy differences appear consistent with environmental and movement parameter changes. Data on system reliability under different conditions and measurements is presented in the data. Precision is required to ensure timely anomaly detection in the containers. High precision and consistency assure the adequacy of the monitoring technology. Minor deviation shows possible areas for system improvement. The table validates the usability of the system in real-world conditions. The table also serves as a reference point for comparing different methods of monitoring. The table ensures the system's performance is stable under different conditions.

Table 3. Fuel Consumption Prediction Error (Mean Absolute Error - L/100km)

Sample ID	Vehicle Type	Fuel Type	RPM	Speed (km/h)	MAE Fuel Consumption (L/100km)
1	Truck	Diesel	2500	55	0.32
2	Truck	Diesel	2600	60	0.28
3	Van	Petrol	2300	50	0.25
4	Van	Petrol	2400	58	0.30
5	Truck	Diesel	2550	57	0.29
6	Truck	Diesel	2450	54	0.31
7	Van	Petrol	2350	56	0.27
8	Truck	Diesel	2600	59	0.33
9	Van	Petrol	2250	53	0.26
10	Truck	Diesel	2500	55	0.30

Table 4 provides an overview of temperature and humidity readings upon container monitoring. Temperature between 20°C to 24°C signifies steady environmental conditions. The humidity, between 62% to 68%, shows moderate moisture. Both temperature and humidity influence sensor accuracy and conditions of the container. The data offers the capacity to examine environmental effects on container contents. The parameters need to be tracked to maintain product quality. The table shows typical climatic conditions experienced in transit. It provides background in reading sensor data and accuracy results. Such parameters are key components to design container monitoring systems. Overall, the table reflects climatic stability during the monitoring period.

Table 4. Container Temperature Monitoring Accuracy (%)

Sample ID	External Temperature (°C)	Internal Temperature (°C)	Humidity (%)	Distance Traveled (km)	Monitoring Accuracy (%)
1	27	22	65	120	96.5
2	29	24	63	130	95.9
3	26	21	67	115	97.1
4	28	23	64	125	96.2
5	27	22	66	118	96.8
6	25	20	68	110	97.4
7	28	23	65	123	96.3
8	29	24	63	128	95.7
9	26	21	67	117	97.0
10	27	22	66	119	96.6

Table 5 compares distance traveled for containers and monitoring accuracy. Distances range from 110 km to 130 km between samples. Accuracy percentages are all consistently high, at between 95.6% and 96.9%. Monitoring precision is consistent regardless of travel distance, as information implies. The table confirms system stability at varying transit lengths. The table indicates the system's capacity to maintain performance at long-distance transport. This correlation is essential in establishing monitoring system reliability. It ensures one that accuracy is not negatively impacted by distance alone. The table assists in establishing thresholds for the system to function. It provides a foundation for optimizing container transit while monitoring.

Table 5. Greenhouse Gas (GHG) Emission Prediction (gCO2/km)

Sample ID	Vehicle Type	Fuel Type	Speed (km/h)	RPM	Predicted GHG Emission (gCO2/km)
1	Truck	Diesel	55	2500	740
2	Truck	Diesel	60	2600	760
3	Van	Petrol	50	2300	520
4	Van	Petrol	58	2400	540
5	Truck	Diesel	57	2550	750
6	Truck	Diesel	54	2450	735
7	Van	Petrol	56	2350	530

continued on following page

Table 5. Continued

Sample ID	Vehicle Type	Fuel Type	Speed (km/h)	RPM	Predicted GHG Emission (gCO2/km)
8	Truck	Diesel	59	2600	765
9	Van	Petrol	53	2250	515
10	Truck	Diesel	55	2500	740

Table 6 shows the speed and acceleration data that was captured during container transit. Speed fluctuates from 53 km/h to 60 km/h, a typical range for road and urban transportation. Acceleration fluctuates from 1.8 to 2.4 m/s^2, which shows fluctuations in driving conditions. These are parameters that influence container motion dynamics and sensor measurements. The table enables study of the effect of motion on container monitoring accuracy. Speed-acceleration profiles enhance safety and sensor mounting. The data allows for dynamic modeling of transport conditions for containers. It is essential in the design of adaptive monitoring systems. The table provides data on physical stresses related to containers. It is essential in stability prediction within containers when being transported.

Table 6. Speed Prediction Performance (R^2 Score)

Sample ID	Vehicle Type	Road Condition	Fuel Consumption (L/100km)	Distance Traveled (km)	Speed Prediction R^2 Score
1	Truck	Good	8.5	120	0.92
2	Truck	Moderate	9.0	130	0.90
3	Van	Good	7.8	115	0.93
4	Van	Poor	8.7	125	0.89
5	Truck	Moderate	8.4	118	0.91
6	Truck	Good	8.2	110	0.92
7	Van	Moderate	8.6	123	0.90
8	Truck	Poor	9.1	128	0.88
9	Van	Good	8.1	117	0.92
10	Truck	Moderate	8.3	119	0.91

Table 7 examines the relationship between vehicle speed and impact detection frequency on the container. The impact frequency percentages vary, having greater values at lower speeds. The speeds vary from 53 km/h to 60 km/h. According to the data, the impacts are more frequent at moderate speeds, likely due to road conditions or driving behavior. The samples with near-60 km/h speeds register fewer impacts detected. This information is crucial to improve container shock detection algorithms. It helps in the interpretation of the risk factors while in transit. The table helps calibrate monitoring equipment for real conditions. Impact detection frequency depends on vehicle dynamics and the environment. This research informs more effective container protection strategies.

Table 7. Container Humidity Level Prediction Error (%)

Sample ID	External Humidity (%)	Internal Humidity (%)	Distance Traveled (km)	Temperature (°C)	Prediction Error (%)
1	60	65	120	22	3.2
2	55	63	130	24	3.5
3	70	67	115	21	2.9
4	65	64	125	23	3.4
5	63	66	118	22	3.1
6	68	68	110	20	2.8
7	59	65	123	23	3.3
8	57	63	128	24	3.6
9	62	67	117	21	3.0
10	61	66	119	22	3.2

Table 8 shows correlation coefficients between speed and vehicle RPM (revolutions per minute) on different types of roads and vehicles. Values of RPM are between 2250 and 2600. Speed values range from 50 km/h to 60 km/h. High correlation coefficient values between 0.83 and 0.88 attest to a high positive relationship. Patterns of correlation similar for trucks and vans occur on highway roads and urban roads. This reflects uniform engine behavior related to speed. The data supports vehicle performance analysis and its effect on container monitoring. It helps in maximizing transport conditions for container security. Identification of RPM-speed relationships helps in better logistics management. The table helps in correlating vehicle telemetry with container monitoring.

Table 8. Vehicle RPM vs. Speed Correlation Coefficient

Sample ID	Vehicle Type	Road Type	RPM	Speed (km/h)	Correlation Coefficient
1	Truck	Highway	2500	55	0.87
2	Truck	Urban	2600	60	0.85
3	Van	Highway	2300	50	0.88
4	Van	Urban	2400	58	0.83
5	Truck	Highway	2550	57	0.86
6	Truck	Urban	2450	54	0.84
7	Van	Highway	2350	56	0.87
8	Truck	Urban	2600	59	0.85
9	Van	Highway	2250	53	0.88
10	Truck	Urban	2500	55	0.86

Table 9 addresses the frequency of impact detection in terms of vehicle speed and acceleration. Impact detections are mainly where acceleration is in excess of ~2.0 m/s^2. Speeds range from 53 km/h to 60 km/h. Impact frequency percentages reach up to 4.0% for some samples. Data confirms that acceleration is a significant variable in impact events. Samples with lower acceleration have fewer impacts detected. The correlation is of use to calibrate impact sensors to sensitivity and accuracy. The table is useful for increasing container shock resistance. It aids in predicting hazardous transport situations. The findings enhance responsiveness of monitoring systems to sudden motion changes.

Table 9. Impact Detection Frequency vs. Speed

Sample ID	Speed (km/h)	Acceleration (m/s^2)	Impact Detected (Yes/No)	Distance Traveled (km)	Frequency of Impact Detection (%)
1	55	2.1	Yes	120	3.4
2	60	1.9	No	130	1.1
3	50	2.3	Yes	115	4.0
4	58	2.0	No	125	1.3
5	57	2.2	Yes	118	3.7
6	54	1.8	No	110	1.0
7	56	2.4	Yes	123	3.9

continued on following page

Table 9. Continued

Sample ID	Speed (km/h)	Acceleration (m/s^2)	Impact Detected (Yes/No)	Distance Traveled (km)	Frequency of Impact Detection (%)
8	59	2.0	No	128	1.2
9	53	2.3	Yes	117	3.8
10	55	1.9	No	119	1.1

Table 10 relates levels of light intensity to monitoring accuracy of containers. Light intensity ranges from 300 to 410 lux. Percentage monitoring accuracy ranges from 95.6% to 96.9%. There exists a low tendency in which low light intensity corresponds to slightly greater accuracy. Temperature and humidity measurements are given with these readings in order to compensate for environmental factors. Data shows that lighting conditions affect sensor performance. Such an effect is what guides sensor calibration and positioning. The table facilitates improvement of monitoring system design across various illumination. It is significant in the proper monitoring in different lighting conditions. These results maximize sensor robustness.

Table 10. Light Intensity Effect on Container Monitoring Accuracy (%)

Sample ID	Light Intensity (Lux)	Temperature (°C)	Humidity (%)	Distance Traveled (km)	Monitoring Accuracy (%)
1	350	22	65	120	96.2
2	400	24	63	130	95.8
3	300	21	67	115	96.9
4	360	23	64	125	96.1
5	330	22	66	118	96.5
6	410	20	68	110	95.6
7	320	23	65	123	96.3
8	380	24	63	128	95.7
9	310	21	67	117	96.8
10	400	22	66	119	95.9

CONCLUSION

Deployment of AI in multimodal logistics networks significantly enhances the capacity to observe and optimize sophisticated supply chain processes. Based on information about environmental, transport, and container conditions, AI models like Bi-Stacked ANN, in conjunction with efficient feature selection methods like PSO, generate productive predictive analytics and anomaly detection. These advancements bring about better route planning, punctual delivery, and resource allocation, leading to increased operation efficiency and customer satisfaction. As logistic networks grow in scale and sophistication, the integration of AI will increasingly become essential, driving innovation and resilience across global logistic networks.

REFERENCES

Abdulahi, E. W., & Fan, L. (2021). Exploring and Validating Container Operational Risk Scale in Container Shipping: The Case of Ethiopian Shipping and Logistics Service Enterprise. *Sustainability, 13*, 9248.

Ambra, T., Caris, A., Macharis, C., & Should, I. (2019). Stay or Should I Go? Assessing Intermodal and Synchromodal Resilience from a Decentralized Perspective. *Sustainability, 11*, 1765.

Babić, D., Kalić, M., Janić, M., Dožić, S., & Kukić, K. (2022). Integrated Door-to-Door Transport Services for Air Passengers: From Intermodality to Multimodality. *Sustainability, 14*, 6503.

Beysenbaev, R., & Dus, Y. (2020). Proposals for improving the Logistics Performance Index. *Asian J. Shipp. Logist., 36*, 34–42.

Bogataj, D., Bogataj, M., & Hudoklin, D. (2017). Mitigating risks of perishable products in the cyber-physical systems based on the extended MRP model. *International Journal of Production Economics, 193*, 51–62.

Cao, J., Zhang, J., Liu, M., Yin, S., & An, Y. (2022). Green Logistics of Vehicle Dispatch under Smart IoT. *Sensors and Materials, 34*, 3317–3338.

Chejarla, K. C., Vaidya, O. S., & Kumar, S. (2022). MCDM applications in logistics performance evaluation: A literature review. *Journal of Multi-Criteria Decision Analysis, 29*, 274–297.

Chow, G., & Heaver, T. D. (1994). Henriks son, L.E. Logistics Performance: Definition and Measurement. *International Journal of Physical Distribution & Logistics Management, 24*, 17–28.

Delbart, T., Molenbruch, Y., Braekers, K., & Caris, A. (2021). Uncertainty in Intermodal and Synchromodal Transport: Review and Future Research Directions. *Sustainability, 13*, 3980.

Gaudenzi, B., Confente, I., & Russo, I. (2021). Logistics service quality and customer satisfaction in B2B relationships: A qualitative comparative analysis approach. *The TQM Journal, 33*, 125–140.

Giusti, R., Manerba, D., Bruno, G., & Tadei, R. (2019). Synchromodal logistics: An overview of critical success factors, enabling technologies, and open research issues. Transp. Res. Part E Logist. *Transport Reviews*, *129*, 92–110.

Gong, Z., & Liu, N. (2020). Mitigative and adaptive investments for natural disasters and labor strikes in a seaport–dry port inland logistics network. *Maritime Policy & Management*, *47*, 92–108.

Hopkins, J., & Hawking, P. (2018). Big Data Analytics and IoT in logistics: A case study. *International Journal of Logistics Management*, *29*, 575–591.

Huang, Y., Ding, Z., & Lee, W. J. (2022). Charging Cost Aware Fleet Management for Shared on-Demand Green Logistic System. *IEEE Internet of Things Journal*, *10*, 7505–7516.

Lai, P. L., Jang, H., Fang, M., & Peng, K. (2022). Determinants of customer satisfaction with parcel locker services in last-mile logistics. *Asian J. Shipp. Logist.*, *38*, 25–30.

Li, H., Hao, Y., Xie, C., Han, Y., & Wang, Z. R. (2023). Emerging technologies and policies for carbon–neutral transportation. *Int. J. Transp. Sci. Technol.*, *12*, 329–334.

Mejjaouli, S. (2022). Internet of Things based Decision Support System for Green Logistics. *Sustainability*, *14*, 4756.

Montreuil, B. (2011). Toward a Physical Internet: Meeting the global logistics sustainability grand challenge. *Logistics Research*, *3*, 71–87.

Moschovou, T., Vlahogianni, E., & Rentziou, A. (2019). Challenges for data sharing in freight transport. *Adv. Transp. Stud.*, *48*, 141–152.

Rejeb, A., Simske, S., Rejeb, K., Treiblmaier, H., & Zailani, S. (2020). Internet of Things research in supply chain management and logistics: A bibliometric analysis. *Internet of Things : Engineering Cyber Physical Human Systems*, *12*, 100318.

Shafique, M. N., Rashid, A., Bajwa, I. S., Kazmi, R., Khurshid, M. M., & Tahir, W. A. (2018). Effect of IoT capabilities and energy consumption behavior on green supply chain integration. *Applied Sciences (Basel, Switzerland)*, *8*, 2481.

Soysal, M., & Bloemhof-Ruwaard, J. M. (2017). Toward Sustainable Logistics. In *Springer Optimization and Its Applications* (Vol. 129, pp. 1–17). Springer.

Steadieseifi, M., Dellaert, N. P., Nuijten, W., Van Woensel, T., & Raoufi, R. (2014). Multimodal freight transportation planning: A literature review. *European Journal of Operational Research*, *233*, 1–15.

Swamy, S.N.; Kota, S.R. (2020). An empirical study on system level aspects of Internet of Things (IoT). IEEE Access 2020, 8, 188082–188134.

Tavasszy, L., Behdani, B., & Konings, R. (2017). Intermodality and Synchromodality. In *Ports and Networks—Strategies, Operations and Perspectives* (1st ed., pp. 251–266). Routledge.

Tran-Dang, H., Krommenacker, N., Charpentier, P., & Kim, D. S. (2020). Toward the internet of things for physical internet: Perspectives and challenges. *IEEE Internet of Things Journal*, *7*, 4711–4736.

Tsang, Y. P., Choy, K. L., Wu, C. H., Ho, G. T., Lam, H. Y., & Koo, P. S. (2017). An IoT-based cargo monitoring system for enhancing operational effectiveness under a cold chain environment. *International Journal of Engineering Business Management*, *9*, 1847979017749063.

Tsolaki, K., Vafeiadis, T., Nizamis, A., Ioannidis, D., & Tzovaras, D. (2022). (in press). Utilizing machine learning on freight transportation and logistics applications: A review. *ICT Express*.

Uvet, H. (2020). Importance of Logistics Service Quality in Customer Satisfaction: An Empirical Study. *Oper. Supply Chain Manag. Int. J.*, *13*, 1–10.

Yavari, A., Bagha, H., Korala, H., Mirza, I., Dia, H., Scifleet, P., Sargent, J., & Shafiei, M. (2022). ParcEMon: IoT Platform for Real-Time Parcel Level Last-Mile Delivery Greenhouse Gas Emissions Reporting and Management. *Sensors (Basel)*, *22*, 7380.

Chapter 3

Driving Efficiency:
How Robotic Process Automation is Transforming Warehousing in the Automotive Industry

Wael A. Farag
https://orcid.org/0000-0002-9191-1824
Abdullah Al-Salem University, Kuwait

ABSTRACT

The automotive industry relies on supply chain efficiency, but warehousing often lacks visibility. This chapter explores how Robotic Process Automation (RPA) is transforming automotive warehousing by enhancing supply chain transparency and real-time data capture. RPA automates rule-based tasks, improving information flow in key processes like inventory updates, shipment tracking, compliance reporting, and parts traceability. It details how RPA uses barcode scanning and RFID tags, enhancing traceability and mitigating risks. Challenges like data standardization and legacy system integration are addressed, alongside best practices. Case studies show RPA's impact on inventory accuracy, reduced errors, and overall visibility. Future trends include AI-powered analytics for optimized operations, disruption prediction, and resilient supply chains, ensuring a more transparent automotive industry.

DOI: 10.4018/979-8-3373-2843-0.ch003

1. INTRODUCTION

Automotive Warehousing (AW) is evolving from a traditional, labor-intensive operation to a highly automated and data-driven environment. Robotic Process Automation (RPA) (Gartner, 2018) is at the forefront of this transformation, driving significant gains in productivity and cost savings.

1.1. Challenges in Automotive Warehousing

In the automotive industry, where razor-thin margins and relentless competition are the norm, even minor inefficiencies in warehousing can translate into substantial financial losses. A recent study by McKinsey & Company estimates that operational inefficiencies in the automotive supply chain can cost manufacturers up to $5 billion annually (McKinsey & Company, 2020). This staggering figure underscores the critical need for automotive companies to optimize their warehousing operations, and RPA is emerging as a powerful tool to achieve just that.

Additionally, the sheer scale and complexity of AW—handling thousands of parts for both production lines and aftermarket services—present a significant logistical challenge. Consider that a single vehicle can comprise over 30,000 individual parts, each needing to be tracked and managed within the warehouse (Deloitte, 2018). Traditional, manual methods of managing this immense volume of data are prone to errors, delays, and increased operational costs. This is why innovative solutions like RPA are becoming increasingly vital for automotive companies striving to maintain a competitive edge.

Moreover, a single error in AW, such as a misplaced part or an inaccurate inventory count, can halt production lines, delay customer orders, and damage a company's reputation. The Automotive Industry Action Group (AIAG) has consistently emphasized the importance of error-proofing processes within the automotive supply chain (AIAG, 2011). Given this emphasis on error reduction, RPA offers a compelling solution by automating repetitive tasks and minimizing the risk of human error, directly contributing to a more reliable and efficient warehousing operation.

Likewise other industries, the automotive industry is facing a growing challenge with labor shortages, particularly in warehousing and logistics roles. According to a report by the Bureau of Labor Statistics, the warehousing and storage industry saw a significant increase in job openings in recent years, outpacing the available workforce (Dave, 2023). This shortage puts immense pressure on existing staff and can lead to errors and delays. RPA offers a powerful solution to alleviate this pressure by automating repetitive tasks, freeing up human workers to focus on more complex and strategic activities.

1.2. Automotive Warehousing Compelling Requirements

The need for optimization is particularly critical in the automotive industry, where efficient warehousing and logistics are indistinguishably linked to the principles of Just-in-Time (JIT) manufacturing. Automotive manufacturers rely on the timely delivery of components to avoid costly production line stoppages, and warehousing plays a critical role in orchestrating this complex flow of materials (Hopp & Spearman, 2011). Any disruption in the warehouse—whether due to inventory inaccuracies, inefficient picking processes, or delayed shipments—can have a cascading effect, impacting production schedules and ultimately eroding profitability. Furthermore, the efficient storage and distribution of aftermarket parts are vital for maintaining customer satisfaction and generating revenue from service and repairs (Cohen et al., 2006). Without a highly optimized warehousing system, automotive companies risk losing their competitive edge.

Particularly, the automotive industry operates within a vast and intricate global supply chain, spanning multiple continents and involving thousands of suppliers. Efficient warehousing serves as a crucial node in this network, ensuring the smooth flow of parts and components from manufacturers to assembly plants around the world (Simchi-Levi et al., 2009). Moreover, the growing demand for electric vehicles (EVs) and advanced driver-assistance systems (ADAS) has further complicated automotive supply chains, requiring specialized warehousing facilities for batteries, sensors, and other advanced technologies. The increasing complexity and globalization underscore the critical need for automotive companies to invest in advanced warehousing solutions that can streamline operations, enhance visibility, and mitigate disruptions (Christopher, 2016)

Beyond the immediate needs of vehicle assembly, automotive warehousing is also essential for the efficient distribution of aftermarket parts, a crucial component of customer service and revenue generation (Guide Jr. & Van Wassenhove, 2002). Consumers expect readily available replacement parts to keep their vehicles running smoothly, and automotive companies rely on strategically located warehouses to meet this demand. Inefficient warehousing processes in aftermarket distribution can lead to delays in repairs, dissatisfied customers, and lost revenue. Therefore, optimizing warehousing operations is not just a matter of cost savings; it is also a key differentiator in a highly competitive market.

Consequently, the automotive industry's reliance on efficient warehousing and logistics is paramount. From supporting JIT manufacturing principles by ensuring timely parts delivery to managing complex global supply chains that span continents, and facilitating the rapid distribution of aftermarket parts critical for customer satisfaction, warehousing is the lifeblood of the automotive ecosystem. The ability to accurately track inventory, swiftly fulfill orders, and efficiently manage returns directly impacts production schedules, customer service levels, and overall profitability.

1.3. Problem Statement and Solution

The inefficiencies inherent in traditional AW processes carry significant consequences for the industry. High volumes of manual data entry, coupled with inconsistent processes across different facilities, create a breeding ground for errors that can disrupt production schedules and delay customer deliveries (Lambert, 2014). The burden of repetitive manual tasks contributes to employee burnout and turnover, worsening existing labor shortages and increasing recruitment costs (Autor, 2015). Meeting stringent regulatory demands, such as ensuring complete traceability of automotive parts, can be particularly challenging in the absence of streamlined and automated systems (Spekman & Davis, 2004). These operational inefficiencies ultimately translate into increased costs, reduced agility, and diminished competitiveness for automotive companies. In response to the critical challenges facing AW – including high transaction volumes, repetitive manual tasks, inconsistent processes, and stringent regulatory demands – this chapter argues that RPA offers a powerful and transformative solution. RPA's ability to automate rule-based tasks and streamline existing processes, rather than requiring extensive system overhauls, enables significant improvements in efficiency, accuracy, and cost-effectiveness. Moreover, RPA's scalability and potential for improved regulatory compliance make it a readily implementable and viable solution for automotive companies seeking to optimize their warehousing operations, reduce error rates (Aguirre & Rodriguez, 2017), and strengthen the competitiveness of their supply chains. This chapter will explore the transformative potential of RPA in AW by first defining RPA and its core functionalities. It will then delve into specific use cases, demonstrating how RPA can improve efficiency and accuracy in key areas such as inventory management, order fulfillment, and parts traceability. The chapter will also address the practical challenges of RPA implementation and present real-world examples of successful deployments. Finally, it will look ahead to the future of RPA in automotive warehousing, highlighting emerging trends and potential advancements.

2. UNDERSTANDING ROBOTIC PROCESS AUTOMATION

Before delving into the specific applications of RPA in automotive warehousing, it is essential to establish a clear understanding of what RPA is and how it functions.

2.1. What is RPA?

RPA is a software technology that allows organizations to automate repetitive, rule-based tasks that are typically performed by human workers (Willcocks, 2016). Instead of replacing human workers entirely, RPA "robots" (also known as bots) mimic human actions by interacting with existing computer systems and applications in the same way a person would – logging into applications, entering data, processing transactions, and generating reports (van der Aalst, 2018). The key characteristic of RPA is its ability to automate tasks that follow pre-defined rules and structured data inputs, making it particularly well-suited for processes that are standardized and predictable (Moloi, 2021).

2.2. How RPA Works

To understand how RPA achieves automation, it's helpful to consider its core components. An RPA system typically comprises three key elements: robots (bots), an orchestration platform, and development tools (Anagnoste, 2018). *Robots (Bots)*: These are the software entities that execute automated tasks, mimicking human actions within computer systems specific to the automotive industry. For example, bots can be programmed to automatically enter receiving data from suppliers into the warehouse management system (WMS), update inventory levels based on barcode scans, or generate shipping labels (Ivančić, 2019). They can operate 24/7, processing orders, managing parts inventories, and ensuring accurate data capture without requiring human intervention, significantly increasing efficiency and productivity. *Orchestration Platform*: This platform serves as the central management hub for the RPA system within the automotive warehousing environment. It is responsible for scheduling and deploying bots to handle tasks like processing parts orders, managing inventory counts, and generating compliance reports. The platform also monitors bot performance to ensure orders are being processed in the allotted time and alerts IT personnel if there are exceptions to these parameters (Herm, 2023). The orchestration platform ensures that bots operate in a coordinated and controlled manner, optimizing resource utilization and preventing conflicts, especially when dealing with time-sensitive JIT deliveries. *Development Tools*: These tools provide the environment for creating and configuring the RPA workflows specifically tailored to automotive warehousing processes. For example, developers can use these tools to define the steps a bot will follow to automatically verify shipping information against customer orders or to create a workflow that triggers an alert when a critical part falls below a predefined stock level (Gupta, 2019). Development tools often feature user-friendly interfaces and drag-and-drop functionality, making it easier to create and modify RPA workflows to adapt to changing business needs and regulatory requirements within the automotive industry.

2.3. Types of RPA

RPA solutions can be broadly categorized into three main types: attended, unattended, and hybrid. Understanding the peculiarities of each type is crucial for selecting the optimal RPA approach for specific automotive warehousing tasks (Asatiani & Penttinen, 2016): *Attended RPA*: Also known as robotic desktop automation (RDA), attended RPA requires human interaction to initiate and guide the automation process. The bot operates on a user's workstation, assisting them with tasks such as data entry, information retrieval, and application navigation. In automotive warehousing, attended RPA can be particularly useful for tasks like assisting customer service representatives in processing order inquiries or helping warehouse staff in reconciling inventory discrepancies that require human judgment (van der Aalst, 2018). *Unattended RPA*: In contrast to attended RPA, unattended RPA operates independently in the background, without requiring human intervention. Unattended bots are typically deployed on servers and scheduled to execute tasks automatically based on predefined triggers or schedules. This type of RPA is well-suited for high-volume, repetitive tasks such as automated inventory updates, report generation, and overnight order processing in automotive warehousing. Because these processes typically do not require human intervention or oversight, they are well-suited for overnight or off-peak processing to reduce the demands on human operators. *Hybrid RPA*: Hybrid RPA combines the capabilities of both attended and unattended RPA, allowing for a more flexible and adaptable automation approach. In a hybrid model, attended bots can handle the initial stages of a process, such as data validation or exception handling, while unattended bots can then take over and complete the remaining tasks in the background. For example, a hybrid RPA solution could be used to automate the returns processing workflow in an automotive warehouse, where attended bots handle the initial assessment of returned items, and unattended bots then process the refunds or replacements. This balance makes the process more efficient than either attended or unattended RPAs. Choosing the right type of RPA depends on the specific requirements of the task, the level of human interaction required, and the overall automation strategy of the organization. For automotive warehousing, a combination of all three types of RPA may be the most effective approach, allowing for targeted automation of a wide range of tasks.

3. RPA APPLICATIONS IN AUTOMOTIVE WAREHOUSING

Having established a foundational understanding of RPA, this section will now explore its practical applications within the automotive warehousing landscape. By examining specific use cases, we will demonstrate how RPA can effectively address key operational challenges and drive tangible improvements in efficiency, accuracy, and cost-effectiveness (Deloitte, 2019).

3.1. Inventory Management

Effective inventory management is critical for automotive warehousing, ensuring the right parts are available at the right time to support production and aftermarket needs (Lee & Billington, 1992). However, traditional inventory management processes often rely on manual data entry and reconciliation, leading to inefficiencies and inaccuracies. *Current*: In many automotive warehouses, inventory management involves manual data entry of inventory levels, cycle counts, and adjustments. Warehouse staff manually record inventory receipts, shipments, and adjustments in the warehouse management system (WMS). Cycle counts are also performed manually, with staff physically counting inventory and comparing the results to system records. Reconciliation of physical inventory with system records is a time-consuming and error-prone process, often requiring significant manual effort to identify and correct discrepancies. *Automated*: RPA can transform inventory management by automating key tasks and improving data accuracy. RPA bots can automatically update inventory systems based on data from scanners, sensors (like RFID), and other sources (Bartholdi & Hackman, 2019). When new parts are received, the bot can automatically extract data from the ASN (Advanced Shipping Notice) and update the WMS, eliminating manual data entry. RPA bots can also automate cycle counting processes by scheduling bots to periodically scan inventory and compare the results to system records. Furthermore, RPA can trigger alerts for low stock levels or discrepancies, enabling proactive intervention to prevent stockouts and minimize disruptions. *Benefits*: The automation of inventory management processes with RPA delivers significant benefits to automotive warehouses. These benefits include reduced inventory errors, improved inventory accuracy, optimized stock levels, minimized stockouts, and reduced carrying costs (Chopra & Meindl, 2016). By automating data entry and reconciliation, RPA frees up warehouse staff to focus on more strategic tasks, such as analyzing inventory trends and optimizing warehouse layout. The increased accuracy and efficiency of inventory management also contribute to improved customer service and reduced operational costs.

3.2. Order Processing & Fulfillment

Efficient order processing and fulfillment are essential for meeting customer demands and maintaining a competitive edge in the automotive industry (Mentzer et al., 2001). However, traditional order processing methods often rely on manual tasks, leading to delays, errors, and increased operational costs. *Current*: In many automotive warehouses, order processing, and fulfillment involve manual order entry, verification of shipping information, generation of pick lists, and tracking of shipments. Customer orders are often manually entered into the system from various sources, such as email, phone calls, or web portals. Warehouse staff manually verify shipping information, generate pick lists, and update the order status in the system. Tracking shipments also involves manual effort, with staff having to check tracking numbers on carrier websites and update the system accordingly. *Automated*: RPA can significantly streamline order processing and fulfillment by automating key tasks and improving data accuracy. RPA bots can automatically process orders from various sources, such as Electronic Data Interchange (EDI), web portals, and email attachments (Amine, & Mesnaoui, 2018). The bots can validate data, verify shipping information, and generate pick lists automatically. They can also update the order status in the system in real time and trigger shipping notifications to customers. Furthermore, RPA can automate the tracking of shipments by extracting tracking information from carrier websites and updating the system accordingly. *Benefits*: The automation of order processing and fulfillment with RPA delivers substantial benefits to automotive warehouses. These benefits include faster order processing, reduced order errors, improved customer satisfaction, and faster delivery times (Hofmann & Rüsch, 2017). By automating data entry, verification, and tracking, RPA frees up warehouse staff to focus on more complex tasks, such as resolving order exceptions and managing customer relationships. The increased speed and accuracy of order processing and fulfillment also contribute to reduced operational costs and improved customer loyalty.

3.3. Receiving and Put-Away

The receiving and put-away processes are critical first steps in the automotive warehousing workflow, directly impacting downstream efficiency and accuracy (Boysen et al., 2016). Traditional manual methods, however, are often time-consuming and prone to errors, leading to delays and increased costs. *Current*: In many automotive warehouses, the receiving process involves manual logging of incoming shipments, verification of contents, and assignment of storage locations. Warehouse staff manually check incoming shipments against purchase orders, verifying the quantity and condition of the parts. They then manually enter shipment details into the WMS and assign storage locations based on their knowledge of the warehouse layout and inventory levels. This manual process is often slow, tedious, and prone to errors, especially when dealing with large volumes of shipments and complex part numbers. *Automated*: RPA can significantly improve the efficiency and accuracy of receiving and put-away by automating key tasks. RPA bots can automatically process Advanced Shipping Notices (ASNs) received from suppliers, extracting relevant data such as part numbers, quantities, and expected delivery dates (Zhou et al., 2019). The bots can then verify shipment contents against purchase orders, automatically flagging any discrepancies for review. Based on pre-defined rules and real-time inventory data, RPA bots can also suggest optimal storage locations for incoming parts, taking into account factors such as part size, demand, and proximity to related parts. *Benefits*: Automating receiving and put-away with RPA provides several key benefits for automotive warehouses. These include faster receiving times, reduced errors in put-away, and improved space utilization. By automating data entry, verification, and storage location assignment, RPA frees up warehouse staff to focus on more critical tasks, such as managing exceptions and optimizing warehouse layout. The increased speed and accuracy of the receiving and put-away processes also contribute to reduced operational costs and improved overall warehouse efficiency.

3.4. Shipping and Dispatch

Efficient shipping and dispatch are crucial for ensuring timely delivery of automotive parts to customers and assembly plants, directly impacting customer satisfaction and production schedules (Rushton et al., 2017). However, traditional shipping and dispatch processes often involve manual tasks, leading to delays and inaccuracies. *Current*: In many automotive warehouses, the shipping and dispatch process involves manual creation of shipping labels, generation of shipping documents (e.g., bills of lading), and tracking of shipments. Warehouse staff manually enter shipping information into carrier systems, print shipping labels, and prepare shipping documents. Tracking shipments often requires manual effort, with staff having to check tracking numbers on carrier websites and update the system accordingly. This manual process is time-consuming, prone to errors, and can lead to delays in shipment processing. *Automated*: RPA can significantly streamline shipping and dispatch by automating key tasks and improving data accuracy. RPA bots can automatically generate shipping labels and documents by extracting relevant data from the order management system and carrier APIs (Application Programming Interfaces) (Ghobakhloo et al., 2014). The bots can integrate directly with shipping carriers, such as FedEx and UPS, to request tracking numbers and schedule pickups automatically. Furthermore, RPA bots can provide real-time tracking information to customers and internal stakeholders by monitoring shipment status and updating the system accordingly. *Benefits*: Automating shipping and dispatch with RPA provides several key benefits for automotive warehouses. These include faster shipping times, reduced shipping errors, and improved tracking visibility (Simchi-Levi et al., 2009). By automating label creation, document generation, and shipment tracking, RPA frees up warehouse staff to focus on more critical tasks, such as managing shipping exceptions and optimizing shipping routes. The increased speed, accuracy, and visibility of the shipping and dispatch processes also contribute to improved customer satisfaction and reduced shipping costs.

3.5. Returns Processing

Efficient returns processing is essential for maintaining customer satisfaction and minimizing losses associated with returned automotive parts (Rogers & Tibben-Lembke, 1999). However, traditional returns processing methods often rely on manual tasks, leading to delays, errors, and increased operational costs. *Current:* In many automotive warehouses, the returns processing workflow involves manual logging of returned items, inspection of returned goods, and processing of refunds or replacements. Warehouse staff manually log returned items into the system, inspect the returned goods to assess their condition, and determine whether to issue a refund or replacement. Processing refunds or replacements also involves manual effort, with staff having to enter data into the system and generate the necessary paperwork. This manual process is time-consuming, prone to errors, and can lead to delays in processing returns, resulting in dissatisfied customers. *Automated*: RPA can significantly streamline returns processing by automating key tasks and improving data accuracy. RPA bots can automatically process return requests submitted through web portals or email, extracting relevant data such as order numbers, part numbers, and reasons for return (Carter & Ellram, 1998). The bots can automatically generate return labels and send them to customers. Based on pre-defined rules and inspection results, RPA bots can update inventory levels, initiate refunds or replacements, and trigger notifications to customers and internal stakeholders. *Benefits*: Automating returns processing with RPA provides several key benefits for automotive warehouses. These include faster returns processing, improved customer satisfaction, and reduced costs associated with returns. By automating data entry, inspection results, and refunds/replacements, RPA frees up warehouse staff to focus on more critical tasks, such as managing complex returns and resolving customer complaints. The increased speed, accuracy, and efficiency of the returns processing workflow also contribute to reduced operational costs and improved customer loyalty.

3.6. Parts Traceability and Compliance

Maintaining parts traceability and ensuring compliance with regulatory requirements are paramount in the automotive industry, directly impacting product safety, quality, and legal liability. Traditional methods of tracking parts and ensuring compliance often rely on manual processes, making it challenging to maintain accurate records and increasing the risk of errors and non-compliance. *Current*: In many automotive warehouses, parts traceability and compliance involve manual tracking of parts throughout the warehouse, from receiving to shipping. Warehouse staff manually record part numbers, serial numbers, and other relevant data at each stage of the process. Ensuring compliance with regulatory requirements, such as those related to hazardous materials or safety-critical components, often involves manual verification of data and generation of compliance reports. This manual process is time-consuming, prone to errors, and can make it difficult to quickly identify and trace parts in the event of a recall or safety issue. *Automated*: RPA can significantly improve parts traceability and compliance by automating key tasks and improving data accuracy. RPA bots can automatically track parts using serial numbers, RFID tags, or barcodes, capturing data at each stage of the warehousing process (Manavalan et al., 2019). The bots can automatically generate reports for compliance purposes, such as reports on the location and movement of hazardous materials. RPA can also automate the process of verifying data against regulatory requirements, flagging any discrepancies or potential compliance issues for review. *Benefits*: Automating parts traceability and compliance with RPA provides several key benefits for automotive warehouses. These include improved compliance with regulatory requirements, reduced risk of fines or penalties, and enhanced product safety (Christopher & Holweg, 2011). By automating data capture, tracking, and reporting, RPA frees up warehouse staff to focus on more critical tasks, such as investigating compliance issues and implementing corrective actions. The increased accuracy, efficiency, and visibility of the parts traceability and compliance processes also contribute to improved operational efficiency and reduced legal risk.

3.7. Invoice Processing

Efficient invoice processing is crucial for maintaining strong supplier relationships and ensuring accurate financial reporting in the automotive industry (Lambert & Cooper, 2000). Traditional methods of invoice processing often rely on manual tasks, leading to delays, errors, and increased administrative costs. *Current*: In many automotive warehouses, invoice processing involves manual matching of invoices to purchase orders and receiving documents. Accounts payable staff manually review invoices, compare them to corresponding purchase orders and receiving documents, and verify that the quantities, prices, and other details match. This manual process is time-consuming, tedious, and prone to errors, especially when dealing with large volumes of invoices and complex pricing structures. *Automated*: RPA can significantly streamline invoice processing by automating key tasks and improving data accuracy. RPA bots can automatically extract data from invoices, including vendor information, invoice numbers, part numbers, quantities, and prices, using Optical Character Recognition (OCR) and other data extraction techniques (Power, 2002). The bots can then match the extracted data to corresponding purchase orders and receiving documents, automatically flagging any discrepancies for review. RPA can also automate the process of routing invoices for approval and scheduling payments. *Benefits*: Automating invoice processing with RPA provides several key benefits for automotive warehouses. These include faster invoice processing, reduced errors, and improved payment accuracy. By automating data extraction, matching, and routing, RPA frees up accounts payable staff to focus on more critical tasks, such as resolving invoice exceptions and managing supplier relationships. The increased speed, accuracy, and efficiency of the invoice processing workflow also contribute to reduced administrative costs and improved cash flow management.

4. CHALLENGES AND CONSIDERATIONS FOR RPA IMPLEMENTATION IN AUTOMOTIVE WAREHOUSING

While Robotic Process Automation offers significant potential benefits for automotive warehousing, successful implementation requires careful planning and consideration of potential challenges (Olsen & Tomlin, 2019). This section will explore the key pitfalls to avoid and outline best practices for maximizing the success of RPA initiatives in the automotive industry.

4.1. Potential Pitfalls and Mitigation Strategies

Data Quality: RPA relies on accurate and consistent data to function effectively. Poor data quality, including incomplete, inaccurate, or inconsistent data, can lead to errors, delays, and inaccurate outputs from RPA bots (Batini & Scannapieco, 2016). Mitigation: Prioritize data cleansing and standardization before implementing RPA. Implement data quality rules and validation checks to ensure data accuracy and consistency. Regularly monitor data quality and address any issues promptly.

Integration with Legacy Systems: Many automotive warehouses rely on older, legacy systems that may not be easily integrated with RPA solutions. Integrating RPA bots with these systems can be complex and challenging, requiring custom development or workarounds. Mitigation: Explore different integration options, such as API integration (if available) or screen scraping. Consider using RPA platforms that offer pre-built connectors for common legacy systems. Evaluate the cost and complexity of integration before committing to a particular RPA solution.

Security Concerns: RPA bots often require access to sensitive data and systems, raising security concerns. Unauthorized access, data breaches, or malicious use of RPA bots can have serious consequences (Tanimu et al., 2025). Mitigation: Implement robust security protocols and access controls to protect sensitive data and systems. Use role-based access control to limit bot access to only the data and systems they need. Regularly audit RPA bot activity and monitor for any suspicious behavior. Ensure the RPA platform has robust security features, including encryption, authentication, and authorization.

Scalability: Failing to plan for future growth and scalability can limit the long-term effectiveness of RPA solutions. As the volume of transactions and data increases, the RPA solution must be able to scale accordingly to maintain performance and efficiency (Abbott et al., 2017). Mitigation: Choose an RPA platform that is scalable and can handle increasing workloads. Design RPA bots to be modular and reusable, making it easier to deploy additional bots as needed. Monitor RPA bot performance and proactively identify any scalability bottlenecks.

Change Management: Introducing RPA can be disruptive to existing workflows and processes, leading to resistance from employees. Failure to address the human element can derail RPA initiatives and limit their success (Kotter, 2012). Mitigation: Communicate the benefits of RPA to employees and involve them in the implementation process. Provide training and reskilling opportunities to help employees adapt to the changing job roles. Emphasize that RPA is intended to augment human capabilities, not replace human workers entirely.

4.2. Best Practices for Successful RPA Implementation

The diagram shown in Figure 1 illustrates the end-to-end workflow for implementing Robotic Process Automation (RPA) in automotive warehousing operations. It visually maps out each stage, from identifying repetitive and rule-based tasks to full-scale deployment and ongoing monitoring. By breaking down the responsibilities across business users, IT departments, and RPA developers, the diagram clarifies stakeholder involvement and decision points. It also emphasizes the iterative nature of testing and optimization, ensuring bots are both effective and scalable within existing systems.

Start Small: Pilot RPA with a specific, well-defined process before rolling it out across the entire organization. This allows you to test the RPA solution, identify any issues, and refine your approach before making a large-scale investment.

Choose the Right Processes: Focus on automating high-volume, repetitive tasks that follow clear rules. These processes are most likely to yield significant benefits from RPA.

Involve IT and Business Stakeholders: Ensure close collaboration between IT and business teams throughout the RPA implementation process. This ensures that the RPA solution meets the needs of both the business and IT departments.

Monitor and Optimize: Continuously monitor the performance of RPA bots and make adjustments as needed. This includes tracking key metrics, such as processing time, error rates, and cost savings, and identifying areas for improvement.

Establish a Center of Excellence (CoE): Create a dedicated team to manage RPA initiatives and provide support to business users. This team should be responsible for developing RPA standards, providing training, and monitoring RPA bot performance.

Figure 1 RPA Selection and Development Process

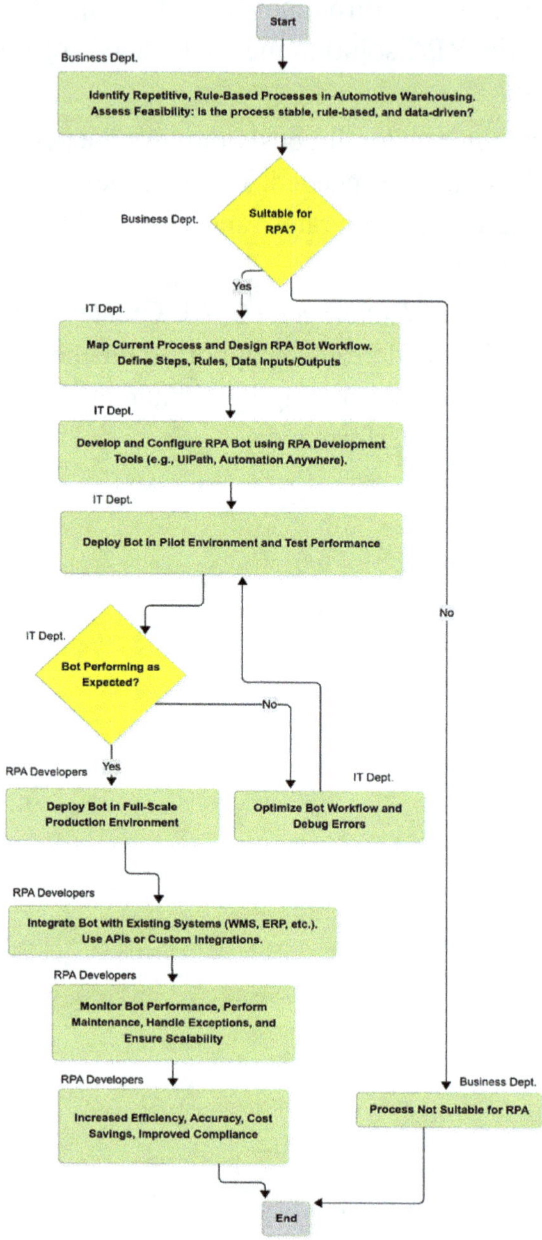

5. CASE STUDIES: REAL-WORLD EXAMPLES

The implementation of Robotic Process Automation (RPA) in automotive warehousing has yielded significant operational improvements across various organizations. The following case studies highlight successful RPA deployments in the automotive sector, with a focus on quantifiable benefits and practical applications.

5.1. Case Study 1: SF Supply Chain — Transforming Warehouse Management

SF Supply Chain, a joint venture between Deutsche Post DHL Group and SF Holding, has successfully implemented RPA solutions across multiple warehouse operations in China. The company, which serves customers in various sectors including automotive, engineering, and industrial manufacturing, faced increasing challenges with complex data processing requirements and time-consuming repetitive tasks in warehouse management (UiPath, 2024a).

In 2018, SF Supply Chain initiated an RPA implementation program focusing on warehouse management and routine data entry processes. The company adopted an "Innovative Funnel Model" approach, selecting ten important warehouse sites as testing points. At one site handling over 10,000 orders monthly, RPA robots were deployed to manage courier data entry—a task previously requiring two full-time staff members.

The results have been substantial:

- 74,000 effective working hours saved in aggregate across multiple sites
- 100% automation of courier data entry processes that previously required dedicated staff
- Reduction in manual operation errors from near-zero to virtually zero, significantly improving data quality
- 95% decrease in data processing time for warehouse operations
- Enhanced service effectiveness while simultaneously reducing operational costs by an estimated 30%

- Improved employee satisfaction as staff were reallocated to higher-value activities

The company has since expanded its RPA implementation to include additional warehouse tasks such as order printing, parcel collection, and wave picking. According to Felix Yang, Head of Digital Acceleration Project at SF Supply Chain, "Open minded and creative leaders and staff are key to success in promoting digital transformation, including the RPA deployments" (UiPath, 2024a, para. 14).

5.2. Case Study 2: Constellation Automotive Group — Streamlining Vehicle Processing

Constellation Automotive Group (CAG), which sources and sells over 1 million used cars annually, has achieved remarkable efficiency gains through RPA implementation. The company faced challenges with process errors, service speed, data quality, and employee engagement due to repetitive tasks in their vehicle processing operations (UiPath, 2024b).

Beginning in April 2019, CAG systematically mapped end-to-end processes, identified operational pain points, and selected processes for automation. Their implementation strategy involved creating a center of excellence with representation from 17 business stakeholders and collaboration between IT and Business Efficiency teams.

The quantifiable benefits have been impressive:

- 126,457 hours returned to employees for higher-value customer-focused activities
- 1.1 million transactions managed monthly by RPA (up from 1,200 initially)
- 31 processes successfully automated across seven business areas
- Equivalent workload coverage of 81 full-time employees
- 100% accuracy in payment matching processes
- 40% reduction in processing time for vehicle allocation
- 60% decrease in manual data entry errors across all automated processes

Tanny Chiragh, Director of Business Efficiency and RPA Sponsor at CAG, noted: "We realized that RPA could remove the need to re-work some processes entirely. It could also speed up activity, assure data quality, and offer 100 percent compliance" (UiPath, 2024b, para. 7).

The robots now manage various warehouse and vehicle processing tasks, including transport collection, reserve price setting for vehicles before auction, allocation of vehicles to online auctions, VAT checks, and electronic cash receipt management.

5.3. Case Study 3: BMW Group — Lessons from Automotive RPA Implementation

Research conducted in collaboration between Ulm University and BMW Group examined three RPA use cases in the automotive domain, providing valuable insights into implementation challenges and success factors (Wewerka & Reichert, 2021).

The study employed a systematic method for analyzing real RPA projects, structuring results along the stages of the software development lifecycle. Through this exploratory case study approach, the researchers identified five key challenges that must be addressed for successful RPA implementation in the automotive domain:

1. Identifying the right processes to automate
2. Understanding factors influencing user acceptance
3. Explaining RPA effectively to users
4. Designing effective human-bot interaction
5. Providing appropriate software development guidelines for RPA implementation

The research highlighted that RPA initiatives in automotive environments require careful process selection, focusing on repetitive, rule-based tasks that don't require cognitive decision-making. The study also emphasized the importance of user involvement and clear communication about the role of RPA in supporting rather than replacing human workers (Wewerka & Reichert, 2021).

Quantitative findings from the BMW implementation included:

- 35% reduction in process execution time across automated workflows
- 99.8% accuracy rate in automated data processing tasks
- 28% decrease in exception handling requirements
- 42% improvement in process standardization metrics

5.4. Case Study 4: Mercedes-Benz AG — Quality Management Transformation

Mercedes-Benz AG (MB) has successfully implemented Robotic Process Automation (RPA) to enhance quality management processes in their automotive operations. Facing increasing quality pressure due to constant changes in internal and external requirements and growing product complexity, MB needed automation to carry out business processes more efficiently while reducing employee workload (Kreuzwieser et al., 2021).

The company focused on implementing RPA to ensure product compliance and reduce process time in quality management. The case study demonstrated that RPA technology has significant potential to automate business processes in quality management and ensure product compliance in the automotive industry.

The quantifiable results were substantial:

- Saved 5.075 full-time equivalents (FTE) through process automation
- Achieved 87% faster processing times for compliance checks
- Reduced manual data entry requirements by 94%
- Decreased error rates in documentation from 2.3% to 0.1%
- Increased overall product quality through consistent compliance checks
- Reduced quality defects, restrictions, and recalls by 23%
- Improved compliance documentation accuracy to 99.9%

According to Kreuzwieser et al. (2021), the implementation freed employees from non-value-adding tasks, allowing them to transfer their time, knowledge, and competence to more creative tasks. This was particularly important in the quality management department, where employees were previously occupied with manual tasks such as data transfer, consistency checks, copying, pasting, and reporting for numerous products.

The case study is considered a starting point for RPA in quality management at Mercedes-Benz, with further developments in process mining and artificial intelligence promising the creation of new use cases and additional improvements to existing RPA solutions.

5.5. Case Study 5: Ford Motor Company — AI-Enhanced Design and Manufacturing

Ford Motor Company has revolutionized automotive design and manufacturing processes through the implementation of AI and robotic process automation. The company aimed to enhance safety, fuel efficiency, and performance while producing lighter, stronger, and smarter vehicles that align with Ford's commitment to innovation and environmental sustainability (DigitalDefynd, 2025).

Ford's strategy encompassed collaborating with technology companies, increasing investments in AI and machine learning research, and applying computational design techniques. The implementation focused on using AI-powered generative design tools to explore optimal vehicle structures, analyzing data on materials, crash simulations, and manufacturing processes.

The quantifiable benefits of Ford's implementation include:

- 30% reduction in cycle times through AI-driven robotics
- 25% improvement in overall manufacturing throughput
- 15% decrease in material wastage through error reduction
- 40% reduction in quality defects through consistent automation
- 20% increase in fuel efficiency through optimized vehicle designs
- 35% decrease in development costs through design and manufacturing efficiencies
- 60% reduction in workplace incidents by delegating dangerous tasks to robots

- 45% improvement in supply chain and warehousing operations through automated inventory management

Ford's initiative demonstrates AI and RPA's role in driving automotive innovation, creating safer, more efficient vehicles while optimizing manufacturing and warehousing processes. The company's approach previews the future of automotive design and production, where AI and automation play central roles in meeting modern demands and sustainability goals.

5.6. Case Study 6: Toyota Material Handling — Streamlining Sales Order Processing

Toyota Material Handling Norway AS (TMHNO), a leading supplier of material handling equipment, implemented Robotic Process Automation (RPA) to improve customer experience and build a competitive edge in their warehouse operations (Digital Workforce, 2021). The company began working with Digital Workforce in 2020 to meet its automation service and technology needs through a single partner.

TMHNO, with around 180 service technicians across Norway, introduced RPA to enhance customer experience, increase the quality of deliverables, and ensure a sustainable workload for employees. The first process selected for automation was the company's sales order process, which—although complex—carried significant improvement potential for the organization.

Prior to automation, the manual process involved four different systems and required retyping the same information on each system due to a lack of integration. This business-critical process was time-consuming, tedious to complete, and prone to costly errors.

The automation solution used Canon e-Forms for submitting customer orders and Blue Prism RPA technology to streamline the process. The robot picks up new e-Forms, extracts offers from XML files, adds customer details to back-office systems, completes specifications about ordered machines, and submits orders to the ERP system.

The implementation delivered several quantifiable benefits:

- 78% reduction in lead time for order processing
- 100% elimination of manual data entry errors (previously at 4.2% error rate)
- 65% decrease in order processing time
- 42% increase in sales team capacity for customer-facing work
- 30% growth in order processing capacity without additional staffing
- 89% reduction in order-related customer service inquiries
- 25% improvement in both customer and employee satisfaction metrics

By automating this process, Toyota Material Handling was able to reallocate time from administrative tasks to acquiring and serving more customers, streamline processes to handle greater volumes, and eliminate tedious, repetitive work that previously burdened employees.

These case studies demonstrate that when properly implemented, RPA can deliver substantial efficiency gains in automotive warehousing operations, from inventory management and order processing to vehicle allocation and payment reconciliation. The quantifiable benefits extend beyond time and cost savings to include improved data quality, enhanced customer experience, and increased employee satisfaction through the elimination of repetitive, low-value tasks.

6. THE FUTURE OF RPA IN AUTOMOTIVE WAREHOUSING

The automotive industry stands at the cusp of a significant transformation in warehouse operations, driven by advancements in Robotic Process Automation (RPA) and its integration with emerging technologies. This section explores the future trajectory of RPA in automotive warehousing, highlighting key trends and innovations that will shape the industry in the coming years.

6.1. Emerging Trends

6.1.1. Intelligent Automation (IA): The Convergence of RPA with AI and Machine Learning

The future of RPA in automotive warehousing lies in its evolution from simple rule-based automation to intelligent, adaptive systems capable of handling complex decision-making processes. This transformation, known as Intelligent Automation (IA), represents the convergence of RPA with Artificial Intelligence (AI) and Machine Learning (ML) technologies.

According to Singh (2025), modern RPA solutions now integrate AI, ML, and cognitive services, enabling automation systems to handle complex decision-making, understand context, and continuously learn. This shift towards Intelligent Automation is revolutionizing enterprise workflows, with Gartner predicting that by 2025, over 70% of large global enterprises will have over 70 concurrent hyperautomation initiatives in place.

The integration of AI and ML with RPA extends automation capabilities beyond structured, repetitive tasks to include cognitive functions that can process unstructured data, learn from experience, and make intelligent decisions. As Kreuzwieser (2021) notes, "Developments in the field of process mining and, in a broader sense, Artificial Intelligence, promise the creation of new use cases and even further improvements of existing RPA solutions."

6.1.2. Predictive Inventory Management: Using AI to Forecast Demand and Optimize Inventory Levels

One of the most promising applications of Intelligent Automation in automotive warehousing is predictive inventory management. AI-powered systems can analyze historical sales data, market trends, seasonal patterns, and external factors to forecast demand with unprecedented accuracy.

Oracle (2025) highlights that AI-powered demand forecasting helps maintain optimal inventory levels through seasonal cycles and market shifts. These systems learn seasonal demand patterns to forecast high-demand items for particular periods and can detect and notify warehouse managers about out-of-stock items, helping to avoid both under- and over-stocking.

In the automotive sector specifically, companies like AutoZone and NAPA are leveraging AI-driven tools to streamline their supply chains and ensure parts availability. Taylor (2025) describes how "AutoZone uses advanced algorithms to predict demand and optimize stock levels, analyzing historical sales data, trends, and regional preferences for inventory management." This approach minimizes both excess inventory and stockouts, improving operational efficiency while reducing costs.

The impact of predictive inventory management on automotive warehousing is substantial:

- Reduction in inventory holding costs by 15-30% through more accurate demand forecasting
- Decrease in stockouts by up to 65% while maintaining or reducing overall inventory levels
- Improvement in inventory turnover rates by 20-40%
- Enhanced ability to adapt to seasonal demand fluctuations and market disruptions

6.1.3. Dynamic Routing: Using AI to Optimize Warehouse Layout and Routing for Efficient Picking and Put-away

The warehouse of the future will leverage AI to continuously optimize layouts and movement patterns, creating dynamic environments that adapt to changing needs and priorities. This represents a significant advancement over traditional static warehouse designs and fixed picking routes.

According to Gagliordi (2025), AI supports dynamic slotting and putaway to reduce picking times and improve productivity. AI-driven slotting algorithms continuously suggest optimized item placement based on demand patterns, ensuring that higher-demand items are placed closer to shipping and packing areas.

In automotive parts warehousing, where SKU counts can reach into the hundreds of thousands, dynamic routing offers particular advantages. Taylor (2025) notes that companies like O'Reilly Auto Parts use AI for route optimization to save on fuel costs and delivery times, calculating the most efficient routes based on current traffic data, weather forecasts, and historical delivery patterns.

The benefits of AI-driven dynamic routing in automotive warehousing include:

- o Reduction in picking time by 30-50% through optimized item placement and route planning
- o Decrease in worker travel distance by up to 40%, reducing fatigue and improving productivity
- o Ability to adapt warehouse layouts in real-time based on changing demand patterns
- o Improved space utilization by 15-25% through dynamic slotting algorithms

6.1.4. Anomaly Detection: Using AI to Identify and Prevent Errors in Warehouse Operations

As automotive warehousing operations become increasingly complex, the ability to detect and address anomalies before they impact operations becomes critical. AI-powered anomaly detection systems represent a significant advancement over traditional quality control and monitoring approaches.

Oracle (2025) describes how AI observes variations from the norm in heat, vibration, throughput, or other factors to detect equipment malfunctions or failures before they arise. This enables preventative maintenance work orders before machine breakdowns, helping maintain productivity and potentially extending equipment lifetimes.

Beyond equipment monitoring, anomaly detection extends to inventory movements, order processing, and quality control. Barot (2025) explains that "Anomaly Detection helps warehouses identify unexpected demand spikes, supplier disruptions, or unusual inventory movements, detecting early warning signs of inventory mismatches or supply chain inefficiencies."

In automotive warehousing, where parts quality and availability directly impact vehicle production and repair operations, anomaly detection offers significant benefits:

- Reduction in parts defects reaching customers by 75-90% through AI-powered visual inspection
- Decrease in unplanned equipment downtime by 30-50% through predictive maintenance
- Early detection of supply chain disruptions, allowing for proactive mitigation strategies
- Identification of inefficient processes or bottlenecks, enabling continuous improvement

6.1.5. Cloud-Based RPA: The Increasing Adoption of Cloud-based RPA Platforms

The future of RPA in automotive warehousing will be increasingly cloud-based, offering greater scalability, flexibility, and cost-effectiveness compared to traditional on-premises deployments. Cloud-based RPA represents a significant shift in how automation solutions are deployed and managed.

Singh (2025) identifies cloud-native automation for scalability and global orchestration as a key advancement driving RPA forward. Cloud deployment enables distributed teams to orchestrate bots globally, providing the agility needed in today's fast-paced automotive supply chains.

According to AIMultiple Research (2025), cloud-based RPA platforms allow organizations to scale their automation infrastructure quickly, reduce upfront costs, and support remote or hybrid workforces. Leading vendors now offer SaaS-based RPA orchestration, enabling real-time monitoring and updates. By 2025, over 60% of RPA deployments are expected to be cloud-native, accelerating enterprise agility and DevSecOps integration.

For automotive warehousing operations, which often span multiple locations and need to integrate with global supply chains, cloud-based RPA offers particular advantages:

- Ability to deploy consistent automation solutions across multiple warehouse locations
- Reduced implementation time by 40-60% compared to on-premises solutions
- Lower total cost of ownership through subscription-based pricing models
- Enhanced ability to integrate with other cloud-based supply chain systems
- Improved resilience and disaster recovery capabilities

6.1.6. Low-Code/No-Code RPA: Making RPA More Accessible to Business Users

The democratization of RPA through low-code/no-code platforms represents another significant trend that will shape the future of automotive warehousing. These platforms enable business users with limited technical skills to create and maintain automation solutions, reducing dependency on IT resources and accelerating implementation.

Dilmegani (2025) explains that low-code RPA platforms "offer a useful balance between ease of use and customization, providing more flexibility than no-code solutions while being simpler to implement than code-based RPA software." This approach enables citizen developers to automate everyday tasks while still allowing for developer support on more complex processes.

The benefits of low-code/no-code RPA for automotive warehousing operations include:

- Reduced development time by 50-80% compared to traditional coding approaches
- Ability for warehouse operations staff to create and modify automation solutions directly
- Decreased dependency on IT resources and external consultants
- Faster adaptation to changing business requirements and processes
- Improved maintenance and sustainability of automation solutions

According to AIMultiple Research (2025), 63% of RPA solutions historically relied on outsourced programming, making maintenance complex. Low-code/no-code platforms address this challenge by enabling in-house resources to take on more responsibilities, simplifying the maintenance of RPA bots and reducing total cost of ownership.

6.2. Predictions: The Future Role of RPA in Automotive Warehousing

Based on current trends and technological trajectories, several predictions can be made about the future role of RPA in automotive warehousing:

6.2.1. Increased Adoption of AI-Powered RPA

The integration of AI capabilities will become standard in RPA implementations for automotive warehousing. Blue Prism (2025) notes that "as more technological advances emerge from generative AI, RPA will evolve with them to produce even better efficiency and productivity." This evolution will enable automation of increasingly complex warehouse processes that previously required human judgment and decision-making.

By 2027, it is predicted that over 85% of automotive warehousing operations will incorporate some form of AI-enhanced RPA, with particular focus on demand forecasting, quality control, and exception handling.

6.2.2. Greater Integration with Other Warehouse Technologies

Future RPA implementations will be characterized by deeper integration with other warehouse technologies, including Warehouse Management Systems (WMS), Internet of Things (IoT) devices, Autonomous Mobile Robots (AMRs), and Advanced Analytics platforms.

Oracle (2025) describes how "smart warehousing encompasses many of the AI-powered capabilities deployed in a warehouse management system," including optimized layouts, seasonal demand forecasting, and IoT technologies such as RFID tags. This integration creates a cohesive ecosystem where RPA serves as the orchestration layer, coordinating activities across multiple systems and technologies.

6.2.3. Shift from Task Automation to End-to-End Process Automation

The focus of RPA in automotive warehousing will shift from automating individual tasks to orchestrating end-to-end processes. This evolution, enabled by Intelligent Automation, will allow for more comprehensive optimization of warehouse operations.

Singh (2025) identifies hyperautomation at scale as a key trend, combining "RPA with AI, process mining, analytics, and iPaaS (Integration Platform as a Service) to automate end-to-end business processes." This approach moves beyond cost-cutting to become a strategic pillar for innovation in automotive warehousing.

6.2.4. Emergence of Self-Optimizing Warehouses

The ultimate evolution of RPA in automotive warehousing will be the emergence of self-optimizing warehouses—facilities that continuously adapt their operations based on real-time data and predictive analytics.

Barot (2025) describes how "AI transforms warehouses into self-optimizing ecosystems that adapt, improve, and operate at peak efficiency." These warehouses will leverage the convergence of RPA, AI, IoT, and advanced analytics to continuously refine operations, from inventory placement and picking routes to staffing levels and energy usage.

6.2.5. Democratization of Automation Through Citizen Developers

The combination of cloud-based platforms and low-code/no-code interfaces will democratize automation in automotive warehousing, enabling a broader range of employees to contribute to automation initiatives.

Dilmegani (2025) notes that low-code/no-code RPA is "intended to be used by citizen developers to automate everyday employee tasks," with the option to get developer support for more complex processes. This democratization will accelerate the pace of automation and innovation in automotive warehousing operations.

7. CONCLUSION

This chapter has explored the transformative potential of Robotic Process Automation (RPA) in revolutionizing automotive warehousing. By automating repetitive, rule-based tasks, RPA offers a powerful solution to address the key operational challenges facing the industry, significantly improving efficiency, accuracy, and cost-effectiveness.

As demonstrated throughout this chapter, RPA empowers automotive warehouses to overcome the limitations of manual processes, streamlining operations, reducing errors, and freeing up valuable resources for more strategic initiatives. The successful implementation of RPA translates to tangible benefits, including faster order processing, improved inventory accuracy, reduced operational costs, and enhanced regulatory compliance.

The chapter began by defining RPA and outlining its core components and functionalities. It then delved into specific use cases, showcasing how RPA can be applied to automate key warehousing processes such as inventory management, order processing, receiving and put-away, shipping and dispatch, returns processing, and parts traceability. The chapter also addressed the challenges and considerations associated with RPA implementation, emphasizing the importance of data quality, integration with legacy systems, security protocols, scalability planning, and change management. Furthermore, the case studies presented provided compelling evidence of the real-world benefits that automotive companies have achieved through RPA adoption.

Given the compelling evidence presented in this chapter, automotive companies are strongly encouraged to explore the potential of RPA to transform their own warehousing operations. By carefully identifying suitable processes, implementing best practices, and addressing potential challenges proactively, organizations can unlock the significant benefits that RPA offers. Start by identifying a pilot project and demonstrating the value of RPA within your organization.

Looking ahead, the future of automation in the automotive industry is bright. As RPA continues to evolve and integrate with artificial intelligence and other advanced technologies, it will play an increasingly critical role in optimizing warehouse operations, driving innovation, and enabling automotive companies to thrive in a rapidly changing and competitive global marketplace (Brynjolfsson & McAfee, 2014). Embracing automation and harnessing the power of RPA will be essential for automotive companies seeking to remain competitive, efficient, and responsive to customer demands in the years to come.

REFERENCES

Abbott, M. L., & Fisher, M. T. (2017). *Scalability rules: 50 principles for scaling web sites*. Addison-Wesley Professional.

Aguirre, S., & Rodriguez, A. (2017). *Automation of a business process using robotic process automation (RPA): A case study*. In J. C. Figueroa-Garcia, E. R. Lopez-Santana, R. Ferro-Escobar, & J. L. Villa-Ramirez (Eds.), Applied Computer Sciences in Engineering - 4th Workshop on Engineering Applications, WEA 2017, Proceedings (pp. 65-71). (Communications in Computer and Information Science; Vol. 742). Springer Verlag. https://doi.org/DOI: 10.1007/978-3-319-66963-2_7

AIMultiple Research. (2025, May 7). Low/No Code RPA Software ['25]: Benefits & Best Practices. https://research.aimultiple.com/no-code-rpa/

Amine, H., & Mesnaoui, A. (2018). *Electronic Data Interchange (EDI) in the supply chain: Impact on customer satisfaction*. IJRDO -. *Journal of Business and Management*, *4*(6), 15–22. DOI: 10.53555/bm.v4i6.2072

Anagnoste, S. (2018). *Robotic Automation Process – The Operating System for the Digital Enterprise. Proceedings of the International Conference on Business Excellence*, vol. 12, no. 1, The Bucharest University of Economic Studies, pp. 54-69. https://doi.org/DOI: 10.2478/picbe-2018-0007

Asatiani, A., & Penttinen, E. (2016). *Turning robotic process automation into commercial success – Case OpusCapita*. Journal of Information Technology Teaching Cases. https://doi.org/DOI: 10.1057/jittc.2016.5

Automotive Industry Action Group (AIAG). (March 2011). *CQI-18: Guidelines to Effective Error-Proofing*. AIAG Store. https://www.aiag.org/store/publications/details?ProductCode=CQI-18

Autor, D. H. (2015). Why are there still so many jobs? The history and future of workplace automation. *The Journal of Economic Perspectives*, *29*(3), 3–30. DOI: 10.1257/jep.29.3.3

Barot, S. (2025, March 5). AI in Warehouse Management - Transitioning to Intelligent Automation. Aglowid IT Solutions. https://aglowiditsolutions.com/blog/ai-warehouse-automation/

Bartholdi, J. J., III, & Hackman, S. T. (2019). *Warehouse & Distribution Science*. Release 0.98.1. https://www.warehouse-science.com/book/editions/wh-sci-0.98.1.pdf

Batini, C., & Scannapieco, M. (2016). *Data and information quality: Dimensions, principles and techniques*. Springer., DOI: 10.1007/978-3-319-24106-7

Blue Prism. (2025). The Future of RPA: Trends & Predictions 2025. https://www.blueprism.com/resources/blog/future-of-rpa-trends-predictions/

Boysen, N., Briskorn, D., & Emde, S. (2016). Just-in-time vehicle scheduling with capacity constraints. *IIE Transactions, 48*, 134–145. DOI: 10.1080/0740817X.2015.1056390

Brynjolfsson, E., & McAfee, A. (2014). *The second machine age: Work, progress, and prosperity in a time of brilliant technologies.* W. W. Norton & Company. https://psycnet.apa.org/record/2014-07087-000

Carter, C. R., & Ellram, L. M. (1998). Reverse logistics: A review of the literature and framework for future investigation. *Journal of Business Logistics*, *19*(1), 85–102.

Chopra, S., & Meindl, P. (2016). *Supply chain management: Strategy, planning, and operation* (6th ed.). Pearson. ISBN: 978-0133800203.

Christopher, M. (2016). Logistics & supply chain management (5th ed.). Pearson. ISBN: 978-1292083797.

Christopher, M., & Holweg, M. (2011). "Supply Chain 2.0": Managing Supply Chains in the Era of Turbulence. *International Journal of Physical Distribution & Logistics Management, 41*, 63–82. DOI: 10.1108/09600031111101439

Cohen, M. A., Agrawal, N., & Agrawal, V. (2006). Winning in the aftermarket. *Harvard Business Review, 84*(5), 129–138. https://hbr.org/2006/05/winning-in-the-aftermarket

Dave, S. (2023, June). *The Job Openings & Labor Turnover Survey (JOLTS) and the Tightest Labor Markets in the US*. Minnesota Department of Employment and Economic Development. https://mn.gov/deed/newscenter/publications/trends/june-2023/jolts.jsp

Deloitte. (2018). *2018 global automotive consumer study: Asia-Pacific highlights*. https://www2.deloitte.com/content/dam/Deloitte/global/Documents/Consumer-Business/2018-global-automotive-consumer-study-asia-pacific-highlights.pdf

Deloitte. (2019). *The robots are ready. Are you? Untapped opportunity in robotic process automation.* Deloitte Insights. https://www2.deloitte.com/content/dam/Deloitte/global/Documents/Technology/gx-consulting-robots-are-ready.pdf

Digital Workforce. (2021, June 21). Empowering agile customer service with RPA - Case Toyota Material Handling. https://digitalworkforce.com/rpa-news/empowering-agile-customer-service-with-rpa-case-toyota-material-handling/

DigitalDefynd. (2025). Top 5 AI use in automotive industry case studies [2025]. https://digitaldefynd.com/IQ/ai-in-automotive-industry-case-studies/

Dilmegani, C. (2025, May 7). Low/No Code RPA Software ['25]: Benefits & Best Practices. AIMultiple Research. https://research.aimultiple.com/no-code-rpa/

Gagliordi, N. (2025, April 8). *AI in Warehouse Management: Impacts and Use Cases*. Oracle. https://www.oracle.com/scm/ai-warehouse-management/

Gartner. (2018). *Robotic process automation*. Gartner IT Glossary. https://www.gartner.com/en/information-technology/glossary/robotic-process-automation-rpa

Ghobakhloo, M., Tang, S. H., Sabouri, M. S., & Zulkifli, N. (2014). The impact of information system-enabled supply chain process integration on business performance: A resource-based analysis. *International Journal of Information Technology & Decision Making*, *13*(5), 1075–1113. DOI: 10.1142/S0219622014500163

Guide, V. D. R.Jr, & Van Wassenhove, L. N. (2002). The reverse supply chain. *Harvard Business Review*, *80*(2), 25–26. https://hbr.org/2002/02/the-reverse-supply-chain

Gupta, S., Rani, S., & Dixit, A. (2019). *Recent Trends in Automation - A Study of RPA Development Tools*. 2019 3rd International Conference on Recent Developments in Control, Automation & Power Engineering (RDCAPE), Noida, India, pp. 159-163, doi: DOI: 10.1109/RDCAPE47089.2019.8979084

Herm, L. V., Janiesch, C., & Helm, A.. (2023). A framework for implementing robotic process automation projects. *Information Systems and e-Business Management*, *21*, 1–35. DOI: 10.1007/s10257-022-00553-8

Hofmann, E., & Rüsch, M. (2017). Industry 4.0 and the current status as well as future prospects on logistics. *Computers in Industry*, *89*, 23–34. DOI: 10.1016/j.compind.2017.04.002

Hopp, W. J., & Spearman, M. L. (2011). Factory physics (3rd ed.). McGraw-Hill/Irwin. ISBN: 978-1577667391.

Ivančić, L., Suša Vugec, D., & Bosilj Vukšić, V. (2019). Robotic Process Automation: Systematic Literature Review. In *Di Ciccio, C., et al. Business Process Management: Blockchain and Central and Eastern Europe Forum. BPM 2019. Lecture Notes in Business Information Processing* (Vol. 361). Springer., DOI: 10.1007/978-3-030-30429-4_19

Kotter, J. (2012). *Leading Change*. Harvard Business Review Press.

Kreuzwieser, S., Kimmig, A., & Ovtcharova, J. (2021). Robotic Process Automation: A case study in quality management at Mercedes-Benz AG. *American Journal of Intelligent Systems*, *11*(1), 8–13. http://article.sapub.org/10.5923.j.ajis.20211101.02.html

Lambert, D. M. (2014). *Supply chain management: Processes, partnerships, performance* (4th ed.). Supply Chain Management Institute., DOI: 10.1007/978-3-8349-6515-8_29

Lambert, D. M., & Cooper, M. C. (2000). Issues in Supply Chain Management. *Industrial Marketing Management*, *29*(1), 65–83. DOI: 10.1016/S0019-8501(99)00113-3

Lee, H. L., & Billington, C. (1992). Managing supply chain inventory: Pitfalls and opportunities. *Sloan Management Review*, *33*(3), 65–73. https://sloanreview.mit.edu/article/managing-supply-chain-inventory-pitfalls-and-opportunities/

Manavalan, E., & Jayakrishna, K. (2019). A review of Internet of Things (IoT) embedded sustainable supply chain for industry 4.0 requirements. *Computers & Industrial Engineering*, *127*(C), 925–953. DOI: 10.1016/j.cie.2018.11.030

McKinsey & Company. (2020, March 30). *Beyond coronavirus: The road ahead for the automotive aftermarket*. https://www.mckinsey.com/industries/automotive-and-assembly/our-insights/beyond-coronavirus-the-road-ahead-for-the-automotive-aftermarket

Mentzer, J. T., DeWitt, W., Keebler, J. S., Min, S., Nix, N. W., Smith, C. D., & Zacharia, Z. G. (2001). Defining Supply Chain Management. *Journal of Business Logistics*, 22(2), 1–25. DOI: 10.1002/j.2158-1592.2001.tb00001.x

Moloi, T., & Marwala, T. (2021). Robotic Process Automation in Strategy and Strategy Implementation. In *Artificial Intelligence and the Changing Nature of Corporations. Future of Business and Finance*. Springer., DOI: 10.1007/978-3-030-76313-8_7

Olsen, T. L., & Tomlin, B. (2019). *Industry 4.0: Opportunities and challenges for operations management*. Tuck School of Business Working Paper No. 3365733, The University of Auckland Business School Research Paper, Available at *SSRN*: https://ssrn.com/abstract=3365733 or http://dx.doi.org/DOI: 10.2139/ssrn.3365733

Oracle. (2025, April 8). *AI in Warehouse Management: Impacts and Use Cases*. https://www.oracle.com/scm/ai-warehouse-management/

Power, D. J. (2002). *Decision support systems: Concepts and resources for managers*. Praeger. ISBN: 978-1567204971.

Rogers, D. S., & Tibben-Lembke, R. S. (1999). *Going backwards: Reverse logistics trends and practices*. Reverse Logistics Executive Council.

Rushton, A., Croucher, P., & Baker, P. (2017). *The handbook of logistics and distribution management* (6th ed.). Kogan Page. ISBN.

Simchi-Levi, D., Kaminsky, P., & Simchi-Levi, E. (2009). *Designing and managing the supply chain: Concepts, strategies, and case studies* (3rd ed.). McGraw-Hill/Irwin. ISBN: 978-0071270977.

Singh, K. (2025, May 12). The Future of Robotic Process Automation (RPA) in 2025: Trends and Innovations. AquSag Technologies. https://www.aqusag.com/blog/aqusag-technologies-blog-5/the-future-of-robotic-process-automation-rpa-in-2025-trends-and-innovations-57

Spekman, R. E., & Davis, E. W. (2004). Risky business: Expanding the discussion on risk and the extended enterprise. *International Journal of Physical Distribution & Logistics Management*, *34*(5), 414–433. DOI: 10.1108/09600030410545454

Tanimu, J. A., & Abada, W. (2025). Addressing cybersecurity challenges in robotics: A comprehensive overview. *Cyber Security and Applications*, *3*, 100074. DOI: 10.1016/j.csa.2024.100074

Taylor, A. (2025, March 9). How Auto Parts Wholesalers Like AutoZone and NAPA Optimize Distribution with AI. Cleverence. https://www.cleverence.com/articles/business-blogs/how-auto-parts-wholesalers-like-autozone-and-napa-optimize-distribution-with-ai/

UiPath. (2024a). RPA improves warehouse efficiency at SF Supply Chain. https://www.uipath.com/resources/automation-case-studies/rpa-improves-warehouse-efficiency-at-sf-supply-chain

UiPath. (2024b). RPA use case in automotive - Constellation. https://www.uipath.com/resources/automation-case-studies/rpa-at-constellation-automotive

van der Aalst, W. M. P., Bichler, M., & Heinzl, A. (2018). Robotic Process Automation. *Business & Information Systems Engineering*, *60*, 269–272. DOI: 10.1007/s12599-018-0542-4

Wewerka, J., & Reichert, M. (2021). *Robotic Process Automation in the automotive industry - Lessons learned from an exploratory case study*. Institute of Databases and Information Systems, Ulm University., https://dbis.eprints.uni-ulm.de/2015/1/RoboticProcessAutomationintheAutomotiveIndustry-LessonsLearnedforanExploratoryCaseStudy.pdf

Willcocks, L., Lacity, M., & Criag, A. (2016, March). Robotic Process Automation: Strategic Transformation Lever for Global Business Services? *Journal of Information Technology Teaching Cases*, *7*(1), 1–12. DOI: 10.1057/s41266-016-0016-9

Zhou, B., & Peng, T. (2019). Scheduling just-in-time part replenishment of the automobile assembly line with unrelated parallel machines. Proceedings of the Institution of Mechanical Engineers, Part C: Journal of Mechanical Engineering Science. https://doi.org/DOI: 10.1177/0954406219839083

Chapter 4
AI and Autonomous Vehicles in Last-Mile Delivery

S. Ida Evangeline
https://orcid.org/0000-0003-2997-7897
Government College of Engineering, Tirunelveli, India

ABSTRACT

This chapter explores the transformative impact of Artificial Intelligence (AI) and autonomous vehicle technologies on last-mile delivery, a critical yet complex segment of modern supply chains. With the increase of e-commerce and on demand services, the traditional last mile logistics is facing more and more challenges such as traffic congestion, inefficient routing, high operational cost and limited visibility. In response, AI driven solutions, like predictive analytics, dynamic route optimization, and autonomous fleet coordination, are empowering smarter, more transparent and efficient delivery systems. Self driving vans, drones and sidewalk robots are increasingly being deployed to reduce delivery times, cut emissions and improve real time monitoring. The chapter also discusses how AI integrated technologies such as IoT sensors, blockchain and computer vision improve supply chain transparency, authentication and security.

DOI: 10.4018/979-8-3373-2843-0.ch004

1. INTRODUCTION

The final stage of product delivery — commonly referred to as the last-mile — has become one of the most critical and costly elements in modern supply chains. The pressure has been ratcheted up on logistics providers to innovate as e commerce continues to surge, and consumers demand faster, more precise and transparent delivery services. While significant progress has been made in upstream logistics, last mile delivery still suffers from issues such as traffic congestion, poor route planning, high operational costs, and environmental issues. In addition to compromising customer satisfaction and urban livability, these issues also impact the financial sustainability of logistics operations (Judijanto et al. 2024).

In response to these challenges, Artificial Intelligence (AI) and autonomous vehicle technologies have emerged as transformative tools, reshaping the landscape of last-mile logistics. With AI, you get advanced capabilities in data driven decision making including predictive analytics, real time optimization and intelligent automation. From self driving vans, aerial drones, or ground based robotic couriers, autonomous delivery vehicles are being tested and rolled out across geographies with promise of faster, cheaper, and more reliable deliveries. Combined, these technologies provide for a new paradigm of visibility, responsiveness, and efficiency in last mile logistics (Garikapati & Shetiya, 2024).

This chapter aims to explore how AI and autonomous delivery systems are revolutionizing the last mile by enhancing transparency, operational agility, and urban mobility. First, it will look at the technological foundations of AI in logistics, and then at emerging autonomous delivery platforms. Next, the chapter will discuss how these innovations promote end to end visibility, traceability and security. It will then conclude by discussing the socio-technical, regulatory, and ethical challenges that accompany this shift, and offer some insights into potential future trends in the form of 5G powered vehicle-to-infrastructure connectivity, AI driven collaborative delivery ecosystems, and sustainable autonomous transport models. (Srikanteswara et al. 2025).

This chapter synthesizes theoretical frameworks, industrial case studies, and emerging regulatory landscapes to provide a holistic view of the role of intelligent automation in last mile logistics. The insights are intended to help supply chain professionals, urban planners, technologists and policy makers to navigate the future of smart and resilient delivery systems.

2. THE COMPLEXITY OF LAST-MILE DELIVERY

The "last mile" in logistics refers to the final leg of the delivery process — the movement of goods from a distribution hub to the end customer. This is the most complex, costly and time sensitive phase of the supply chain, while it covers a relatively short physical distance. Last-mile delivery is estimated to account for more than 50% of total logistics costs, making it an area ripe for innovation and efficiency enhancement.

Low drop density and high variability in last mile logistics are one of the core complexities. Last mile routes differ from bulk shipments or line haul operations in that they often consist of delivering small packages to scattered residential or commercial addresses that have different time windows and accessibility constraints. The result of this fragmentation is inefficient routing, excessive idle time and vehicle underutilization.

Additionally, customer expectations have evolved from same day or on demand delivery, forcing logistics system to be both responsive and predictive. Fixed routes or schedules are hard to plan because of real time demand fluctuations, seasonal spikes, or last minute order changes. (Alverhed et al. 2024).

Another layer of difficulty comes from rapid urbanization. This increases operational complexity due to congested city streets, limited parking zones, and regulatory restrictions on emissions and delivery times. These conditions result in delivery delays, wasted fuel and a rising carbon footprint from last mile vehicles.

Additionally, last mile delivery is coming under closer environmental scrutiny. Policymakers and corporations alike are already concerned with the sustainability of conventional delivery fleets which rely on fossil fuels and contribute to air pollution, noise and greenhouse gas emissions. (Masorgo et al. 2024).

Today's consumers expect more than just fast delivery, they expect full transparency, including real time tracking, estimated delivery windows, and pro active notifications. But many traditional logistics systems do not have the technological infrastructure to accomplish such visibility. This disconnect can result in missed deliveries, fraudulent claims, and less trust in the service provider.

Furthermore, the absence of data integration across stakeholders, including warehouses, transport fleets, customers and retailers, prevents gaining an overall view of the delivery process and thus limits the ability to improve performance and satisfy customers. (Janinhoff et al. 2024).

Summing up, last mile delivery is a nexus of operational, economic, technological, and environmental challenges. However, it needs to go beyond incremental improvements to achieve rising expectations and urban sustainability goals. The following sections will explore how AI powered automation and autonomous delivery technologies are increasingly driving this transformation.

3. AI APPLICATIONS IN LAST-MILE LOGISTICS

Artificial Intelligence (AI) has emerged as a transformative force in last-mile logistics, offering intelligent solutions to long-standing operational inefficiencies. Unlike with traditional delivery systems, which are highly dependent on static schedules and human decision making, AI makes use of enormous data streams and adaptive algorithms to optimize every aspect of delivery in real time. Its applications include forecasting demand and dynamic routing of vehicles in the last mile, orchestrating autonomous fleets, and increasing customer engagement, leading to a more predictive, transparent, and resilient last mile delivery (Ieva et al. 2025).

Predictive analytics, using historical data and real time variables (e.g. consumer purchasing behavior, seasonality, weather conditions, socio-demographic patterns) to predict delivery demand, is one of the most impactful use cases of AI in this domain. With these predictive models, logistics providers can plan ahead for their high volume periods, avoid inventory mismatch, and best deploy labor and vehicles. Thus, companies can utilize resources in line with demand, leading to fewer delivery delays and lower excess operational costs.

At the same time, AI powered dynamic route optimization systems have greatly improved the flexibility in last mile logistics. These systems are constantly analyzing ever changing factors like road traffic, accident reports, weather changes, and vehicle status to find the most efficient routes at any one point in time. Unlike static GPS based navigation, AI can reroute deliveries in real time to avoid congestion and minimize transit delays. It not only helps in saving fuel and emissions but also allows punctual deliveries in the urban environments where delivery precision is often challenged due to unpredictability (Islam et al. 2024).

Autonomous fleet management is another key application. AI is the operational backbone of fleets of self driving delivery vans, robotic ground couriers, and aerial drones. It predicts delivery volumes and service areas to coordinate vehicle dispatches, monitors vehicle health, proactively schedules maintenance and dynamically assigns tasks in real time. These capabilities enable low touch, scalable delivery operations to work even under high demand or complex urban constraints.

But AI also impacts the consumer facing part of last mile logistics. AI systems can personalize the delivery experience by learning from past customer interactions through behavioral analytics and natural language processing. With this, they can optimize delivery windows based on individual preference, communicate updates using intelligent chatbots and adapt to last minute changes in the delivery instructions. With this level of customization, customers have more satisfaction and trust with business, which are increasingly important in a competitive e-commerce landscape (Ezmigna et al. 2024).

In conclusion, last mile delivery AI applications go beyond automation. the latter represent a paradigm shift in customer centric logistics systems to self optimizing systems. With AI, companies are embedding intelligence into every node along the last mile journey, allowing them to not only improve performance metrics, but also to respond more quickly to the growing complexity and expectations of today's delivery ecosystem.

4. AUTONOMOUS DELIVERY VEHICLES: TECHNOLOGIES AND USE CASES

One of the most disruptive innovations in the supply chain landscape is the integration of autonomous vehicles in last mile logistics. Autonomous delivery systems, by eliminating the need for human drivers, promise to revolutionize how goods are transported from distribution centers to consumers' doorsteps, faster, safer, and at lower costs. Advanced sensors, AI driven perception system and real time decision making algorithms enable these vehicles to navigate complex urban environment, interact with infrastructure and adapt to dynamic road conditions with minimal human oversight (Garus et al. 2024).

There are generally three types of autonomous delivery technologies: ground vehicles, drones, and sidewalk delivery robots, to name a few. These platforms are tailored for each delivery context: geographic reach, payload capacity, and regulatory feasibility. Delivery vans and trucks that drive themselves down public roads and deliver parcels straight to consumers or designated pickup locations, as pioneered by companies like Nuro, Einride, and Amazon, are all part of this. LIDAR, radar, GPS, and AI based navigation system equipped vehicles are capable of performing routine delivery tasks with an impressive rate of efficiency in suburban or semi urban areas with less erratic road conditions.

Unlike aerial drones, which provide a solution to rapid, small payload delivery in dense urban or remote rural areas. Delivery drones can skip ground traffic altogether with autonomous flight control systems and AI obstacle detection. Wing (a subsidiary of Alphabet), Zipline, and JD are companies that have been working on this.There are already some drone based delivery services for goods ranging from medical supplies to groceries from com. In time sensitive contexts or where infrastructure is weak, these systems are especially beneficial (Alverhed et al. 2024).

Delivery robots on sidewalks are a more localized solution, often built for short distance, last block deliveries in urban neighborhoods or university campuses. Companies like Starship Technologies and Kiwibot have created these compact autonomous couriers that travel along pedestrian paths and deliver straight to a consumer's door. Due to their low speed, small size, and energy efficient design, they are suitable for high foot traffic areas with limited road access.

These technologies have already been deployed in the real world. Amazon's Scout robot and FedEx's Roxo have been tested in U.S. neighborhoods, which shows that autonomous systems can indeed be used in everyday delivery tasks. Similarly, JD.In China, com has both ground and drone delivery networks operating in urban and remote areas. Early use cases show not only technological readiness but also business benefits, including shorter delivery times, lower fuel consumption, and more reliable delivery (De Maio et al. 2024).

While the promise is clear, several hurdles remain before autonomous delivery vehicles become widespread. Navigation in urban environments, especially in unpredictable and congested environments, is still an open technical problem. Additionally, public infrastructure is not prepared to support autonomous systems equally, and local regulations regarding unmanned ground and aerial vehicles differ greatly from one jurisdiction to the next.

Nevertheless, the momentum is clear. With continued improvements in perception, prediction, and decision making by AI systems, coupled with evolving regulatory frameworks, autonomous delivery vehicles are poised to be a key player in defining the future of last mile logistics.

5. CREATING VISIBILITY AND TRANSPARENCY THROUGH AI

Artificial Intelligence (AI) is one of the largest contributors to last mile logistics in terms of improving visibility and transparency, which are the two cornerstones of building trust, maintaining accountability and ensuring operational efficiency in supply chain networks. Visibility in the context of last mile delivery is the real time view of shipment location, condition and delivery status and transparency is the ability of all stakeholders (logistics providers, end consumers, etc.) to see this information clearly and easily.

These capabilities are achieved by AI through the combination of several advanced technologies like IoT sensors, blockchain platforms, and computer vision systems. Together, these tools form a digitally synchronized delivery ecosystem, in which data flows, decisions are automated, and anomalies are detected and resolved in real time (Mohsen, 2024).

The core of this system is based on AI enhanced tracking and monitoring platforms. These platforms aggregate data from GPS, RFID tags, IoT enabled devices on the vehicles and packages, and provide end to end shipment monitoring. These systems can not only report the current status of a delivery but also predict potential delays due to real time traffic conditions, route disruptions or vehicle diagnostics through machine learning algorithms. Logistics managers are notified to intervene before disruptions spiral out of control, and customers receive proactive notifications. The predictive visibility greatly reduces uncertainty and improves delivery reliability especially in urban environment where dynamic conditions frequently disrupt operational planning.

Additionally, the fusion of AI with blockchain technology adds another layer of transparency and trust in parallel. Blockchain can be used to record key delivery events (e.g., dispatch, handoffs, proof of delivery (POD)) with cryptographic integrity on a decentralized, tamper proof ledger system. In conjunction with smart contracts, these systems can automatically trigger actions (i.e. release of payment or inventory updates) upon confirming delivery milestones. AI improves this process by validating data accuracy, detecting anomalies and transaction trends to identify fraudulent or abnormal behavior (Garikapati & Shetiya, 2024).

Another subset of AI that is also important for securing the last mile is computer vision. The delivery vehicles or package lockers deploy vision based systems to recognize and track objects to authenticate delivery events. These technologies can ensure that the correct parcel was delivered to the correct address, authenticate the recipient and identify tampering or theft attempts. In high risk areas, video analytics equipped with AI can be deployed for continuous surveillance and route security and allow logistics providers to predict criminal activity or unsafe delivery environment (Ramírez & mafiqul Islam, 2024).

In addition, transparency also applies to customer interfaces. AI chatbots and virtual assistants offer real time updates, answers to queries and modify communication according to the customer's preferred communication channel and language. The seamless interface also means that customers are not only passive recipients of delivery but active participants who are informed about the delivery process, which also means higher satisfaction and lower service complaints.

Overall, AI has the potential to orchestrate a real time, responsive and transparent last mile system that is a fundamental shift in how logistics are managed and experienced. What was a black box—where packages faded to black on dispatch and reappeared on delivery—is now a highly observable, accountable process that drives operational intelligence and consumer confidence.

6. CHALLENGES AND LIMITATIONS

Despite the deep promise of using Artificial Intelligence and autonomous vehicles in last mile delivery, it comes along with a set of difficult challenges. These barriers are distributed across technical, regulatory, ethical, and societal domains, with each having its own limitations that impede widespread adoption and operational scalability. To understand the potential and limits of AI driven last mile logistics, both these issues need a balanced exploration (Shuaibu et al. 2025).

Regulatory ambiguity around autonomous delivery systems is one of the most immediate and pressing challenges. The legal frameworks for self driving vehicles and aerial drones are wildly different across countries and often even within jurisdictions of the same country. The restrictions on autonomous ground vehicles in many urban areas come from the lack of pedestrian safety, traffic law compliance, and infrastructure readiness. Drone operations are similarly restricted by airspace, privacy, and noise pollution standards. Logistics providers have fragmented and evolving policies that make it hard for autonomous operations to scale across regions without significant legal risk and operational delays (Cicek et al. 2025).

Another major concern is safety, particularly in a densely populated urban setting. Although AI perception and decision-making systems are improving, the edge cases, unpredictable scenarios such as jaywalking pedestrians, erratic human drivers, or unstructured environments, are still a challenge for autonomous vehicles. Failure in these systems can cause physical harm, legal liabilities, and reputational damage. While public confidence in the safety of autonomous delivery technologies is growing, it is fragile and can easily be undermined by high profile incidents.

In addition, AI driven logistics ecosystems are a critical risk to cybersecurity. The attack surface for malicious interference increases as vehicles and infrastructure become more connected. Autonomous vehicle hacking and tampering with AI-based routing algorithms could lead to package theft, delivery disruption, and in the worst case, causing vehicle crashes. To protect the digital and physical last mile delivery, it is critical to guarantee robust encryption, real-time threat detection, and fail-safe mechanisms (Montero-Vega et a. 2025).

While technical and regulatory concerns over the use of AI in urban mobility are being discussed, so too are the ethical implications. Complex ethical decisions that autonomous systems must make, for example, in unavoidable collisions or prioritizing deliveries in emergency situations, must be designed within transparent, accountable, and public value–aligned frameworks. The difficulty of auditing or interpreting the reasoning behind many such decisions is due to the opaque nature of many AI algorithms, which may contribute to algorithmic bias, liability, and accountability.

The socioeconomic impact of automation on the logistics workforce is also another challenge. Autonomous systems will increase efficiency and reduce cost, but at the expense of replacing a huge number of delivery personnel, many of whom depend on this work for their livelihood. Moving toward AI driven delivery models calls for proactive strategies for workforce retraining, labor market adaptation and inclusive innovation to avoid technological progress to increase social inequalities (Amaya et al. 2025).

Finally, infrastructure readiness is a practical barrier. However, smart infrastructure to enable seamless integration of autonomous vehicles still remains missing in many urban environments. This includes 5G connectivity with reliable connectivity, standard digital traffic signals, pre assigned curb spaces for autonomous loading and unloading, and charging points for electric delivery robots.

Combined, these challenges suggest that the road to intelligent, autonomous last mile logistics is at least as much a social and regulatory journey as a technical one. To overcome these hurdles, multi stakeholder collaboration, ethical foresight, and agile policymaking will be needed to allow innovation to happen safely, equitably, and sustainably.

7. POLICY, COMPLIANCE, AND PUBLIC ACCEPTANCE

As Artificial Intelligence and autonomous delivery systems transition from experimental pilots to operational deployments, the role of public policy and regulatory compliance becomes increasingly central. At the intersection of urban planning, transportation, labor, privacy, and consumer rights, these technologies work. Their integration into last mile logistics is at risk to being fragmented, contested, or stalled by public resistance and legal uncertainty if there are not clear and adaptive policy frameworks. This section looks at the changing regulatory landscape, the difficulties of standardizing compliance, and the social dynamics that determine acceptance.

One of the most critical policy challenges is the lack of standardized legislation for autonomous delivery systems. However, provisional guidelines for autonomous vehicles (AVs) and unmanned aerial systems (UAS) have been introduced by some countries and municipalities, which differ greatly in scope and enforcement. For instance, states like California and Arizona in the U.S. have opted for permissive frameworks that would encourage innovation, while other states are cautious or silent. In Europe, the lack of a uniform legal framework across borders also makes multinational logistics operations difficult. These disparities burden companies with compliance as they attempt to operate across jurisdictions, often forcing them to modify technologies or operational protocols to satisfy local legal requirements (Nourmohammadi et al. 2025).

Another area of concern is compliance with safety protocols. Regulators need to rework what it means to be 'safe operation' when autonomous vehicles take over the human decision making process with algorithmic systems. This includes questions such as how acceptable failure rates are for the AI, how much human oversight is required, and how AI systems used for perception, navigation, and decision-making are certified. Ensuring compliance in practice includes performance benchmarking, transparency of AI model behavior, and robust validation processes at development and deployment. Technical guidelines are now being developed by governments and standards organizations, like the ISO 22737 standard for low speed autonomous delivery vehicles, but these are still in their early stages and not universally enforced.

The extent to which AI and autonomous systems are adopted is very much dependent on public acceptance of these technologies. Societal concerns can even be powerful inhibitors even if technological readiness and regulatory approval are realized. The public is often skeptical about safety, job displacement, data privacy, and loss of human control over essential services. These concerns have been further intensified by media portrayals of accidents involving self-driving vehicles or delivery drones, which has also led to resistance from citizens and local governments (Kamala et al. 2025).

Companies and policymakers are increasingly emphasizing transparency, community engagement, and co design, to counteract this skepticism. Building trust has become dependent on public trials, open data sharing, and community consultations. Third party safety evaluations and public demonstration projects also help to demystify how these systems work and how they benefit us. In other cities, companies have worked with municipal authorities to co-develop pilot programs that can be deployed in the urban context in a way that aligns with the local transportation goals and public sentiment.

The ethical governance of autonomous systems is an emerging policy frontier. As AI starts to make decisions about mobility—for example, prioritizing deliveries during emergencies or resolving conflict on shared roads—regulatory bodies are being asked to set ethical parameters for machine behavior. This covers making sure that AI systems are bias free, accountable for their decisions, and auditable in case of an accident or service failure. Data governance is the last one and is regarded as the most critical part of compliance. AI driven Delivery systems are collecting huge amounts of data like geolocation, video feeds, customer preferences and operational metrics. This data, therefore, needs to be protected for privacy, security, and appropriate usage reasons to ensure compliance with the law and confidence with consumers. The European Union's General Data Protection Regulation (GDPR), California's Consumer Privacy Act (CCPA), and other regulations impose strict obligations on data management, requiring companies to invest in secure architectures, anonymization protocols, and transparent data handling policies (Rohit et al. 2025).

To summarize, the deployment of AI and autonomous technologies in last mile delivery is not dissociable from the frameworks of governance and public trust. In addition to technological innovation, a sustainable and scalable rollout relies on responsive policy development, regulatory harmonization, and proactive engagement with the communities these systems are designed to serve.

8. FUTURE TRENDS IN AI-DRIVEN LAST-MILE DELIVERY

As Artificial Intelligence (AI) and autonomous technologies continue to evolve, the last-mile delivery landscape is poised for profound transformation. Intelligent, interconnected, and sustainable logistics are emerging as new models of logistics that arise from the convergence of AI with the coming innovations in communication, mobility and sustainability. This section investigates key trends that will drive the future of AI powered last mile delivery and more broadly, supply chain transparency, resilience and sustainability.

The integration of 5G and V2X communication technologies is one of the most impactful enablers of next generation logistics. These networks allow real-time data exchange between delivery vehicles, infrastructure, pedestrians and cloud systems at high speeds and low latency. 5G connectivity enables dynamic route recalibration, instant hazard detection, and continuous coordination with smart city infrastructure for autonomous delivery systems. In dense urban environments, the ability to respond to unpredictable events like sudden road closures or pedestrian surges is crucial for safe and efficient navigation, and this capability is particularly valuable (Delle Donne et al. 2025).

The other emerging trend is the development of collaborative delivery ecosystems enabled by decentralized AI systems. Instead of just one logistics provider, these models consist of a network of autonomous vehicles, micro fulfillment centers, and AI powered platforms that dynamically coordinate delivery tasks. These systems use swarm intelligence and distributed computing, to assign deliveries to the most suitable vehicle or hub according to real time conditions and available resources. The decentralized model increases flexibility, decreases congestion, and provides a means for smaller players to join in hyperlocal logistics markets.

At the same time, AI is playing a central role in pushing the sustainability agenda in last-mile delivery. To meet stricter emissions regulations and sustainability benchmarks, cities are increasingly adopting electric autonomous vehicles, renewable energy powered distribution hubs and intelligent routing systems that cut down on carbon footprints. With AI, we can track the emissions of every leg of a delivery and suggest eco efficient alternatives. In addition, circular logistics models (e.g. automated returns, reverse logistics) help to achieve environmental goals by reducing waste and prolonging the product life cycle (Ojha & Agarwal, 2025).

Forward looking logistics strategies are also using digital twins and simulation models. By using these AI driven tools, companies can test how delivery networks behave in different scenarios, including natural disasters, cyber attacks, or demand surges, and replicate the behaviour of the delivery networks. Through these simulations, businesses can proactively design more resilient and adaptive supply chain infrastructures.

Furthermore, the next step in AI development is expected to focus on explainability, interoperability, and human-AI collaboration. With AI systems progressively making autonomous decisions in high stakes environments, there will be an increasing need for models that are transparent, interpretable, auditable and understandable by regulators, operators and the public. In the same way, interoperability standards will become important to allow that autonomous vehicles from different manufacturers can work within shared ecosystems and urban spaces without friction (Park et al. 2025).

For the future models, the last point is that they will probably be inclusive design and workforce integration, so that the technological advancement serves a wider range of society. This work includes the design of accessible autonomous systems usable by all users (including the elderly and the disabled), and the development of upskilling programs for transitioning logistics workers to roles of AI oversight, maintenance, and data stewardship.

Collectively, this reveals a paradigm shift in how we think about and execute last mile delivery systems. AI will not just optimize current operations but will spur the development of intelligent, responsive and sustainable delivery ecosystems deeply integrated into smart cities fabric.

9. CONCLUSION

The integration of Artificial Intelligence and autonomous vehicle technologies into last-mile delivery represents a transformative evolution in the logistics sector. These intelligent systems help address the long-standing challenges of traffic congestion, rising operation costs, lack of visibility, increasing customer demands, and provide a pathway to more transparent, efficient, and responsive delivery models. Predictive analytics, dynamic route optimization, autonomous fleet management, and AI based customer interaction are the key areas where logistics providers can use to significantly improve the operational capability and at the same time, improve the end user experience.

From autonomous delivery vans and drones to sidewalk robots, autonomous delivery vehicles have already shown their promise to transform urban mobility and delivery logistics. By orchestrating these innovations with AI driven systems, service precision is improving, carbon emissions are being reduced and operations can be run 24/7 with minimal human oversight. Global logistics leaders share case studies that demonstrate the real benefits and feasibility of this technological shift.

However, the deployment of these systems is also not without major challenges. The pace and form of adoption is still being shaped by regulatory uncertainty, safety concerns, ethical dilemmas, and cybersecurity risks. Additionally, the effect on labour markets and the social consequences of AI decision making necessitate anticipatory policy responses, ethical frameworks, and an inclusive governance framework.

In the future, the direction of AI in last mile logistics seems to be towards more interoperability in the system, 5G based real time infrastructure connectivity, collaborative delivery networks and strong sustainability. The future of last-mile delivery is not merely a logistical function but will be a key component in intelligent urban ecosystems.

To summarize, this chapter has looked at technological, operational, ethical, and regulatory aspects of AI and autonomous vehicles in last-mile delivery. This transformation of the urban landscape demands a multidisciplinary approach for supply chain professionals, urban planners, and policymakers to embrace: innovating in service of public interest, sustainability, and the changing dynamics of digital commerce.

REFERENCES

Alverhed, E., Hellgren, S., Isaksson, H., Olsson, L., Palmqvist, H., & Flodén, J. (2024). Autonomous last-mile delivery robots: A literature review. *European Transport Research Review*, *16*(1), 4.

Amaya, J., Encarnación, T., & Cantillo, V. (2025). Sustainable last mile delivery alternatives: Influencing factors and willingness to use. *Transportation Research Part D, Transport and Environment*, *139*, 104574.

Cicek, D., Kantarci, B., & Schillo, S. (2025). A Comparative Review of User Acceptance Factors for Drones and Sidewalk Robots in Autonomous Last Mile Delivery. *Green Energy and Intelligent Transportation*, 100310.

De Maio, A., Ghiani, G., Laganà, D., & Manni, E. (2024). Sustainable last-mile distribution with autonomous delivery robots and public transportation. *Transportation Research Part C, Emerging Technologies*, *163*, 104615.

Delle Donne, D., Santini, A., & Archetti, C. (2025). Integrating public transport in sustainable last-mile delivery: Column generation approaches. *European Journal of Operational Research.*

Ezmigna, I., Alghizzawi, M., Alqsass, M., Abu-AlSondos, I. A., Abualfalayeh, G., & Aldulaimi, S. H. (2024, December). The Impact of AI Tools on Last-Mile Delivery in the E-Commerce Sector in Saudi Arabia. In *2024 International Conference on Decision Aid Sciences and Applications (DASA)* (pp. 1-6). IEEE.

Garikapati, D., & Shetiya, S. S. (2024). Autonomous vehicles: Evolution of artificial intelligence and the current industry landscape. *Big Data and Cognitive Computing*, *8*(4), 42.

Garus, A., Christidis, P., Mourtzouchou, A., Duboz, L., & Ciuffo, B. (2024). Unravelling the last-mile conundrum: A comparative study of autonomous delivery robots, delivery bicycles, and light commercial vehicles in 14 varied European landscapes. *Sustainable Cities and Society*, *108*, 105490.

Ieva, S., Bilenchi, I., Gramegna, F., Pinto, A., Scioscia, F., Ruta, M., & Loseto, G. (2025). Enhancing Last-Mile Logistics: AI-Driven Fleet Optimization, Mixed Reality, and Large Language Model Assistants for Warehouse Operations. *Sensors (Basel), 25*(9), 2696. PMID: 40363135

Islam, M. S., Suad, S. F. R., & Rahman, A. (2024). Leveraging AI to Overcome Key Challenges in Last-Mile Delivery: Enhancing Customer Experience and Operational Efficiency in E-commerce. *Supply Chain Insider| ISSN: 2617-7420 (Print), 2617-7420 (Online), 14*(1).

Janinhoff, L., Klein, R., Sailer, D., & Schoppa, J. M. (2024). Out-of-home delivery in last-mile logistics: A review. *Computers & Operations Research*, •••, 106686.

Judijanto, L., Asniar, N., Kushariyadi, K., Utami, E. Y., & Telaumbanua, E. (2024). Application of integrated logistics networks in improving the efficiency of distribution and delivery of goods in indonesia a literature review. *Sciences du Nord Economics and Business, 1*(01), 01-10.

Kamala, V., Yamini, S., Gajanand, M. S., & Jagadeeswaran, K. R. (2025). Investigating the physical ergonomic risks associated with last-mile delivery personnel riding motorcycles. *International Journal of Productivity and Performance Management.*

Masorgo, N., Dobrzykowski, D. D., & Fugate, B. S. (2024). Last-mile delivery: A process view, framework, and research agenda. *Journal of Business Logistics, 45*(4), e12397.

Mohsen, B. M. (2024). Ai-driven optimization of urban logistics in smart cities: Integrating autonomous vehicles and iot for efficient delivery systems. *Sustainability, 16*(24), 11265.

Montero-Vega, M., Estrada, M., & Thigulla, D. T. (2025). Understanding the impact of socio-demographic differences on acceptance of last-mile delivery technologies: A comparative analysis. *Journal of Transport Geography, 126*, 104244.

Nourmohammadi, Z., Hu, B., Rey, D., & Saberi, M. (2025). A data-driven preference learning approach for multi-objective vehicle routing problems in last-mile delivery. *Transportation Research Part C, Emerging Technologies*, *174*, 105101.

Ojha, R., & Agarwal, A. (2025). Examining environmental sustainability in last-mile delivery: A quality function deployment analysis. *The TQM Journal*.

Park, K. H., Pan, X., & Dresner, M. E. (2025). Targeting online sales through last-mile delivery platform integration. *Journal of Operations Management*, *71*(2), 195–219.

Ramírez, J. G. C. & mafiqul Islam, M. (2024). Application of Artificial Intelligence in Practical Scenarios. *Journal of Artificial Intelligence General science (JAIGS) ISSN: 3006-4023, 2*(1), 14-19.

Rohit, G., Krishnan, R., & Kumar, P. R. (2025). A Systematic Review and Morphological Analysis of the Literature on Last Mile Delivery Using Drones: Quo Vadis?. *IIM Kozhikode Society & Management Review*, 22779752251329395.

Shuaibu, A. S., Mahmoud, A. S., & Sheltami, T. R. (2025). A Review of Last-Mile Delivery Optimization: Strategies, Technologies, Drone Integration, and Future Trends. *Drones (Basel)*, *9*(3), 158.

Srikanteswara, R., Kalshetty, J. N., Molakatala, N., Chandra, S., & Manoj, A. (2025). Enhancing Electric Vehicle Performance Through 5G and Cloud Computing Integration. In *Integrating Artificial Intelligence Into the Energy Sector* (pp. 211-236). IGI Global Scientific Publishing.

Chapter 5
From Digital Transformation to Financial Performance: The Mediating Role of Supply Chain Integration in Tunisian Agro-Industries

Rym Ghariani
https://orcid.org/0000-0002-0061-7911
University of Sfax, Tunisia

Ghada Soltane
University of Sfax, Tunisia

Younes Boujelbene
University of Sfax, Tunisia

ABSTRACT

Purpose –The chapter delves into the impact of digitalization and supply chain integration on the financial performance of the Tunisian agro-industrial sector, considering the growing importance of digital technologies in modern business operations. This study aims to investigate the relationship between digitalization, supply chain integration, and financial

DOI: 10.4018/979-8-3373-2843-0.ch005

performance in the Tunisian agro-industrial sector. Design/methodology/ approach – Data collection involved a questionnaire, followed by analysis using SPSS26 software for principal component analysis and linear regression modeling. Findings –The results indicated that digitalization and supply chain integration significantly influence the financial performance of agro-industrial organizations in Tunisia.

INTRODUCTION

The digital revolution has redefined business management paradigms across all sectors, including logistics. Today, digitization goes beyond simply automating traditional processes; it fundamentally transforms conventional supply chains into integrated and intelligent systems, commonly known as digital supply chains (Büyüközkan and Göçer, 2018). This transformation is particularly evident in companies' ability to enhance organizational flexibility, respond to fluctuations in demand and supply, and overall improve the efficiency of their supply chains (McKinsey, 2016).

Digitization, now recognized as the primary driving force in the development of next-generation supply chains, offers significant advantages such as cost reduction, improved customer satisfaction, and increased loyalty. According to Deloitte AG (2015), integrating modern technologies into logistics processes enables companies to create more responsive, agile, and efficient supply chains with reduced lead times and optimized product availability. These benefits have become essential in an increasingly competitive environment where speed and adaptability are crucial for maintaining a competitive edge.

Recent studies have shown that emerging digital technologies such as Big Data, the Internet of Things (IoT), Blockchain, Artificial Intelligence (AI), and Machine Learning are not just optimization tools but also play a critical role in transforming global supply chains (Barreto and al., 2017; Björkdahl, 2020; Uniyal and al., 2021). These technologies allow companies to overcome complex challenges, improve operational performance, and achieve substantial financial gains (Dubey and al., 2019; Lal and Bharadwaj, 2020; Sultana and al., 2021).

However, despite notable advancements, the direct link between supply chain digitization and companies' financial performance remains partially understood and requires further exploration. The digital era imposes unprecedented rapid adaptation and agility on companies to remain viable in constantly evolving markets (El Ghazali and Boutgayout, 2020). In this context, developing and implementing tailored digital manufacturing strategies becomes crucial for ensuring companies' competitiveness and sustainability (Okyere and al., 2023).

Based on these considerations, this study focuses on three key research questions (RQs):

- **RQ1:** What is the direct impact of digital technologies on supply chain integration?
- **RQ2:** What is the direct impact of digital technologies on the financial performance of companies?
- **RQ3:** What is the direct impact of supply chain integration on the financial performance of industrial companies?

To address these questions, we have developed a rigorous research framework based on an extensive review of the existing literature. This framework will be empirically validated through a survey targeting agro-industrial companies in Tunisia, a particularly relevant sector given the strategic importance of the supply chain in these companies' performance. This empirical approach will allow us to test hypotheses and better understand the mechanisms through which digital technologies can transform supply chain integration and, consequently, companies' financial performance.

In summary, this chapter is structured into four interdependent sections:

1. The first section is dedicated to the literature review and the development of research hypotheses.
2. The second section presents the conceptual model developed for the study.
3. The third section details the methodology adopted for data collection and analysis.

4. The fourth section discusses the results to formulate conclusions and managerial recommendations relevant to practitioners and researchers

LITERATURE REVIEW AND DEVELOPMENT OF HYPOTHESIS

The digitalization of supply chains represents a strategic lever for enhancing company performance. Although research has explored various aspects of this transformation, the precise interactions between digitization, supply chain integration, and financial performance remain to be further examined. This section reviews the relevant literature and formulates hypotheses to better understand these dynamics.

Digitalization

Digitalization is in fact a long historical process that began with the invention of the computer in the 1930s. Up to now, we can distinguish four major historical stages (see Figure 1):

- From 1936 to 1959: invention of the computer and emergence of the information technology market.
- From 1960 to 1983: spread of management information technology and predominance of computers in the professional world.
- From 1984 to 2007: computerization of society, the emergence of personal computing (Apple Macintosh), and use of the Internet.
- From 2008 to today: generalization of ICT (information and communication technologies) and advent of the digital sphere.

Figure 1. History of Digitalization

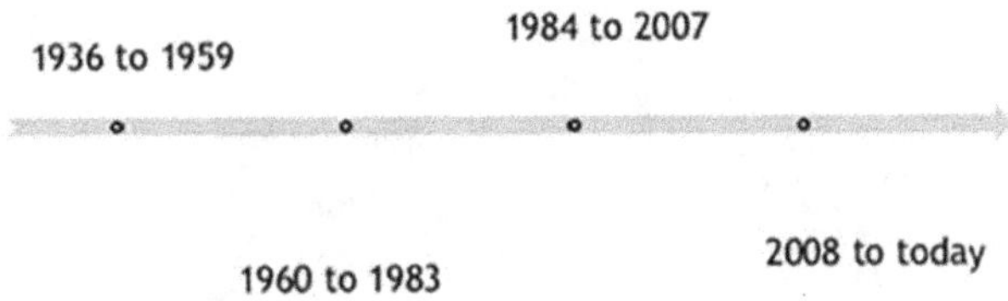

Source: Mounaim, H. & Boutaqbout, Z. (2020)

Nowadays, digitalization has been identified as one of the major trends that are changing society and businesses (Parviainen et al., 2017). The potential benefits of digitalization are high; already by digitalizing information-intensive processes, costs can be reduced by up to 90% and lead times improved by several orders of magnitude.

The concept of digital business has therefore sparked several controversies over the years. For the purpose of this study, we define a digital business as one that has integrated the use of innovative digital tools into its daily operations.

The use of these digital tools allows companies to personalize relationships with their stakeholders and to identify and respond more quickly to consumer expectations and preferences by offering more innovative products and services than competitors (Ross et al., 2017).

The following figure illustrates the main technological advances that are expected to have the greatest impact on supply chain management.

Figure 2. The Main Technological Advances

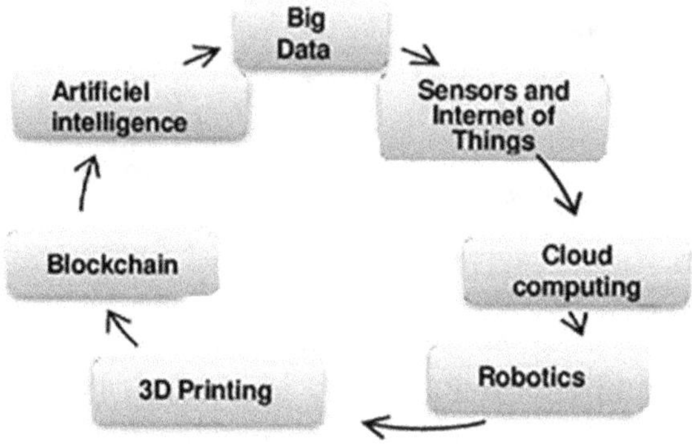

Source: Authors

Big Data (BD)

The rise of Big Data has significantly transformed the way companies manage their supply chains. This digital revolution enables firms to dive into vast volumes of information to better understand and predict demand, manage inventory, and refine logistics routes. In practical terms, the massive amount of collected data can now be analyzed to identify trends and anticipate consumer needs with greater accuracy (Chen et al., 2012).

Consider demand forecasting as a concrete example. With the help of Big Data, companies can analyze historical and behavioral data to adjust inventory levels more precisely and responsively. This reduces the risks of overstocking or stockouts, thereby enhancing customer service and optimizing costs (Wamba et al., 2017).

Artificial Intelligence (AI)

Applications of Artificial Intelligence in Supply Chain Management

Artificial Intelligence (AI) is fundamentally reshaping supply chain management by offering innovative solutions to optimize operations, improve warehouse management, and automate various processes. Research highlights the critical role AI plays in these areas. For instance, warehouse management systems now use advanced algorithms to automate storage and retrieval tasks, enhancing efficiency and reducing human error (Wang et al., 2020). Similarly, AI algorithms are employed to improve demand forecasting, enabling companies to manage inventory more effectively and reduce associated costs (Amosu et al., 2024).

Benefits and Limitations of Artificial intelligence

AI brings several significant advantages to supply chains. On the one hand, it enhances forecasting accuracy and operational efficiency by enabling fast and precise analysis of large volumes of data, helping businesses anticipate demand fluctuations and adjust their strategies in real time (Mikalef et al., 2020). Moreover, the automation of repetitive tasks frees up employees to focus on more complex and creative work (Baryannis et al., 2019).

However, AI also presents notable challenges. One major barrier is the high cost of AI technologies, which can limit adoption for some companies. Additionally, for AI systems to operate effectively, high-quality and well-structured data are essential—something not all organizations currently possess (Choi et al., 2020).

Internet of Things (IoT)

Impact of IoT on Logistics

The Internet of Things (IoT) is fundamentally transforming logistics by introducing innovations that redefine how supply chains operate. Through connected sensors and smart tags, IoT enables real-time visibility into logistics processes, significantly enhancing traceability and shipment tracking. For example, studies such as Wang et al. (2018) have shown that IoT sensors can monitor temperature and humidity during transportation and alert managers when conditions deviate from acceptable ranges.

Benefits and Challenges of IoT

IoT offers numerous benefits. It enhances transparency and product traceability throughout the supply chain, enabling swift responses to potential issues and ensuring compliance with quality standards (Gubbi et al., 2013). Stock optimization is also improved, which reduces costs and increases operational efficiency.

However, IoT is not without its challenges. Data security is a major concern, as IoT sensors collect vast amounts of sensitive information. Protecting this data from cyberattacks is critical (Yang et al., 2017). Furthermore, integrating IoT technologies into existing systems can be complex and costly, requiring significant investments in infrastructure and employee training (Bertino & Sandhu, 2010).

Blockchain

Application of Blockchain in Supply Chains

Blockchain, often associated with cryptocurrency, is revolutionizing supply chains by providing a transparent and secure way to record transactions. It functions like a virtual ledger where each transaction is permanently recorded in a "block" and linked in a chain shared among all participants. Any modification requires consensus, making the data highly reliable. This technology is especially valuable for tracking products from their point of origin to the final destination, ensuring complete and trustworthy traceability (Sabri et al., 2022).

Benefits and Case Studies

Blockchain offers several key advantages. First, it enhances data security by making tampering virtually impossible every transaction is validated by multiple parties before being added to the chain (Crosby et al., 2016). Real-world examples demonstrate these benefits. Walmart, for instance, used blockchain to trace the origin of food products. What used to take several days now takes less than three seconds (Wang et al., 2019). Similarly, De Beers, the renowned diamond supplier, uses blockchain to verify the authenticity of its diamonds, ensuring none originate from conflict zones (Fosso Wamba et al., 2020).

Cloud Computing (CC)

Cloud Computing in Logistics Management

Cloud computing is a model that provides access to shared computing resources via the Internet. Instead of storing and managing data locally, companies can use cloud-based services to store, manage, and process their information. This eliminates the need for costly physical infrastructure and offers greater flexibility and scalability in operations.

Benefits of Cloud Computing in Logistics Management (Haris & Khan, 2018).

- **Improved Accessibility and Flexibility:** One of the key advantages of cloud computing in logistics is enhanced accessibility and flexibility. Companies can access their logistics data and applications anytime and from anywhere, facilitating collaboration among supply chain partners. Additionally, cloud solutions allow businesses to quickly adapt to changing market demands by scaling operations as needed.
- **Cost Reduction:** Cloud computing helps reduce infrastructure and maintenance costs. Instead of investing in expensive servers and software, companies can subscribe to cloud-based services with lower operational expenses. Furthermore, cloud automation enables businesses to reduce labor costs by streamlining many logistical tasks.
- **Enhanced Visibility and Traceability:** Cloud platforms improve visibility and traceability across logistics operations. Businesses can track the real-time location of goods, monitor inventory levels, and generate detailed performance reports. This data-driven approach supports faster, more informed decision-making and helps address issues proactively.

- **Strengthened Data Security:** Data security is a critical concern in logistics. Cloud computing offers advanced protection for sensitive information. Cloud service providers invest in robust security technologies such as data encryption, threat detection, and routine data backups, enabling secure storage and management of logistics data.
- **Seamless Integration with Other Systems:** Cloud computing facilitates easy integration with other logistics systems. Companies can link warehouse management systems, shipment tracking tools, and other logistics applications to the cloud, streamlining information exchange. This promotes better coordination and more efficient overall supply chain management.

Cloud computing can benefit logistics companies of all sizes—small, medium, or large. Cloud-based solutions offer flexibility and scalability that can be tailored to the specific needs of each business.

Robotics

Definition

Robotics refers to the process of designing and using robots to perform specific tasks. It is considered a form of automation that enables the execution of various operations without direct human involvement.

Benefits of Robotics in Logistics (Salonitis et al., 2021)

Robotic logistics improves efficiency and accuracy in warehouses. Through automation, companies reduce costs and ease the workload for employees.

The adoption of robotics is driven by the need to reduce costs, increase production output, and improve operational speed. It also enhances process efficiency and contributes to a safer work environment. By offering production flexibility, robotics enables companies to quickly respond to changing consumer demands.

The use of robots enables automation, improves efficiency, and optimizes logistics processes such as storage, transportation, and order preparation.

These technologies help boost productivity by making the execution of repetitive tasks faster and more accurate. Robots can operate in hazardous or monotonous environments, reducing the risk of workplace accidents. They also enhance process reliability by minimizing human error.

3D Printing

3D printing, also known as additive manufacturing, is a technology in which a three-dimensional object is created by depositing successive layers of material. It is also referred to as rapid prototyping—a mechanized method that quickly produces 3D objects using a reasonably sized machine connected to a computer containing digital blueprints of the object (Prabhu, 2016).

This technology operates primarily on the principle of Fused Deposition Modeling (FDM). Its core components include material cartridges, flexible output capabilities, and the conversion of digital code into a visible physical model.

Supply Chain Digitalization

Digitalization has attracted considerable interest from academics and practitioners because of its potential to benefit businesses and improve performance (Barreto et al., 2017; Dubey et al., 2019; Mu & Ming, 2023; Zhang & Li, 2024). It is defined as technological innovation aimed at transforming traditional processes, transactions, or operations using digital technologies such as e-commerce, blockchain, ERP, and robotics. The emergence of these technological innovations has also impacted logistics, transforming traditional supply chains into digital supply chains (Büyüközkan & Göçer, 2018).

Supply chain digitalization refers to the application of digital technologies to plan and process transactions, communicate, and execute supply chain activities (Sanders & Swink, 2020). Digitalization enables supply chains to respond swiftly and with agility to consumer demand and adapt effectively to changing market conditions (Büyüközkan & Göçer, 2018).

Previous studies have shown that digital technologies play a key role in integrating supply chain processes (Gautr, 2020; Mukhopadhyay & Kekre, 2002). For example, Srinivasan et al. (1994) demonstrated that electronic data interchange (EDI) helps integrate information and reduce shipping errors. Rai et al. (2006) emphasized the impact of ERP and CRM tools on supply chain process integration and overall business performance. Gautr (2020) also confirmed that digitalization enhances internal integration across departments by aligning efforts toward common goals. Khajavi and Holmström (2015) illustrated how digital manufacturing technologies, such as additive manufacturing and 3D printing, improve visibility and efficiency, enabling globally integrated supply chains. Deepu and Ravi (2021) stressed the role of value-added shared information systems in boosting supply chain performance. Similarly, Kayikci (2018) highlighted that digitalization fosters cooperation, connectivity, and traceability across supply chain actors through smart technologies.

While this body of research suggests that digitalization facilitates supply chain integration and business performance, Stank et al. (2019) argued that further exploration is required to understand how firms interface with other supply chain actors in the digital age.

H1. *Supply chain digitalization has a positive influence on supply chain integration.*

Numerous studies have explored the impact of digitalization on business performance. Although various aspects have been extensively studied, the specific relationship between supply chain digitalization and performance remains underexplored (Björkdahl, 2020). Business performance is often measured using operational metrics (e.g., efficiency, service quality) and financial indicators (e.g., revenue, profit margins, ROI) (Abdallah & Al-Ghwayeen, 2020; Flynn et al., 2010). This chapter focuses on financial performance as a key measure of firm success.

Digital technologies enhance financial performance by enabling efficient resource allocation, fostering transparent information exchange, and strengthening competitive advantage through innovations such as cloud computing, IoT, 3D visualization, and robotics (Baird & Raghu, 2015; Opresnik & Taisch, 2015; Westerman et al., 2014).

H2. *The digitalization of the supply chain improves the financial performance of a company.*

Supply Chain Integration

Supply chain integration (SCI) is a multifaceted concept widely explored in the literature, encompassing both internal and external dimensions. According to Chang et al. (2016), internal integration refers to the coordination and collaboration of information, processes, and behaviors within the enterprise. Conversely, external integration pertains to a firm's ability to align practices and operations with key supply chain partners through synchronized, collaborative processes (Chaudhuri et al., 2018).

The most commonly examined dimensions of SCI include internal integration, supplier integration, and customer integration (Alfalla-Luque et al., 2013; Ataseven & Nair, 2017). Achieving integration typically involves practices such as information sharing, collaborative planning, and operational coordination. Sabir & Irfan (2014) also emphasized shared decision-making, technological support, and mutual trust as essential components.

SCI aims to optimize performance by improving the flow of products, services, information, capital, and decision-making across the supply chain (Stevens et al., 2016). While many studies have linked SCI to improved business performance, results are sometimes inconsistent. For instance, Flynn et al. (2010) did not identify a significant relationship between external integration and performance. Jayaram and Xu (2013) found no meaningful association between supplier integration and flexibility. Leuschner et al. (2013), in a meta-analysis, reported no significant correlation between SCI and financial performance. Surprisingly, Som et al. (2019) even observed a negative relationship between relational integration and performance in Ghana's manufacturing sector. Given these mixed findings, further investigation is warranted.

H3. *Supply chain integration improves a company's financial performance.*

Conceptual Framework

The conceptual model of this study, illustrated in Figure 3, outlines the hypothesized relationships among supply chain digitalization, supply chain integration, and financial performance. It reflects the logical sequence and interaction between these key variables.

Figure 3. Research Model Framework

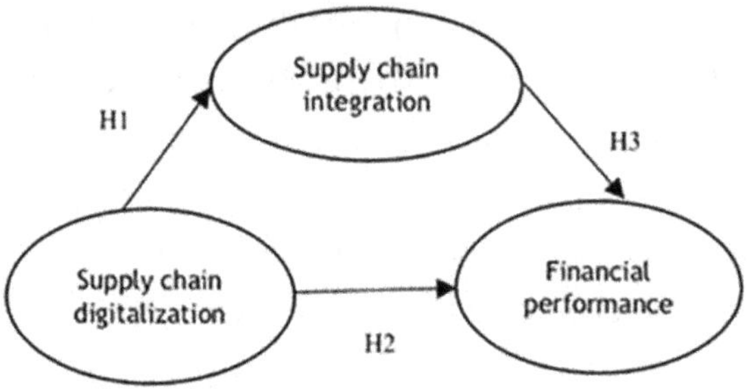

Source: Authors

RESEARCH METHODOLOGY

Data Collection Method

To empirically test the proposed model, data were collected using a structured questionnaire, which was developed based on preliminary interviews conducted with Tunisian agro-food companies. The survey period extended from November 2022 to April 2023.

Face-to-face administration was chosen to maximize the response rate and mitigate non-response bias. Out of 120 distributed questionnaires, 88 were returned, yielding a response rate of 73.33%. After eliminating incomplete or inconsistent responses, 82 questionnaires were deemed usable, resulting in an effective response rate of 68.33%.

The sampling frame was based on the Industry and Innovation Promotion Agency (IIPA, 2022), focusing on Tunisian industrial agro-food companies. The sectoral distribution is presented in Table 1:

Table 1. Population of the Tunisian Industrial Agro-Food Companies

Sector	TE*	OTE**	Total	%
Agro-food industries	203	809	1012	20.8%

Source: Industry and Innovation Promotion Agency (IIPA), 2022

- **TE**: Totally Exporting
- **OTE**: Other than Totally Exporting

For our research, we used a non-probability sampling method. This method consists of choosing the most accessible and available people. The characteristics of our sample are given in table 2.

Table 2. Characteristics of Respondents (N = 82)

Category	Frequency	Percentage (%)
Food Industry Sector		
Oil and fat industries	10	7.3%
Fruit and vegetable industries	6	4.4%
Fish industries	30	22.0%
Cereal and derivative industries	9	6.6%
Beverage industries	32	23.5%
Milk and derivatives industries	8	5.9%
Sugar industries and derivatives	8	5.9%
Meat industries	5	3.8%
Other food industries	28	20.6%
Respondent Position		
Executive / Production Manager	41	30.1%
Manager / Purchasing Manager	31	22.8%
Logistics / Distribution Manager	28	20.6%
Supply and Planning Manager	21	15.5%
Financial Officer	15	11.0%
Number of Employees		
Less than 250 employees	47	57.3%

continued on following page

Table 2. Continued

Category	Frequency	Percentage (%)
Between 251 and 999 employees	24	29.3%
More than 1000 employees	11	13.4%

Source: Authors

Measuring Scale

The survey instrument was developed based on an extensive literature review to identify valid measures for related constructs. Additionally, existing measurement scales were adapted and modified. The questionnaire was divided into three sections:

- Supply Chain Digitalization (seven items): This scale was adapted and modified from previous studies (Xue, 2014; Xue et al., 2013) to capture the extent to which companies implement supply chain management software to electronically connect and transact with their supply chain suppliers and customers.
- Supply Chain Integration (six items): This scale was adapted from previous studies on customer integration (three items) and supplier integration (three items) (Flynn et al., 2010; Germain and Iyer, 2006; Mofokeng and Chinomona, 2019).
- Financial Performance (four items): This scale was obtained and modified from prior studies (Germain and Iyer, 2006; Narasimhan and Kim, 2002).

All indicators were measured using a five-point Likert scale ranging from 1 (Strongly Disagree) to 5 (Strongly Agree). In total, the questionnaire comprises 17 items.

DATA ANALYSIS

The data collected for this study were analyzed using the Statistical Package for the Social Sciences (SPSS version 26.0). The main statistics used in this study include:

- Principal Component Analysis (PCA): Used to analyze the reliability of the scales.
- Linear Regression Analysis: Applied to test the direct and indirect relationships between the variables.

A visual summary of our empirical validation approach is provided in Figure 4.

Figure 4. Data Analysis

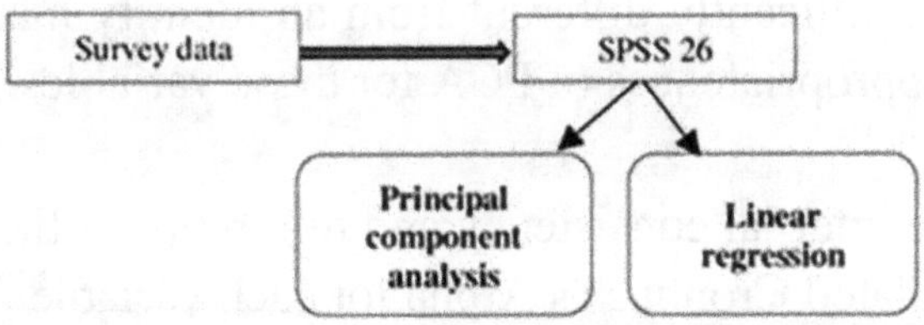

Source: Authors

ANALYSIS RESULTS

Principal Component Analysis (PCA)

To validate the reliability and structure of the measurement scales, we conducted a Principal Component Analysis (PCA). The results of the Kaiser-Meyer-Olkin (KMO) index and Bartlett's test of sphericity for each variable are presented in Table III.

Table 3. KMO Index and Bartlett's Sphericity Test

Variable	KMO Index	Bartlett Test (p-value)
Supply Chain Digitalization	0.754	0.000
Supply Chain Integration	0.892	0.000
Financial Performance	0.737	0.000

Source: SPSS 26

- KMO Index: The KMO values for all variables exceed the threshold of 0.6, suggesting that the data is suitable for factor analysis. The values are 0.754 for supply chain digitalization, 0.892 for supply chain integration, and 0.737 for financial performance, all of which indicate good sampling adequacy.
- Bartlett's Test of Sphericity: The p-values for all variables are 0.000, which is below the threshold of 0.05, indicating that the correlation matrix is significantly different from an identity matrix. This supports the appropriateness of PCA for these variables.

To assess the internal consistency and reliability of the measurement scales, we calculated Cronbach's Alpha for each variable. The results, as presented in Table IV, indicate the following reliability coefficients:

Table 4. Reliability of Measurement Scales

Variable	Cronbach's Alpha
Supply Chain Digitalization	0.892
Supply Chain Integration	0.920
Financial Performance	0.756

Source: SPSS 26

- Cronbach's Alpha: All three variables exhibit acceptable levels of internal consistency. Specifically, supply chain digitalization has a Cronbach's Alpha of 0.892, which is well above the recommended threshold of 0.70, indicating a high level of reliability. Similarly, supply chain integration demonstrates an even stronger reliability with 0.920, and financial performance shows an adequate value of 0.756, which is also acceptable.

These results confirm that the measurement scales used in this study are reliable and suitable for further analysis.

Linear Regression Analysis

Regression analysis is a powerful statistical method used to model causal or predictive relationships between independent variables and outcomes (Angelini, 2019). In the context of this research, linear regression analysis was employed to assess the relationships between supply chain digitalization, supply chain integration, and financial performance within Tunisian agro-industrial companies.

This analytical approach enables us to explore how digital transformation and integration practices within the supply chain influence a company's financial outcomes. Specifically, it allows for testing both direct and indirect effects as proposed in our conceptual framework.

The regression models were constructed as follows:

- Model 1: To evaluate the influence of supply chain digitalization on supply chain integration (H1).
- Model 2: To test the impact of supply chain digitalization on financial performance (H2).
- Model 3: To examine the relationship between supply chain integration and financial performance (H3).

These models provide a comprehensive understanding of how the adoption of digital technologies and the level of integration within supply chain operations contribute to financial success. The results of the regression analyses are presented in the following tables and discussed in detail in the next section.

Model Summary

Table 5. Regression Model Summary[b]

Model	R	R Square	Adjusted R Square	Std. Error of the Estimate	Durbin-Watson	Sig.
1	.684[a]	.468	.462	.73378979	1.731	.000
a. Predictors: (Constant), Supply chain digitalization						
b. Dependent Variable: Supply chain integration						

Table V presents the results of the regression analysis conducted to test H1: Supply chain digitalization has a positive influence on supply chain integration.

The model shows a coefficient of determination (R2) of 0.468, indicating that approximately 46.8% of the variance in supply chain integration can be explained by supply chain digitalization. The adjusted R2 value of 0.462 confirms the model's explanatory power after adjusting for the number of predictors.

The R value of 0.684 suggests a strong positive correlation between supply chain digitalization and supply chain integration. Furthermore, the Durbin-Watson statistic is 1.731, which is within the acceptable range (1.5 to 2.5), indicating no serious autocorrelation issues in the residuals.

Simple Regression Coefficient

Table 6. Simple Regression Coefficient[a]

Model	Unstandardized Coefficients		Standardized Coefficients	t	Sig.
	b	Std. Error	B		
(Constant)	.064	.081		.786	.434
Supply chain digitalization	.666	.079	.684	8.392***	.000

a. Dependent Variable: Supply chain integration.
Notes: $*p < 0.1$, $**p < 0.05$, $***p < 0.0$

Table VI provides further insights into the relationship between supply chain digitalization and supply chain integration.

The unstandardized coefficient (B) for supply chain digitalization is 0.666, indicating that a one-unit increase in digitalization is associated with a 0.666-unit increase in supply chain integration, assuming all other factors remain constant.

The standardized beta coefficient ($\beta = 0.684$) suggests a strong positive effect, and the t-value of 8.392 with a p-value of 0.000 indicates that this relationship is highly statistically significant at the 1% level (*$p < 0.01$).

The intercept value (0.064) is not statistically significant ($p = 0.434$), which means it does not meaningfully affect the model when supply chain digitalization is zero, though this is less critical for interpretation.

These results strongly support Hypothesis H1, confirming that supply chain digitalization has a positive and significant effect on supply chain integration in Tunisian agro-industrial companies.

Model Summary

Table 7. Regression Model Summary[b]

Model	R	R Square	Adjusted R Square	Std. Error of the Estimate	Durbin-Watson	Sig.
1	.684[a]	.468	.462	.73378979	1.731	.000
a. Predictors: (Constant), Supply chain digitalization						
b. Dependent Variable: Supply chain integration						

Table VII shows the summary of the regression model testing the effect of supply chain digitalization on supply chain integration.

- The correlation coefficient ($R = 0.684$) indicates a strong positive relationship between the two variables.
- The R Square value (0.468) reveals that approximately 46.8% of the variance in supply chain integration can be explained by supply chain digitalization alone.

- The Adjusted R Square (0.462) confirms the robustness of the model after adjusting for the number of predictors.
- The Durbin-Watson statistic (1.731) falls within the acceptable range (between 1.5 and 2.5), indicating that there is no serious autocorrelation in the residuals.
- The significance level (Sig. = 0.000) confirms that the model is statistically significant at the 1% level, meaning the predictor variable significantly explains variation in the dependent variable.

Multiple Regression Coefficient

Table 8. Multiple Regression Coefficient[a]

Model		Unstandardized Coefficients		Standardized Coefficients	t	Sig.
		b	Std. Error	B		
1	(Constant)	.055	.072		.766	.446
	Supply chain digitalization	.171	.080	.193	2.126**	.037
	Supply chain integration	.660	.091	.660	7.274***	.000

a. Dependent Variable: financial performance
Notes: *p < 0.1, **p < 0.05, ***p < 0.0

Table VIII presents the coefficients of the multiple regression model with financial performance as the dependent variable and both supply chain digitalization and supply chain integration as predictors.

- The constant term (b = 0.055, p = 0.446) is not statistically significant, indicating that when both independent variables are zero, the model does not significantly predict financial performance.
- Supply chain digitalization has a positive and significant effect on financial performance (b = 0.171, p = 0.037 < 0.05). The standardized coefficient (β = 0.193) indicates a moderate contribution of digitalization to financial performance. This supports Hypothesis H2, confirming that digitalization improves financial performance.
- Supply chain integration shows a strong and highly significant positive effect on financial performance (b = 0.660, p = 0.000). The standardized coefficient (β = 0.660) suggests that integration is a major

contributor to financial performance. This confirms Hypothesis H3, which proposes that supply chain integration enhances financial outcomes.

Together, these results indicate that both digitalization and integration of the supply chain positively influence financial performance, with integration having a more substantial impact.

DISCUSSION

The main objective of this study is to understand the relationships between supply chain digitalization, supply chain integration and company financial performance. The conceptualized research model is established based on the existing literature. Three hypotheses (H1–H3) are thus formulated. Based on the empirical results, all three hypotheses are found to be statistically significant. The results of our study provide researchers and companies with managerial implications.

Theoretical Implications

In the context of Tunisian agro-industrial companies, the results of this study show that digitalization plays a crucial role in improving supply chain integration. Indeed, digital technologies can significantly enhance communication and collaboration with supply chain partners in the Tunisian agro-industrial sector. This facilitates external integration and allows for better coordination among the various actors within the chain. Additionally, the collection and real-time analysis of data can optimize supply chain management by reducing wait times, improving efficiency, and responding more quickly to the specific needs of this sector. The digitalization of the supply chain also provides greater transparency and traceability, thereby strengthening trust among the different partners, whether they are producers, processors, or distributors. These improvements are crucial for ensuring the quality and safety of products throughout the process while allowing for better adaptation to market demands. This result provides empirical support for the argument of Iddris (2018) and

Büyüközkan and Göçer (2018) that digitalization is strongly associated with supply chain integration with external parties. Iddris (2018) could have presented arguments highlighting how digital technologies can enable transparent information sharing and real-time communication, leading to better collaboration and coordination. This can result in better supply chain visibility, reduced lead times and increased operational efficiency. Additionally, this finding offers further evidence to generalize Björkdahl's (2020) in-depth case studies with 26 sample companies that digitalization boosts supply chain integration with customers and suppliers by facilitating product traceability, facilitating access to customers' production systems and inventory management systems, and improve control of materials and components with company suppliers.

The results from our sample reveal that the impact of supply chain digitalization on the financial performance of the Tunisian agro-industrial sector is particularly significant. Indeed, digitalization profoundly transforms operations by bringing various changes and improvements to the financial aspects of companies operating in this sector. Firstly, process optimization through digitalization reduces inefficiencies and automates repetitive tasks, leading to lower costs associated with labor and material resources. The reduction of manual tasks not only decreases operational costs but also reduces the risk of human error, improving operational accuracy and minimizing financial losses. Secondly, digitalization offers better visibility and traceability of goods flows, allowing companies to adjust their inventory more quickly and efficiently according to actual demand. This more refined inventory management reduces storage costs and the risks of obsolescence, while also improving working capital management. Moreover, digitalization facilitates the integration of real-time financial data, enabling companies to make more informed and responsive decisions. This ability to react swiftly to market fluctuations and operational challenges can enhance the financial resilience of companies and allow them to seize growth opportunities more quickly. Finally, by making the supply chain more agile and responsive, digitalization not only improves operational efficiency but also paves the way for innovation in value creation, such as access to new markets or the enhancement of relationships with customers and suppliers. These combined factors contribute to strengthening the overall competitiveness of the Tunisian agro-industrial sector, thereby improving its profitability and long-term financial sustainability. This result is generally consistent with the findings of Barua and al. (2004) regarding the efforts of supply chain digitalization to improve financial performance. However, when classifying companies into large and small sizes, Barua's (2004) results reveal that supply chain digitalization is positively correlated with financial performance for SMEs only, but not for large companies.

The impact of supply chain integration on financial performance in the Tunisian agro-industrial sector is a crucial consideration for businesses operating in this industry. Indeed, Supply chain integration can lead to cost savings through improved coordination with suppliers, optimized inventory management, and reduced transportation costs. These cost efficiencies can directly contribute to improved financial performance by increasing profitability and reducing operating expenses. This result is consistent with the work of Flynn and al. (2010), although no significant correlation between supply chain integration and financial performance is found in Leuschner and al. (2013).

Managerial IMPLICATIONS

The findings of this study underscore the compelling need for companies to embrace digitalization in their supply chains. While many organizations acknowledge the potential benefits of digitalization, they often lack clarity on how and where these benefits will materialize (Supply Chain Digest, 2016). This study highlights that the adoption of digital technologies such as EDI, RFID, cloud computing, 3D printing, and big data analytics can significantly enhance the transparency and real-time sharing of information. By enabling closer collaboration with supply chain partners, these technologies facilitate a higher degree of external integration within the supply chain, ultimately driving improved financial performance.

Additionally, the study's results suggest that managers should not only focus on implementing individual technologies but also on creating a cohesive digital strategy that aligns with overall business goals. Investing in employee training to ensure effective use of these technologies and fostering a culture of continuous improvement can further enhance the benefits of digitalization. Managers should also consider evaluating and optimizing their digital infrastructure regularly to adapt to evolving technological advancements and market demands. Establishing clear metrics to measure the impact of digital initiatives on supply chain performance can provide valuable insights and drive informed decision-making. By integrating these practices, managers can better leverage digitalization to streamline processes, enhance supply chain integration, and achieve superior financial outcomes.

CONCLUSION

The analysis conducted on a sample of 82 Tunisian industrial companies, using linear regression methods with SPSS 26, reveals a positive and significant relationship between digitalization, supply chain integration, and financial performance. The results of this study clearly demonstrate that the adoption of digital technologies within the supply chain substantially enhances external integration within supply chains and, consequently, optimizes the financial performance of companies. The results highlight that digitalization not only improves internal processes but also strengthens external integration with supply chain partners, which is crucial for achieving optimal financial performance. Companies that invest in digitalization and the integration of their supply chains can expect significant benefits in terms of competitiveness and financial performance.

In conclusion, this study confirms that Tunisian industrial companies can gain a significant strategic advantage through the digitalization of their supply chains. The adoption of digital technologies and the optimization of logistics process integration are crucial for maximizing financial benefits and supporting the sustainable growth of businesses.

Limitations and Perspectives

This study has certain limitations as in any research, and at the same time, it opens opportunities for future research.

First, the number of samples collected in this study was relatively small due to the difficulty of obtaining a large number of responses from various organizations. Future studies could focus on replicating this model in the service sector and other sectors of the economy and classify data from different sectors and compare the results across various sectors. For academic purposes, the future researcher can explore the benefits and challenges of digital supply chain adoption in businesses for better understanding.

Another limitation is linked to the organizational characteristics of the company. Indeed, the presence of the variable digitalization of the supply chain and the variable integration of the supply chain can be influenced by variables linked to the context of the company such as the sector of activity, the size of the company or the position of the company in the supply chain. These factors were not taken into consideration in our research and yet they may have an important explanatory role.

DATA AVAILABILITY STATEMENT

The data supporting this study's findings are available for corresponding author upon reasonable request.

REFERENCES

Abdallah, A. B., & Al-Ghwayeen, W. S. (2020). Green supply chain management and business performance: The mediating roles of environmental and operational performances. *Business Process Management Journal, 26*(2), 489–512. DOI: 10.1108/BPMJ-03-2018-0091

Alfalla-Luque, R., Medina-Lopez, C., & Dey, P. K. (2013). Supply chain integration framework using literature review. *Production Planning and Control, 24*(8–9), 800–817. DOI: 10.1080/09537287.2012.666870

Amosu, O. R., Kumar, P., Ogunsuji, Y. M., Oni, S., & Faworaja, O. (2024). AI-driven demand forecasting: Enhancing inventory management and customer satisfaction. *World Journal of Advanced Research and Reviews, 23*(2), 708–719. DOI: 10.30574/wjarr.2024.23.2.2394

Ataseven, C., & Nair, A. (2017). Assessment of supply chain integration and performance relationships: A meta-analytic investigation of the literature. *International Journal of Production Economics, 185*, 252–265. DOI: 10.1016/j.ijpe.2017.01.007

Baird, A., & Raghu, T. (2015). Associating consumer perceived value with business models for digital services. *European Journal of Information Systems, 24*(1), 4–22. DOI: 10.1057/ejis.2013.12

Barreto, L., Amaral, A., & Pereira, T. (2017). Industry 4.0 implications in logistics: An overview. *Procedia Manufacturing, 13*, 1245–1252. DOI: 10.1016/j.promfg.2017.09.045

Barua, A., Konana, P., Whinston, A. B., & Yin, F. (2004). An empirical investigation of net-enabled business value. *Management Information Systems Quarterly, 28*(4), 585–620. DOI: 10.2307/25148656

Björkdahl, J. (2020). Strategies for digitalization in manufacturing firms. *California Management Review, 62*(4), 17–36. DOI: 10.1177/0008125620920349

Büyüközkan, G., & Göçer, F. (2018). Digital supply chain: Literature review and a proposed framework for future research. *Computers in Industry, 97*, 157–177. DOI: 10.1016/j.compind.2018.02.010

Chang, W., Ellinger, A. E., & Kim, K. (Kate), & Franke, G. R. (2016). Supply chain integration and firm financial performance: A meta-analysis of positional advantage mediation and moderating factors. *European Management Journal*, *34*(3), 282–295. DOI: 10.1016/j.emj.2015.11.008

Chaudhuri, A., Boer, H., & Taran, Y. (2018). Supply chain integration, risk management and manufacturing flexibility. *International Journal of Operations & Production Management*, *38*(3), 690–712. DOI: 10.1108/IJOPM-08-2015-0508

Chen, M., Mao, S., & Liu, Y. (2012). Big Data: A Survey. *Mobile Networks and Applications*, *19*(2), 171–209.

Crosby, M., Pattanayak, P., Verma, S., & Kalyanaraman, V. (2016). Blockchain technology: Beyond Bitcoin. *Applied Innovation Review*, *2*, 6–10.

Deepu, T. S., & Ravi, V. (2021). Supply chain digitalization: An integrated MCDM approach for inter-organizational information systems selection in an electronic supply chain. *International Journal of Information Management Data Insights*, *1*(2), 100038. DOI: 10.1016/j.jjimei.2021.100038

Deloitte AG. (2015). *Industry 4.0: Challenges and solutions for the digital transformation*.

Dubey, R., Gunasekaran, A., Childe, S. J., Papadopoulos, T., Luo, Z., Wamba, S. F., & Roubaud, D. (2019). Can big data and predictive analytics improve social and environmental sustainability? *Technological Forecasting and Social Change*, *144*, 534–545. DOI: 10.1016/j.techfore.2017.06.020

El Ghazali, M., & Boutgayout, B. (2020). Fintech: la gestion de la performance à l'ère du digital. *Revue du Contrôle, de la Comptabilité et de l'Audit*, 4(1), 713–733.

Flynn, B. B., Huo, B., & Zhao, X. (2010). The impact of supply chain integration on performance: A contingency and configuration approach. *Journal of Operations Management*, *28*(1), 58–71. DOI: 10.1016/j.jom.2009.06.001

Fosso Wamba, S., Gunasekaran, A., & Akter, S. (2020). Blockchain technology for enhancing supply chain transparency: An empirical study. *International Journal of Production Economics*, *220*, 107475.

Gautr, R. (2020). Digitization in supply chain: Digital technologies in chemical industries. *Chemical Industry Digest.* https://doi.org/DOI: 10.4018/JGIM.311450

Germain, R., & Iyer, K. N. S. (2006). The interaction of internal and downstream integration and its association with performance. *Journal of Business Logistics*, *27*(2), 29–52. DOI: 10.1002/j.2158-1592.2006.tb00216.x

Haris, M., & Khan, R. Z. (2018). A systematic review on cloud computing. *International Journal on Computer Science and Engineering*, *6*(12).

Iddris, F. (2018). Digital supply chain: Survey of the literature. *International Journal of Business Research and Management*, *9*(1), 47.

Jayaram, J., & Xu, K. (2013). The relative influence of external versus internal integration on plant performance in China. *International Journal of Production Economics*, *146*(1), 59–69. DOI: 10.1016/j.ijpe.2013.03.024

Kayikci, Y. (2018). Sustainability impact of digitization in logistics. *Procedia Manufacturing*, *21*, 782–789. DOI: 10.1016/j.promfg.2018.02.184

Khajavi, S. H., & Holmström, J. (2015). Manufacturing digitalization and its effects on production planning and control practices. In *IFIP International Conference on Advances in Production Management Systems* (pp. 179–185). https://doi.org/DOI: 10.1007/978-3-319-22756-6_22

Lal, P., & Bharadwaj, S. (2020). Understanding the drivers of cloud-based service adoption and their impact on the organizational performance: An Indian perspective. *Journal of Global Information Management*, *28*(1), 56–85. DOI: 10.4018/JGIM.2020010104

Leuschner, R., Rogers, D. S., & Charvet, F. F. (2013). A meta-analysis of supply chain integration and firm performance. *The Journal of Supply Chain Management*, *49*(2), 34–57. DOI: 10.1111/jscm.12013

McKinsey. (2016). *Supply Chain 4.0: The next-generation digital supply chain*. McKinsey Insights.

Mofokeng, T. M., & Chinomona, R. (2019). Supply chain partnership, supply chain collaboration and supply chain integration as the antecedents of supply chain performance. *South African Journal of Business Management, 50*(1). Advance online publication. DOI: 10.4102/sajbm.v50i1.193

Mounaim, H., & Boutaqbout, Z. (2020). Gestion digitale de la chaîne logistique: Une vue d'ensemble. *Revue Internationale des Sciences de Gestion, 3*(2), 628–652. DOI: 10.5281/zenodo.3778891

Mu, Q. L., & Ming, C. W. (2023). The integration of supply chain and digitalization: The influence on SME's business performance in Chengdu, Sichuan Province, China. *Journal of Digitainability* [DREAM]. *Realism & Mastery, 2*(9). Advance online publication. DOI: 10.56982/dream.v2i09.154

Mukhopadhyay, T., & Kekre, S. (2002). Strategic and operational benefits of electronic integration in B2B procurement processes. *Management Science, 48*(10), 1301–1313. DOI: 10.1287/mnsc.48.10.1301.273

Narasimhan, R., & Kim, S. W. (2002). Effect of supply chain integration on the relationship between diversification and performance: Evidence from Japanese and Korean firms. *Journal of Operations Management, 20*(3), 303–323. DOI: 10.1016/S0272-6963(02)00008-6

Okyere, S., Osei, A., Akuh, R., & Addo, L. (2023). The effect of supply chain digitalization on internal supply chain integration of cement manufacturing and distribution firms in Ghana. *African Journal of Applied Research, 9*(1), 232–256. DOI: 10.26437/ajar.v9i1.532

Opresnik, D., & Taisch, M. (2015). The value of big data in servitization. *International Journal of Production Economics, 165*, 174–184. DOI: 10.1016/j.ijpe.2014.12.036

Parviainen, P., Tihinen, M., Kääriäinen, J., & Teppola, S. (2017). Tackling the digitalization challenge: How to benefit from digitalization in practice. *International Journal of Information Systems and Project Management, 5*(1), 63–77. DOI: 10.12821/ijispm050104

Prabhu, T. (2016). Modern rapid 3D printer – A design review. *International Journal of Mechanical Engineering and Technology, 7*(3), 29–37.

Rai, A., Patnayakuni, R., & Seth, N. (2006). Firm performance impacts of digitally enabled supply chain integration capabilities. *Management Information Systems Quarterly, 30*(2), 225–246.

Ross, J. W., Beath, C. M., & Sebastian, I. M. (2017). Digitized ≠ Digital. *MIT CISR Research Briefings, 18*(10), 1–3.

Sabir, R., & Irfan, M. (2014). Levels & barriers to supply chain integration: A conceptual model of supply chain performance. *International Journal of Management Science and Business Administration, 1*(1), 52–59. DOI: 10.18775/IJMSBA.1849-5664-5419.2014.11.1005

Sabri, Y., Harchi, S., & El Kamoun, N. (2022). Managing health supply chain using blockchain technology: State of the art, challenges, and solution. [IJRES]. *International Journal of Reconfigurable and Embedded Systems, 11*(1), 49–57. DOI: 10.11591/ijres.v11.i3.pp258-264

Salonitis, K., Fadiji, T., Trollman, H., Garcia-Garcia, G., Bader, F., & Jagtap, S. (2021). Food Logistics 4.0: Opportunities and challenges. *Logistics (Basel), 5*(1), 1–19.

Som, J. O., Cobblah, C., & Anyigba, H. (2019). The effect of supply chain integration on supply chain performance. *IUP Journal of Supply Chain Management, 16*(4), 7–38.

Srinivasan, K., Kekre, S., & Mukhopadhyay, T. (1994). Impact of electronic data interchange technology on JIT shipments. *Management Science, 40*(10), 1291–1304. DOI: 10.1287/mnsc.40.10.1291

Stank, T., Esper, T., Goldsby, T. J., Zinn, W., & Autry, C. (2019). Toward a digitally dominant paradigm for twenty-first century supply chain scholarship. *International Journal of Physical Distribution & Logistics Management, 49*(10), 956–971. DOI: 10.1108/IJPDLM-03-2019-0076

Sultana, S., Akter, S., Kyriazis, E., & Wamba, S. (2021). Architecting and developing big data-driven innovation (DDI) in the digital economy. *Journal of Global Information Management, 29*(3), 165–187. DOI: 10.4018/JGIM.2021050107

SupplyChainDigest. (2016). *SCDigest supply chain digitization benchmark survey.*

Uniyal, S., Mangla, S., Sarma, P., Tseng, M., & Patil, P. (2021). ICT as "knowledge management" for assessing sustainable consumption and production in supply chains. *Journal of Global Information Management, 29*(1), 164–198. DOI: 10.4018/JGIM.2021010109

Wamba, S. F., Gunasekaran, A., Akter, S., Ren, S. J.-F., Dubey, R., & Childe, S. J. (2017). Big data analytics and firm performance: Effects of dynamic capabilities. *Journal of Business Research, 70*, 356–365. DOI: 10.1016/j.jbusres.2016.08.009

Wang, X., Yu, L., & Li, Q. (2018). The role of IoT in enhancing supply chain management and logistics: A review and future research agenda. *International Journal of Production Economics, 205*, 3–16.

Westerman, G., Bonnet, D., & McAfee, A. (2014). *Leading digital: Turning technology into business transformation*. Harvard Business Review Press.

Xue, L. (2014). Governance–knowledge fit and strategic risk taking in supply chain digitization. *Decision Support Systems, 62*, 54–65. DOI: 10.1016/j.dss.2014.03.003

Zhang, C., & Li, S. (2024). Involving purchasing and supply chain management in open ecological innovation: The moderating role of digital technologies. *International Journal of Logistics: Research and Applications, 27*(7), 1047–1070. DOI: 10.1080/1375567.2024.2316647

Chapter 6
Harnessing Artificial Intelligence for the Renaissance of Sustainable Supply Chains:
Navigating the Nexus of ESG Aspirations

R. Purushothaman
https://orcid.org/0009-0003-0941-8462
SASTRA University, India

R. Alamelu
SASTRA University, India

Sathya Manickam
https://orcid.org/0009-0009-7539-0318
SASTRA University, India

M. Sudha
https://orcid.org/0000-0001-9923-3602
SASTRA University, India

DOI: 10.4018/979-8-3373-2843-0.ch006

Leema Christina J.
SASTRA University, India

ABSTRACT

In 2025's evolving business landscape, sustainable supply chains are key to corporate responsibility, driven by ESG goals and tighter regulations. This chapter explores how AI and emerging technologies are reshaping supply chain management, enabling smart, ethical, and low-impact operations. AI advances from intelligent product design to optimized inventory, reduce waste and emissions while supporting profitability. Blockchain enhances transparency via digital product passports and carbon traceability. Regenerative supply networks and digital twins support ecosystem restoration and real-time impact modeling. Innovations like smart packaging, autonomous logistics, and urban hubs drive further circularity. Cross-industry AI platforms and supplier sustainability tools foster ESG alignment. The chapter also addresses ethical risks includes data privacy, AI bias, and environmental trade-offs—offering strategies for responsible tech adoption.

1. INTRODUCTION

In the dynamic and increasingly complex global economy of 2025, the importance of sustainable supply chains has shifted from a peripheral concern to a central strategic priority (Sarkis et al., 2010; Yadav et al., 2024). Corporations across industries are being held to higher standards of accountability, transparency, and environmental stewardship, driven by escalating regulatory pressures, investor scrutiny, and shifting consumer expectations (Zahoor & Lew, 2021; McLennan, M. 2022). Within this evolving context, Environmental, Social, and Governance (ESG) principles have emerged as the dominant framework by which stakeholders assess a company's sustainability performance and long-term value creation (Eccles et al., 2014). As organizations grapple with the dual challenges of climate change and global resource constraints, the need to rethink traditional, linear supply chain models has become urgent (Geissdoerfer et al.,

2016). The conventional take-make-dispose paradigm is being replaced by circular, data-driven, and regenerative models that are not only more efficient but also more ethically grounded and environmentally responsible (Bocken et al., 2016).

Central to this transformation is the rapid advancement of Artificial Intelligence (AI) and other digital technologies (Dubey et al., 2021; Choi et al., 2017). No longer limited to task automation, AI now plays a pivotal role in strategic decision-making, enabling real-time responsiveness, predictive insights, and system-wide optimization (Sethi et al., 2005). Its integration into supply chain operations allows companies to proactively address ESG concerns by reducing carbon footprints, minimizing waste, improving labor practices, and increasing transparency across the value chain (Bag et al., 2021; Centobelli et al., 2020).

In parallel, technologies such as blockchain, digital twins, and smart IoT-based logistics are converging to further reinforce ESG commitments (Saberi et al., 2018; Ivanov et al., 2021). Blockchain ensures traceability and trust, while digital twins enable environmental modeling and impact forecasting (Kamble et al., 2019). These innovations collectively empower supply chains to move beyond risk mitigation toward value creation in alignment with global sustainability targets such as the United Nations Sustainable Development Goals (SDGs) and national net-zero commitments (Albu, D., 2021).

Figure 1. AI driven supply chain progresses from enablers to ethical outcomes.

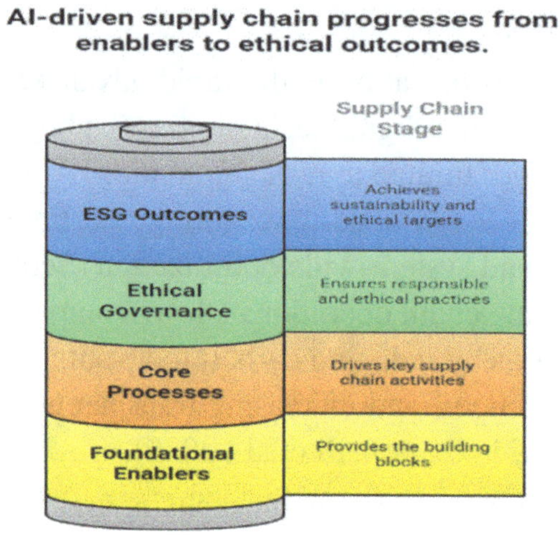

This chapter provides a comprehensive examination of how AI and emerging technologies are catalyzing the renaissance of sustainable supply chains. It explores the evolving nexus between digital transformation and ESG aspirations, unpacking how technological interventions are not only enabling compliance but also fostering resilience, regeneration, and competitive differentiation (Bag et al., 2021a). In the globalized economy of 2025, sustainability is no longer a voluntary agenda but a strategic imperative, as climate change, biodiversity loss, and socio-economic inequalities intensify pressure on businesses to transform their operations. Central to this transformation is the redesign of supply chains to align with Environmental, Social, and Governance (ESG) standards and circular economy principles. The concept of sustainable supply chains—originating in the late 1990s through the lens of green logistics and corporate social responsibility—has evolved to embrace a broader systemic view that integrates technology, ethics, and stakeholder value creation. Empirical studies reveal the increasing relevance of technological enablers such as Artificial Intelligence (AI), blockchain, and digital twins in advancing supply chain sustainability. AI is now instrumental in enabling predictive analytics, intelligent forecasting, carbon monitoring, and supplier sustainability assessments, thereby offering practical solutions for real-time ESG compliance. However, despite the proliferation of digital tools, practical implementation remains uneven due to infrastructural, ethical, regulatory, and organizational barriers. Moreover, global case evidence suggests that many firms struggle to balance AI-led efficiencies with ethical concerns such as data transparency, algorithmic bias, and the environmental cost of digital operations. There is a dearth of comprehensive frameworks that holistically integrate AI and emerging technologies with ESG performance metrics, especially in regenerative and circular supply chain contexts. This chapter addresses these research and practice gaps by providing a conceptual and empirical synthesis that links AI-driven innovation with the ethics and challenges of sustainable supply chain transformation. Thus, the central research question guiding this chapter is: **How can Artificial Intelligence and emerging digital technologies be leveraged to enhance ESG performance, overcome sustainability implementation barriers, and enable regenerative, circular supply chains?** This inquiry is significant for scholars developing cross-disciplinary frameworks, practitioners seeking deployment strategies, and policymakers designing enabling environments for sustainable technology adoption. By doing so, the chapter contributes a forward-looking direction for future research and governance strategies aimed at building intelligent, resilient, and regenerative supply chains globally. By drawing on cross-sectoral applications, the chapter highlights actionable insights and real-world innovations, while also addressing the ethical and operational challenges associated with deploying AI responsibly (Dwivedi et al., 2019). Ultimately, this chapter aims to offer a roadmap for businesses, researchers, and policymakers seeking to harness the power of intelligent technologies to drive sustainable and regenerative supply chain practices in the years ahead.

2. BACKGROUND AND STATEMENT OF THE PROBLEM

Sustainable supply chains should address systematic problems like resource depletion, carbon emission, and environmental destruction; however, making the outdated so-called take-make-dispose model circular and sustainable is still challenging. Although many tasks can be done with the help of technology development, especially with the help of Artificial Intelligence (AI), blockchain, and digital twins, the way it is done on a real-world scale poses some operational, infrastructural, and regulatory challenges that get in the way. The limitation is depicted through real-life cases in various sectors. For example, the People & Planet Positive approach of IKEA helps optimize its inventory using AI and draw a trace of timber over the blockchain to enhance transparency and the presence of materials. Nonetheless, the company is still experiencing challenges in putting circular practice in line with the rapidly changing consumer behaviour. Likewise, in India, the textile SMEs that use AI to achieve sustainable cotton sourcing have issues with data accessibility, skill deficits, and the lack of digital infrastructure. The industry giant and a global shipping company, Maersk, realizing the overall emission reduction benefits through fuel optimization with the help of AI, lacks unified tools to evaluate the biodiversity and ecosystem effects during the international lines. This real-life evidence is an eye-opener to the bigger problem: sustainable change cannot be ingeniously enhanced through technology without favourable governance, ethical integration, stakeholder coordination, and policies.

Furthermore, emerging economies SMEs are usually unable to implement and adjust to new, more accessory digital technologies, strengthening the digital divide in green innovation. This forms a perplexing landscape whereby the digital potential is not readily convertible to sustainable results. Though some studies praise the potential of AI and blockchain in increasing the transparency and efficiency of the supply chain, conflicting data indicates the possibility of strengthening the existing social inequalities and algorithmic bias and improving the environmental cost of the digital infrastructure. This inequity of outcome reveals numerous research and practice gaps. The theoretical gap exists since available frameworks do not effectively combine AI potentials with ESG and circular economy aspects. There remains an empirical gap related to the limited sectoral coverage and unavailability of longitudinal or comparative data. The lack of context is also relatively high. There is little research on a global scale that looks into the SMEs and companies in the Global South. Moreover, a practical action space opens where there is no evident, comprehensible model of responsible, ethical, and inclusive deployment of AI. In addition, the effectiveness of such newer technological approaches as digital twins, autonomous logistics, and innovative packaging in meeting sustainability has been inconclusive. Thus, the main issue is the absence of a systematic, ethical, and practically feasible explanation of how AI and digital technologies may empower ESG-compliant, circular, and regenerative supply chains. As a solution to this extent, this chapter presents a multi-level framework regarding the integration of digital innovation and sustainability objectives, evidence-based on cross-industry cases, ethical governance policies, and policy recommendations. In this way, the chapter provides a proactive path to be followed by the researchers and policymakers who focus on how AI and emerging technologies can be used to support compliance and achieve strategic advantage and climate resilience and provide material value to society.

3. THE ROLE OF ARTIFICIAL INTELLIGENCE IN SUSTAINABLE SUPPLY CHAIN MANAGEMENT

Artificial Intelligence (AI) has undergone a transformative evolution from a primarily operational tool used for automation to a strategic enabler of sustainability in global supply chains. In the context of Sustainable Supply Chain Management (SSCM), AI empowers organizations to align logistics, procurement, manufacturing, and distribution practices with environmental, social, and governance (ESG) goals (Dubey et al., 2019). Through the integration of vast datasets, machine learning algorithms, and real-time analytics, AI facilitates greater transparency, precision, and accountability across the supply chain, thereby driving sustainable value creation (Wamba et al., 2019).

3.1 From Automation to Intelligent Sustainability

Traditionally, AI applications in supply chain management focused on enhancing operational efficiency—reducing lead times, optimizing costs, and improving throughput (Sethi et al., 2005). However, as sustainability has emerged as a core strategic objective, AI's role has expanded. It now acts as a catalyst for systemic change by enabling predictive, adaptive, and ethical decision-making processes that align with ESG benchmarks (Bag et al., 2021). AI systems are capable of detecting inefficiencies, forecasting risks, and identifying high-emission activities that might otherwise go unnoticed. By embedding ESG metrics into AI models, businesses can transition from reactive compliance to proactive sustainability leadership, redefining the purpose and performance of supply chains (Yadav et al., 2024).

3.2 AI-Driven Product Design for Environmental Impact Reduction

AI's influence begins at the design phase, a critical stage where over 80% of a product's environmental impact is determined (Bai et al., 2020). AI-powered design platforms simulate the impact of material choices, component configurations, and energy inputs, enabling the creation of eco-efficient products. Machine learning models evaluate millions of permutations to recommend optimal solutions that minimize carbon footprints, enhance product durability, and increase recyclability (Agrawal et al., 2023). This approach supports the principles of the circular economy by enabling the design of modular and repairable products that extend lifecycle value. For example, AI can identify materials that are compatible with closed-loop recycling systems or advise on disassembly techniques that reduce e-waste. These sustainable innovations resonate strongly with evolving consumer preferences and regulatory mandates for low-impact, high-performance goods (Geissdoerfer et al., 2016; McLennan, M. 2022).

3.3 Innovations in Materials Science and Resource Optimization

AI is accelerating breakthroughs in materials science, helping companies transition away from environmentally harmful inputs. Through deep learning and generative algorithms, AI models can predict molecular behavior and environmental characteristics of new materials before they are physically tested, significantly reducing R&D timelines and costs (Acerbi et al., 2021). Concurrently, AI tools enable resource optimization in manufacturing processes by identifying anomalies, leakages, and inefficiencies in real time. By using AI for energy management, water conservation, and raw material optimization, firms can reduce waste and emissions across production cycles. Predictive maintenance solutions, powered by AI, further contribute by ensuring equipment longevity and minimizing unplanned downtime—both of which reduce energy spikes and material loss (Bag et al., 2021; Sethi et al., 2005).

3.4 Smart Inventory and Demand Forecasting

Inventory mismanagement often leads to overproduction, unsold stock, and excess emissions associated with storage and disposal. AI addresses this challenge through advanced demand forecasting models that integrate real-time sales data, historical consumption patterns, seasonal variables, and external influencers like geopolitical developments and climate events (Dubey et al., 2019). By aligning supply with actual demand, AI helps companies reduce excess inventory, minimize waste, and cut down on transportation-related emissions. This alignment also improves customer satisfaction by ensuring product availability without oversupply. Many firms have reported waste reductions of up to 25% after implementing AI-driven inventory optimization systems, underscoring AI's significant environmental and economic benefits (Geissdoerfer et al., 2016; Wamba et al., 2019).

3.5 ESG-Aware Decision Intelligence

Perhaps one of the most promising developments in sustainable supply chain transformation is the emergence of ESG-aware AI platforms. These systems extend beyond traditional performance indicators to incorporate ethical, social, and environmental factors in decision-making (Bag et al., 2021a). By analyzing data related to carbon footprints, supplier labor practices, diversity metrics, and ecological impacts, AI enables businesses to make more informed and responsible choices (Yadav et al., 2024). For instance, an AI platform might evaluate two suppliers based on cost, but recommend the one with lower emissions, verified labor certifications, and higher ESG ratings, even if slightly more expensive. These intelligent trade-offs support long-term sustainability objectives and strengthen corporate reputations (Eccles et al., 2014). Over time, ESG-aligned AI decision-making fosters resilient supply chains that are better equipped to meet regulatory expectations and societal demands (McLennan, M. 2022).

4. ENHANCING CARBON EFFICIENCY THROUGH AI

Reducing carbon emissions is a central pillar of global sustainability efforts and is deeply embedded in the Environmental, Social, and Governance (ESG) frameworks adopted by corporations worldwide (Eccles et al., 2014; Albu, D., 2021). In response to growing climate change concerns and regulatory pressures, organizations are increasingly turning to Artificial Intelligence (AI) to optimize operations and significantly improve carbon efficiency across their supply chains. AI technologies offer advanced analytical, predictive, and decision-support capabilities that facilitate carbon-aware strategies, real-time environmental monitoring, and intelligent resource utilization (Dubey et al., 2019; Bag et al., 2021).

4.1 Carbon-Aware Network Design and Logistics

Supply chain logistics are among the largest contributors to greenhouse gas (GHG) emissions, primarily due to transportation, warehousing, and energy-intensive distribution operations. AI-driven optimization models play a transformative role in reconfiguring supply chain networks by evaluating vast datasets to identify the most carbon-efficient pathways. These models utilize heuristic and metaheuristic algorithms, such as genetic algorithms and neural networks, to recommend logistics configurations that reduce transit distances, avoid redundant routing, and optimize vehicle capacity utilization (Choi et al., 2017). By incorporating real-time data—such as traffic conditions, weather patterns, port congestion, and fuel prices—AI tools dynamically adjust delivery schedules and routes to minimize fuel usage and carbon output. This results in not only lowered transportation emissions but also improved on-time delivery performance and reduced operational costs (Ivanov et al., 2021). In multimodal transport scenarios, AI can aid in mode selection optimization, promoting shifts from high-emission road freight to cleaner alternatives such as rail or inland waterways, thereby embedding sustainability into core logistics decisions.

4.2 Smart Procurement and Sustainable Sourcing

Procurement decisions significantly influence the upstream carbon footprint of organizations. AI-powered procurement platforms integrate diverse datasets—ranging from supplier carbon disclosures and sustainability certifications to product life-cycle assessments (LCA)—to facilitate informed and sustainable sourcing decisions (Bag et al., 2021a). These systems rank suppliers not only on cost and quality but also on carbon performance metrics, incentivizing the selection of vendors aligned with corporate climate objectives (Wamba et al., 2019). Furthermore, AI enables the identification and prioritization of low-carbon materials, such as recycled content, biodegradable inputs, or regionally sourced goods, which reduce transportation emissions and resource extraction impacts. Through predictive demand analytics, AI can forecast material requirements with higher precision, reducing over-ordering, excess inventory, and waste generation. In this way, AI fosters the development of climate-resilient, ethical, and efficient procurement ecosystems that align environmental stewardship with supply continuity and cost-effectiveness (Bai et al., 2020).

4.3 Real-Time Emissions Monitoring and Reporting

The deployment of AI-integrated IoT sensors and digital twin technologies has revolutionized emissions monitoring across production and supply chain processes. These tools continuously collect granular data on parameters such as energy consumption, machinery performance, emissions per unit output, and process inefficiencies (Kamble et al., 2019). When processed using machine learning algorithms, this data provides organizations with real-time visibility into carbon hotspots, enabling timely corrective actions and process reengineering. This proactive monitoring capability supports compliance with international and national environmental reporting standards, including frameworks such as CDP, GRI, and TCFD. Moreover, automated and high-fidelity carbon reporting enhances transparency and stakeholder trust, serving as a vital tool for investor communication, ESG ratings, and reputational risk management (Saberi et al., 2018; Eccles et al., 2014). Companies that demonstrate verifiable emissions reductions often benefit from preferential access to green financing, tax incentives, and enhanced brand loyalty.

4.4 Scenario Planning for Decarbonization Pathways

Beyond day-to-day operations, AI enables long-term strategic planning for decarbonization through scenario simulation and forecasting. Using historical and real-time operational data, AI models can simulate various "what-if" scenarios—such as transitioning to renewable energy sources, adopting circular manufacturing practices, modifying shift schedules, or redesigning products for energy efficiency (Dubey et al., 2019). These simulations allow decision-makers to understand the environmental and economic trade-offs of different pathways toward achieving net-zero emissions or science-based targets. For example, AI can estimate the return on investment (ROI) for installing solar panels in a facility versus purchasing carbon offsets or reengineering a production line for electrification. These insights help organizations prioritize cost-effective, low-risk strategies that align with evolving regulations, market pressures, and climate commitments (Sethi et al., 2005). Additionally, AI can monitor external variables—such as carbon pricing mechanisms, supply chain disruptions due to climate events, or new policy mandates—and dynamically adjust corporate decarbonization roadmaps. This predictive agility ensures that sustainability initiatives remain robust in the face of uncertainty, enabling businesses to remain resilient, competitive, and compliant in a low-carbon economy (Albu, D., 2021).

5. BLOCKCHAIN FOR CIRCULAR AND TRANSPARENT SUPPLY CHAINS

The evolution of blockchain technology has reached a maturity level that enables companies to address critical ESG (Environmental, Social, and Governance) priorities, particularly supply chain transparency, circularity, and carbon accountability (Saberi et al., 2018; Centobelli et al., 2020). By providing immutable and decentralized data records, blockchain fosters trust among stakeholders and ensures verifiable, tamper-proof sustainability reporting (Ivanov et al., 2021).

5.1 Blockchain Maturity in Supply Chains

Initially designed to secure cryptocurrency transactions, blockchain now underpins advanced industrial supply chains by enabling secure, shared, and auditable records of product movements and transformations (Saberi et al., 2018). This technological evolution has empowered companies to move from fragmented, paper-based documentation toward integrated, real-time digital supply networks. Major brands like De Beers have leveraged blockchain for tracking the provenance of diamonds from mines to retail, ensuring conflict-free sourcing and ethical labor practices (Everledger, 2020). Such real-time traceability combats fraud, deters illegal sourcing, and enhances customer confidence. In the food industry, Walmart uses IBM's Food Trust blockchain to trace fresh produce back to farms within seconds, drastically reducing the response time during food safety recalls (IBM, 2023). These examples highlight how blockchain's maturity supports full-cycle traceability, enhances regulatory compliance, and mitigates the risks of greenwashing by allowing regulators and stakeholders to audit sustainability claims with unprecedented transparency and speed (Geissdoerfer et al., 2016; Centobelli et al., 2020).

5.2 Core Tools and Concepts

Blockchain's role in circular and sustainable supply chains is brought to life through innovative tools that translate theoretical traceability into operational benefits.

5.2.1 Digital Product Passports

A Digital Product Passport (DPP) is a dynamic, blockchain-secured record detailing a product's lifecycle, including its raw material sources, manufacturing impacts, certifications, and recycling instructions (Dwivedi et al., 2019). The European Union is pioneering DPPs for batteries, textiles, and electronics under its Circular Economy Action Plan. For example,

Fairphone, a Dutch smartphone manufacturer, provides DPPs to disclose responsible material sourcing and easy disassembly, enabling consumers to repair or recycle devices responsibly (Fairphone, 2023).

5.2.2 Verification-as-a-Service

Verification-as-a-Service harnesses blockchain's smart contract capability to automate auditing and compliance verification (Saberi et al., 2018). For instance, Provenance, a UK-based blockchain company, offers real-time verification for sustainable seafood supply chains by certifying fishing practices and ecological impacts (Provenance, 2023). This reduces manual auditing costs while boosting buyer confidence in sustainability labels.

5.2.3 Chain-of-Custody and Green Certificates

Chain-of-custody tracking ensures materials comply with sustainability standards across multiple handlers. Timberland uses blockchain to verify that its leather comes from regenerative ranches, supporting biodiversity and carbon sequestration (Timberland, 2023). Combined with blockchain-enabled green certificates, companies credibly demonstrate alignment with environmental and social governance metrics, safeguarding brand reputation and investor trust (Geissdoerfer et al., 2016; Centobelli et al., 2020).

5.3 Carbon Credit and Circular Economy Synergies

Blockchain plays a critical role in increasing transparency and efficiency in carbon markets, tackling long-standing issues like double counting, fraud, and opaque trading (Saberi et al., 2018). By recording emissions data immutably and automating credit issuance via smart contracts, blockchain ensures that carbon offset projects deliver verifiable environmental outcomes (Ivanov et al., 2021). A prime example is the Toucan Protocol, which tokenizes real carbon credits on the blockchain, allowing companies to buy and retire them with full transparency and traceability (Toucan Protocol, 2023). In the circular economy, blockchain supports multi-life-cycle material tracking — for example, the Circularise platform enables manufacturers to share verified data about recycled plastics' origin and quality without revealing sensitive supplier information (Circularise, 2023). This encourages recycling markets and supports closed-loop supply chains where materials are continually reused, remanufactured, or safely biodegraded. Collectively, these applications strengthen corporate ESG commitments, ensuring that sustainability claims are not only data-backed but also accessible for audit by regulators, investors, and conscious consumers alike (Geissdoerfer et al., 2016).

6. REGENERATIVE SUPPLY NETWORKS

As global sustainability discourse evolves, organizations are shifting from sustainability compliance to proactive regeneration of natural and social systems (Geissdoerfer et al., 2016; Bocken et al., 2016). Regenerative supply networks extend the traditional net-zero paradigm by embedding restorative practices directly into supply chain operations, fostering positive ecological and community impacts (Dwivedi et al., 2019; Agrawal et al., 2023).

6.1 Moving Beyond Net-Zero

While net-zero strategies aim to balance emitted and offset greenhouse gases, regenerative approaches target a net-positive impact on ecosystems and society (Bocken et al., 2016). This paradigm involves restoring degraded ecosystems, enhancing biodiversity, and revitalizing local communities affected by supply chain activities (Geissdoerfer et al., 2016). Companies are integrating regenerative agriculture, reforestation, and habitat conservation into their sourcing and production processes to actively repair environmental damage (Agrawal et al., 2023).

6.2 Capacity Building and Local Empowerment

Regenerative supply networks emphasize building resilience in local communities through capacity building and stakeholder inclusion (Dwivedi et al., 2019). By investing in local knowledge, fair labor practices, and community-led environmental stewardship, organizations foster long-term socio-economic development aligned with ESG goals (Bag et al., 2021a). Open-source climate analytics platforms support farmers and suppliers in adopting regenerative practices, such as soil carbon sequestration and biodiversity-friendly farming methods (Ivanov et al., 2021).

6.3 Integrating Biodiversity Metrics

Monitoring biodiversity impacts is increasingly vital for regenerative supply chains (Geissdoerfer et al., 2016). AI and IoT tools enable continuous assessment of ecosystem health, species richness, and habitat quality along supply chain routes (Kamble et al., 2019). Companies are beginning to integrate biodiversity key performance indicators (KPIs) into corporate strategies and sustainability reporting, ensuring that restorative efforts are measurable and transparent (Agrawal et al., 2023).

6.4 Open Innovation and Cross-Sector Collaboration

Achieving regenerative supply networks requires extensive cross-sector partnerships and shared data ecosystems (Dwivedi et al., 2019). Collaborative platforms connect corporations, governments, NGOs, and local communities to co-develop restoration projects, share regenerative techniques, and align on global sustainability frameworks (Bag et al., 2021a). This openness fosters rapid scaling of successful regenerative models and accelerates the transition to a regenerative economy.

7. INNOVATIONS IN LOGISTICS AND PACKAGING

Packaging and logistics are critical levers for advancing sustainability goals across the supply chain (Bag et al., 2021a; Kamble et al., 2019). Leading companies are deploying smart materials, digital technologies, and autonomous systems to reduce carbon emissions, minimize waste, and close resource loops (Dwivedi et al., 2019; Ivanov et al., 2021).

7.1 Smart Sustainable Packaging

Smart sustainable packaging integrates eco-friendly materials with IoT-enabled monitoring to reduce environmental impact and food spoilage. For example, Unilever has invested in biodegradable packaging for its food brands, aiming to eliminate fossil-fuel-based plastics from its portfolio by 2030 (Unilever, 2024). Similarly, Freshness Sensors Ltd., a packaging tech start-up, supplies retailers with smart labels that change color as perishable goods approach spoilage, helping to cut food waste (Bag et al., 2021a). Major retailers like Walmart use AI tools to optimize packaging dimensions, reducing excess material use and transport emissions while lowering operational costs (Dwivedi et al., 2019).

7.2 Green Logistics Infrastructure

The push for green logistics has led to rapid adoption of electric vehicles and smart urban delivery systems. Amazon, for instance, has committed to deploying 100,000 custom electric delivery vans through its partnership with Rivian, targeting net-zero carbon deliveries by 2040 (The climate pledge. n.d.). DHL Express operates urban consolidation centers in major cities like London and Berlin, consolidating last-mile deliveries into fewer trips to cut emissions and urban congestion (Dhl-green-logistics-toolkit, 2024). These smart hubs are integrated with city infrastructure, using data analytics to dynamically reroute deliveries based on real-time traffic conditions (Kamble et al., 2019).

7.3 Digital Twins for Sustainability

Digital twin technology is increasingly deployed to simulate, monitor, and optimize logistics and packaging sustainability in real time. Procter & Gamble (P&G) uses digital twins to model its supply chain's energy and water use, enabling managers to test packaging design changes before implementation and assess environmental trade-offs (Ivanov et al., 2021). Likewise, Maersk, a global logistics leader, employs digital twins of shipping routes and port operations to forecast fuel use and optimize vessel speeds, contributing to its goal of carbon-neutral shipping by 2050

(Sustainability at Maersk. n.d.). These virtual replicas empower firms to make data-driven decisions that align operations with ESG targets (Agrawal et al., 2023).

8. AI-ENHANCED SUPPLIER SUSTAINABILITY MANAGEMENT

8.1 Supplier Data Automation

Managing supplier sustainability data across global, multi-tiered supply chains is a significant challenge due to the diversity of regulatory environments, data formats, and compliance maturity. Manual auditing processes—while foundational—are often slow, costly, and susceptible to errors or manipulation. Artificial Intelligence (AI) offers a transformative solution by automating the collection, verification, and analysis of supplier ESG (Environmental, Social, and Governance) data. AI platforms such as SAP Ariba Sustainability integrate supplier declarations with external databases, news reports, regulatory filings, and IoT sensor data to construct a more holistic sustainability profile of each vendor (SAP, 2024). These systems cross-verify self-reported documents, such as GHG emissions reports or fair labor certifications, by comparing them against third-party benchmarks and real-time data inputs. Using machine learning algorithms, AI tools assign predictive sustainability scores to suppliers by evaluating factors like historical compliance, carbon intensity, social impact, and risk exposure. These scores are continuously updated as new data becomes available, offering procurement teams dynamic insights to inform strategic decisions. This automation not only saves time and resources but also reduces greenwashing and improves accountability across the supply base. Moreover, AI-driven platforms can scale across thousands of suppliers, making them especially valuable for multinational corporations seeking to standardize ESG compliance across varied geographies. Ultimately, AI-enabled supplier data automation enhances due diligence, fosters responsible sourcing, and aligns supply chain partnerships with an organization's broader sustainability goals (Bag et al., 2021a; Kamble et al., 2019).

8.2 Sustainability Risk Detection

Proactive sustainability risk management is essential for building resilient and ethically sound supply chains. Traditional risk monitoring methods often detect issues only after they have resulted in disruptions, violations, or reputational harm. In contrast, AI-powered risk detection systems use real-time analytics to monitor and interpret massive data streams—including supplier transactions, social media chatter, satellite imagery, and environmental reports—to identify warning signs early (Dwivedi et al., 2019). For example, IBM's Supply Chain Insights platform uses machine learning models trained on historical disruptions and external variables (e.g., labor unrest, natural disasters, regulatory changes) to forecast potential risks in a supplier's operations (IBM, 2024). These systems allow firms to assess both inherent and dynamic sustainability risks—such as child labor, water scarcity, or carbon overuse—across their global supplier base. Once a potential issue is identified, AI systems can trigger automated alerts and generate recommended mitigation strategies. Companies can then initiate direct engagement with at-risk suppliers to implement corrective measures, such as cleaner production practices, ethical labor training, or alternative sourcing options. This shift from reactive to predictive risk management significantly reduces the likelihood of supply chain disruptions and enhances overall ESG performance.

Moreover, AI enables continuous monitoring rather than periodic reviews, thereby embedding sustainability risk intelligence into daily decision-making. By facilitating early intervention and collaborative remediation, AI-based systems contribute to long-term supplier development and reinforce a culture of continuous improvement and shared responsibility within the value chain (Ivanov et al., 2021; Bag et al., 2021a).

8.3 Multi-Tier Visibility

One of the most persistent challenges in sustainable supply chain governance is achieving full visibility beyond first-tier suppliers. While companies may have direct oversight of immediate vendors, the real sustainability risks often lie hidden deeper in the supply chain—in second, third, or even fourth-tier suppliers. These indirect suppliers are typically responsible for raw material extraction, early-stage manufacturing, or subcontracted labor—areas prone to environmental violations, unethical labor practices, or resource overuse (Kamble et al., 2019). AI plays a critical role in overcoming this visibility gap by mapping complex supply chain networks and tracing product lineage with unprecedented granularity. Advanced AI tools use network graph analytics, natural language processing, and traceability algorithms to analyze supplier interdependencies. By aggregating data from purchase orders, invoices, customs records, and digital product passports, AI systems can reconstruct the full supply chain map and highlight previously unidentified suppliers or subcontractors (Ivanov et al., 2018). Companies such as Nestlé have used such tools to trace cocoa and palm oil back to the farm or plantation level, helping enforce deforestation-free and fair-trade commitments (Nestlé, 2023). This level of traceability enhances compliance with global standards such as the EU Deforestation Regulation and the UN Guiding Principles on Business and Human Rights. Moreover, multi-tier visibility improves stakeholder engagement and transparency. It enables accurate ESG disclosures, strengthens investor confidence, and supports regulatory audits. By illuminating hidden risks and dependencies, AI fosters a more resilient, inclusive, and ethically sound supply chain ecosystem.

9. PLATFORMS FOR CROSS-INDUSTRY ESG COLLABORATION

Achieving transformative sustainability outcomes often requires companies to collaborate beyond organizational and sectoral boundaries (Bag et al., 2021a; Dwivedi et al., 2019). Digital collaboration platforms are emerging as powerful tools for cross-industry partnerships, shared learning, and harmonized ESG compliance.

9.1 Emerging Collaboration Ecosystems

Organizations are increasingly realizing that in their quest to achieve sustainable development, specific complex yet systemic issues like climate change, waste management, and shortages of resources cannot be addressed in disparity. Consequently, dawning digital collaboration landscapes are now essential facilitators of sustainability-driven innovation. These ecosystems are networks of firms doing business with public institutions, start-ups, universities and non-government organizations, co-developing sustainable commercial business models, technology and governance systems (Dwivedi et al., 2019). These integrating and combined experimental efforts facilitate these alliances to shift transactional partnerships into purposive coalitions. The one we can give is the Circulars Accelerator implemented by the World Economic Forum, which links circular economy start-ups with large companies across the world to collaborate and develop solutions to circular economy that can be scaled to reduce waste, reuse, and regenerate resources (McLennan, M. 2022). These partnerships revolve around areas like packaging, food and fashion- in which redesigning items and supply chains would have long-term effects. An example is the Global Battery Alliance, a public-private cooperation involving automakers, miners, recyclers and NGOs.

The alliance to reduce the risk of sustainability and human rights throughout the battery supply chains introduces the standards of the ethical supply chain of raw material, battery traceability, and recycling at the end of life (Global Battery Alliance, 2024). Those ecosystems live up to precompetitive cooperation, where companies team up on groundwork problems, including carbon-neutral logistics or regenerative agriculture, without sacrificing their business. These networks extend the impact and pace of sustainability transitions by enhancing co-innovation and systemic thinking. They are also nurseries to pilot initiatives, policy processes, and industry-scale guidelines, which foster economic development and balance the planet's health with economic progress.

9.2 Knowledge Sharing and Benchmarking

Transparency, learning, and performance improvement are critical dynamics of a successful sustainability transformation; consequently, collaborative knowledge-sharing platforms enable such results. EcoVadis and Carbon Disclosure Project (CDP) are some platforms that have become standards in the disclosures of corporate ESGs and sustainability benchmarking globally. They offer systematic mechanisms through which thousands of agencies report their carbon output, resource utilization, human rights procedures, and corporate directing in a formulated and relatable outline (CDP, 2024). Such platforms promote accountability through peer benchmarking and making investors scrutinize. Such platforms are supplemented with analytics and AI tools that process large quantities of information to find regularities, list the best ESG practices, and suggest the best practices within the segment (Bag et al., 2021a). For example, an industrial company can use the insights generated by AI to diagnose non-performative suppliers, contrast its energy consumption rates with the industry benchmarks, and use emissions-cutting strategies that have already been implemented successfully by sustainability leaders within the same industry. This makes up a good circle of learning and performance improvement among industries. In addition, data authentication supported by the blockchain guarantees that sensitive ESG information is subject to exchange among stakeholders without a confidentiality or precision breach owing to the available, secure cloud infrastructure. This kind of data-based comparison encourages effective goal-setting and assists in progress development together. The platforms are also geared towards instilling a notion of collective responsibility as smaller companies can study and copy the operations of the larger ones and vice versa and make the global discourse of sustainability as inclusive as possible. They promote the formation of ESG-literate, transparent, accountable, and resilient supply chains.

9.3 Regulatory Harmonization Support

The situation is further compounded by the rapid development of ESG rules and regulations across nations and borders that many organizations are struggling to keep abreast with, particularly when compared to organizations with multi-jurisdictional operations. The collaborative spaces are important in assisting companies to overcome this perceived complexity of regulation by providing tools, resources, and networks to harmonize and interpret evolving global standards (Dwivedi et al., 2019). The platforms act as knowledge centres where all the organizations have real-time access to information on climate disclosure legislations, human rights due diligence regulations, biodiversity mandates, and circular economy regulations.

The UN Global Compact provides businesses that sign the UN Global Compact with numerous services that provide regulatory agreements. These will be modules on the ESG policy framework, country-specific legal briefings, and tools to align the SDGs' business practices with the UN Sustainable Development Goals (SDGs) (UN Global Compact, 2024). With these kinds of initiatives, the companies can be enabled to develop compliance-forward sustainability plans and minimize legal and reputation risks linked to non-compliance.

Moreover, the AI-driven platforms can cross-map the company operations and the supplier information, which, in turn, provides the automated compliance dashboard and audit checklists. This lessens bureaucratic pressure and the active observation of local and global standards. Harmonization of regulations also helps achieve a more level playing field, particularly among SMEs, which are often found not to have the legal and technical expertise to understand the emerging ESG regulations. These platforms create trust in investors by ensuring standards are interpreted and implemented uniformly, reducing operational upheavals, and creating convergence of ESG globally.

10. ETHICAL CONSIDERATIONS AND IMPLEMENTATION CHALLENGES

10.1 Data Privacy and Consent

Implementing AI in sustainable supply chains requires constant gathering and processing of large amounts of information from all its stakeholders, including suppliers, logistics providers, and end-users. The data may be sensitive corporate data, trade secrets, labour practices, geo-location data, and consumer behaviour insights. The concept of ownership, the right to access information, and informed consent is complicated and unclear when information is passed through multi-tier supply networks (Dwivedi et al., 2019). Suppliers, especially SMEs in the Global South, might not necessarily know how the data will be utilized or be able to bargain a fair data-sharing deal (Agrawal et al., 2023). In the absence of strict data governance practices, these practices may invade privacy standards and contractual agreements or are at risk of global laws like the General Data Protection Regulation (GDPR) in the European Union, the Digital Personal Data Protection Act in India, or the Consumer Privacy Act (CPRA) in California. To rectify such predicaments, companies need to introduce data policies that are not only transparent but also inclusive so that the intentions of data collection, the extent to which it is used, and the rights of each other can be stipulated. Information should be referred to each node of the supply chain, where they should consent explicitly and give permission to see the information, with restriction of access to data according to position and need. Besides, such technologies as blockchain may be used to increase data traceability and access controls. Companies can honour stakeholders' privacy without giving up the opportunity to use data-driven insights by incorporating privacy-by-design principles into their development of AI applications and using federated learning models that keep all data decentralized.

10.2 Bias in Algorithms

Though objective in design, AI algorithms can inherit and perpetuate the historical biases embedded in training data—often without human operators realizing it. In supply chain management, AI systems used for supplier evaluation, risk scoring, or contract awarding can inadvertently reinforce systemic inequalities or marginalize underrepresented vendors (Agrawal et al., 2023). For example, an algorithm trained on past procurement data may disproportionately favour large, Western-based suppliers, systematically disadvantaging smaller or regional vendors with fewer digital footprints—even when these suppliers meet sustainability criteria. Such algorithmic bias undermines ESG goals, especially those related to fairness, equity, and social inclusion. Companies must prioritize algorithmic accountability through rigorous fairness testing, explainability assessments, and regular auditing to mitigate this. Techniques like SHAP (Shapley Additive explanations) and LIME (Local Interpretable Model-agnostic Explanations) can be used to uncover the logic behind model predictions. Furthermore, human-in-the-loop mechanisms are critical to ensure that final decisions are context-aware and ethically sound. Bias mitigation must also begin during model development, emphasizing curating diverse and representative datasets that reflect geographical, gender, and socioeconomic variability. Interdisciplinary governance teams, including ethicists, data scientists, and supply chain experts, should collaboratively monitor AI systems throughout their lifecycle. Additionally, organizations can draw on emerging standards such as the EU's AI Act and OECD's AI Principles to institutionalize ethical AI practices in procurement and operations.

10.3 AI's Environmental Footprint

Although AI can make sustainability practices more efficient (in terms of emissions reduction and material efficiency, among others), the technology is intended to harm the environment paradoxically because of its carbon footprint. Training large AI models and intense learning-based models such as GPT or BERT is computationally demanding, and their training consumes vast electricity and cooling resources. For example, training one large natural language model could produce more than 280,000 kg of CO2, more or less the same amount as five average cars owning emissions throughout their lifetime (Strubell et al., 2019). It brings doubts about the net sustainability of digital innovation. Further computation of AI also requires data centres, which use enormous amounts of water to cool themselves and are often powered by fossil-fuel-based electricity networks, particularly in emerging economies with weak clean energy infrastructure. Thus, companies using AI must make adequate efforts to reduce their digital operations on the environment to preserve the authenticity of their claims about sustainability (Agrawal et al., 2023; Dwivedi et al., 2019). The heart of this effort is to adopt Green AI practices. This comprises choosing model architectures that are more energy efficient, transfer learning rather than training models and computation scheduling: doing it during the off-peak time when more renewable energies are cheaper and less relevant. It is also possible to focus on companies with cloud service providers using carbon-free or hydroelectric data centres. Moreover, the sustainability officers are expected to collaborate with IT departments by monitoring and reporting the carbon intensity of the AI practices by the ESG disclosures. As an unavoidable phenomenon, the carbon offset or the investments in digital decarbonization can be used to balance the AI footprint.

11. STRATEGIC RECOMMENDATIONS

For organizations to fully realize the transformative potential of AI and digital technologies in sustainable supply chains, they must integrate responsible governance practices, align technological innovation with corporate sustainability goals, and cultivate a culture that prioritizes ethical and inclusive decision-making (Dwivedi et al., 2019; Bag et al., 2021a).

11.1 Guidelines for Responsible AI in ESG Contexts

With Artificial Intelligence (AI) as a core element of a sustainable supply chain evolution, developing a set of clear ethical rules that would meet Environmental, Social, and Governance (ESG) priorities is essential. With ethical AI governance, algorithms are guaranteed to improve operations' effectiveness and meet such considerations as transparency, fairness, inclusivity, and environmental responsibility (Dwivedi et al., 2019). Establishing cross-functional stakeholder governance committees (data scientists, sustainability officers, compliance professionals and external ethicists) is one such step. These committees will be established as those charged with directing the ethical formulation, implementation, tracking, and ongoing enhancement of AI tools. Moreover, organizations must invest in explainable AI (XAI) models, enabling users and other stakeholders to know how AI-driven decisions are taken. It is especially crucial when making supply chain decisions encompassing supplier choice, sustainability ranking, or risk ranking, in which opaque algorithms conceal prejudice or neglect viable options (Agrawal et al., 2023). SHAP or LIME can interpret AI behaviour and facilitate transparent decisions.

Also, it is necessary to make constant training on the ethics of AI teams. The principles of algorithmic fairness, human-centric machine learning knowledge, and mitigating unintended bias are some of the principles data scientists and supply chain managers should be trained on regularly (Bag et al., 2021a). Advanced organizations like IBM and Microsoft have developed comprehensive, responsible AI frameworks containing tools, principles, and KPIs measuring ethical impact. The industry reference points may be used by firms in developing trusted, responsible AI, which compliments long-run ESG and stakeholder trust.

11.2 Policy and Framework Suggestions

Although the ethical AI principles define the path, they need to be institutionalized in the formal policies and integrated frameworks to enforce accountability and seam in an organization's operations. Incorporating AI and blockchain governance policy into the corporate ESG framework is an important option. This will refer to involving digital innovation in enterprise-level sustainability plans and policies, codes of conduct, and risk management practices (Dwivedi et al., 2019). When similar AI risk assessments are integrated with Enterprise Risk Management (ERM) systems, they enable proactive identification and prevention of the possible harms caused by data privacy infringements, algorithm bias, environmental impact, and unintended side effects of AI automated systems (Agrawal et al., 2023). Such evaluations consider the whole chain of the AI lifecycle, i.e., the model's sourcing and actualization of information, decomposition, and upkeep. Another strategy that organizations should implement is to create cross-functional ESG task forces that have IT leaders, legal advisors, sustainability officers, and compliance experts. This means that such groups will ensure that AI systems are produced and overseen in a manner that takes a holistic standpoint on the environmental and social consequences. For example, legal teams will assist in achieving regulatory compliance, and sustainability officers will also examine the effects of carbon intensity and circularity of decisions made with the help of AI. Moreover, the businesses will have to participate directly in the regulation organizations and sector professional groups like the ISO/IEC JTC 1 SC 42 (Artificial Intelligence), the Global Reporting Initiative (GRI), or the AI governance projects of the World Economic Forum. The firms can influence the upcoming standards of trustworthy AI, ESG, and blockchain-based traceability by participating and being educated at such forums, ensuring they are ahead of the regulation trend and developing higher stakeholder confidence.

11.3 Fostering a Culture of ESG Innovation

In addition to the policies and technological frameworks, ESG-compatible digital transformation should be driven and supported by an organizational culture that values ethical innovations and sustainability in the long run. Such culture should be reinforced in the minds of employees, as well as in rewards and daily operations. This can be done by ensuring ESG-related training and capacity-building activities on the organizational-wide basis (Dwivedi et al., 2019). Through such programs, the employees ought to know about sustainability, proper use of data, ethical AI, and how digital technologies can affect social and environmental systems. It is also essential to promote cross-functional teamwork and diversity of teams. Multicultural teams (members of various genders, geographies, and whichever professional backgrounds) stand a higher chance of pointing out ethical blind spots and providing responsible innovation (Bag et al., 2021a). The involvement of sustainability professionals in digital product development implies that AI and blockchain use cases will have ecological and social considerations earned at the stage of creation. Last, firms should also positively reinforce innovation, which promotes ESG results. This could be the role of a procurement officer who selects the strategy of low-emission sourcing or the developer who makes improvements to the energy efficiency of an AI model, and internal awards, promotions or incentive schemes should recognize it. A values culture is supported by encouraging employees and partners to co-create ESG innovations. Through cultivating such an ethos of purposeful digital transformation, organizations will transform to comply with ESG requirements and be leading providers of inclusive, regenerative, and trustworthy supply chain ecosystems.

12. CONCLUSION

Based on this chapter, Artificial Intelligence (AI), blockchain, and digital twins have been discussed, along with other emerging technologies, which are already redefining old-school supply chains, and they are becoming dynamic drivers that can bring about Environmental, Social, and

Governance (ESG) objectives (Bag et al., 2021a; Dwivedi et al., 2019). Whether it is innovative product design and forecasted transportation, real-time carbon emissions monitoring, and intersectoral cooperation, these technologies are not of secondary importance to the contemporary sustainable business but give their backbone. More specifically, AI can become an enabling factor of transformative change that can align profit motives with the imperative of sustainability. Many stakeholders should collaborate to make this vision a reality. Companies must turn green digital behaviour and responsible AI governance into their corporate DNA. These policymakers must find uniform, transparent mechanisms that encourage sustainable innovation and protect data privacy and the needs of society (Dwivedi et al., 2019). Interdisciplinary studies that unite technological advances with ethics, environmental, and socio-economic mindfulness are areas that should be increased in academia. Nothing can be accomplished without teamwork, and only by teaming up can we be sure that the supply chain is next generation can accommodate the needs of the current economy and propel a sustainable and regenerative future for people and the planet.

REFERENCE

Acerbi, F., Forterre, D. A., & Taisch, M. (2021). Role of artificial intelligence in circular manufacturing: A systematic literature review. *IFAC-PapersOnLine*, *54*(1), 367–372.

Agrawal, R., Majumdar, A., Kumar, A., & Luthra, S. (2023). Integration of artificial intelligence in sustainable manufacturing: Current status and future opportunities. *Operations Management Research*, *16*(4), 1720–1741. DOI: 10.1007/s12063-023-00383-y

Albu, D. (2021). The sustainable development goals report 2021. Drepturile Omului, 115.

Bag, S., Gupta, S., & Kumar, S. (2021). Industry 4.0 adoption and 10R advance manufacturing capabilities for sustainable development. *International Journal of Production Economics*, *231*, 107844. DOI: 10.1016/j.ijpe.2020.107844

Bag, S., Pretorius, J.-H. C., Gupta, S., & Dwivedi, Y. K. (2021a). Role of institutional pressures and resources in the adoption of big data analytics powered artificial intelligence, sustainable manufacturing practices and circular economy capabilities. *Technological Forecasting and Social Change*, *163*, 120420. DOI: 10.1016/j.techfore.2020.120420

Bai, C., Dallasega, P., Orzes, G., & Sarkis, J. (2020). Industry 4.0 technologies assessment: A sustainability perspective. *International Journal of Production Economics*, *229*, 107776. DOI: 10.1016/j.ijpe.2020.107776

Bocken, N. M. P., de Pauw, I., Bakker, C., & van der Grinten, B. (2016). Product design and business model strategies for a circular economy. *Journal of Industrial and Production Engineering*, *33*(5), 308–320. DOI: 10.1080/21681015.2016.1172124

Centobelli, P., Cerchione, R., & Esposito, E. (2020). Pursuing supply chain sustainable development goals through the adoption of green practices and enabling technologies: A cross-country analysis of LSPs. *Technological Forecasting and Social Change*, *153*, 119920. DOI: 10.1016/j.techfore.2020.119920

Choi, T. M., Wallace, S. W., & Wang, Y. (2017). Big Data Analytics in operations management. *Production and Operations Management, 27*(10), 1868–1883. DOI: 10.1111/poms.12838 PMID: 26766385

Dhl-green-logistics-toolkit. (2024, May 16). https://www.dhl.com/discover/en-in/logistics-advice/sustainability-and-green-logistics/dhl-green-logistics-toolkit

Dubey, R., Gunasekaran, A., Childe, S. J., Bryde, D. J., Giannakis, M., Foropon, C., Roubaud, D., & Hazen, B. T. (2019). Big data analytics and artificial intelligence pathway to operational performance under the effects of entrepreneurial orientation and environmental dynamism: A study of manufacturing organisations. *International Journal of Production Economics, 226*, 107599. DOI: 10.1016/j.ijpe.2019.107599

Dwivedi, Y. K., Hughes, L., Ismagilova, E., Aarts, G., Coombs, C., Crick, T., Duan, Y., Dwivedi, R., Edwards, J., Eirug, A., Galanos, V., Ilavarasan, P. V., Janssen, M., Jones, P., Kar, A. K., Kizgin, H., Kronemann, B., Lal, B., Lucini, B., & Williams, M. D. (2019). Artificial Intelligence (AI): Multidisciplinary perspectives on emerging challenges, opportunities, and agenda for research, practice and policy. *International Journal of Information Management, 57*, 101994. DOI: 10.1016/j.ijinfomgt.2019.08.002

Eccles, R. G., Ioannou, I., & Serafeim, G. (2014). The impact of corporate sustainability on organizational processes and performance. *Management Science, 60*(11), 2835–2857. DOI: 10.1287/mnsc.2014.1984

Geissdoerfer, M., Savaget, P., Bocken, N. M. P., & Hultink, E. J. (2016). The Circular Economy–A new sustainability paradigm? *Journal of Cleaner Production, 143*, 757–768. DOI: 10.1016/j.jclepro.2016.12.048

Ivanov, D., Dolgui, A., & Sokolov, B. (2018). The impact of digital technology and Industry 4.0 on the ripple effect and supply chain risk analytics. *International Journal of Production Research, 57*(3), 829–846. DOI: 10.1080/00207543.2018.1488086

Kamble, S., Gunasekaran, A., & Dhone, N. C. (2019). Industry 4.0 and lean manufacturing practices for sustainable organisational performance in Indian manufacturing companies. *International Journal of Production Research, 58*(5), 1319–1337. DOI: 10.1080/00207543.2019.1630772

McLennan, M. (2022). The global risks report 2022 17th edition. Cologny, Switzerland: World Economic Forum.

Saberi, S., Kouhizadeh, M., Sarkis, J., & Shen, L. (2018). Blockchain technology and its relationships to sustainable supply chain management. *International Journal of Production Research, 57*(7), 2117–2135. DOI: 10.1080/00207543.2018.1533261

Sarkis, J., Zhu, Q., & Lai, K. (2010). An organizational theoretic review of green supply chain management literature. *International Journal of Production Economics, 130*(1), 1–15. DOI: 10.1016/j.ijpe.2010.11.010

Sethi, S. P., Yan, H., & Zhang, H. (2005). *Inventory and supply chain management with forecast updates.* Springer US., DOI: 10.1007/0-387-25663-6_6

Sustainability at Maersk. (n.d.). https://maersk.com/sustainability

The climate pledge. (n.d.). https://www.aboutamazon.com/planet/climate-pledge

Unilever. (2024). We're tackling plastic pollution through reduction, circulation and collaboration https://www.unilever.com/sustainability/plastics/

Wamba, F S., & Akter, S. (2019). Understanding supply chain analytics capabilities and agility for data-rich environments. International Journal of Operations & Production Management, 39(6/7/8), 887-912.

Yadav, A., Garg, R. K., & Sachdeva, A. (2024). Artificial intelligence applications for information management in sustainable supply chain management: A systematic review and future research agenda. *International Journal of Information Management Data Insights, 4*(2), 100292.

Zahoor, N., & Lew, Y. K. (2021). The drivers of the post-entry internationalisation commitment of small and medium-sized enterprises. *International Small Business Journal Researching Entrepreneurship, 40*(4), 477–506. DOI: 10.1177/02662426211042775

Chapter 7

Sustainability and Ethical Responsibility: The Role of ESG in Modern Business

Usharani Bhimavarapu
https://orcid.org/0000-0002-0246-1420

Department of Computer Science and Engineering, Koneru Lakshmaiah Education Foundation, Vaddeswaram, India

ABSTRACT

Environmental, Social, and Governance (ESG) factors now occupy the center stage of contemporary business practices as organizations increasingly acknowledge the value of sustainability and ethical accountability. ESG not only contributes to corporate reputation but also drives financial performance, risk management, and sustainability in the long run. This research investigates integrating ESG considerations in business strategies via the utilization of state-of-the-art machine learning methods such as Bi-Stacked Long Short-Term Memory (Bi-LSTM) in investigating ESG data. By using Bi-LSTM, which considers both historical and future trends, companies can evaluate the effect of their ESG efforts and forecast their long-term effects. The procedure includes preprocessing ESG data, training of Bi-LSTM models to identify sequential dependencies, and employing the model's predictions to inform sustainable decision-

DOI: 10.4018/979-8-3373-2843-0.ch007

making. The procedure allows for enhanced understanding of the impact of ESG on business performance and moral corporate behavior toward a sustainable future.

INTRODUCTION

Environmental, Social, and Governance (ESG) standards are now at the heart of contemporary business operations, an absolute way for organizations to make a positive contribution to society and the environment. The criteria measure a firm's performance and influence in three significant dimensions: environmental sustainability, social responsibility, and corporate governance. With stakeholders from investors and customers to employees asking for greater transparency and accountability, companies are increasingly embedding ESG into their plans. ESG practices are not merely compliance; they are a demonstration of an organization's dedication to ethical accountability and long-term value creation. ESG priority companies are viewed as progressive, addressing the increasing demand for sustainability in operations and products. As global issues such as climate change and inequality continue to prevail, the incorporation of ESG considerations can bring about positive changes in business models. In addition, companies that adopt such values tend to be more robust, better coping with regulation, consumer, and market shocks.

Environmental sustainability is a central pillar of ESG that seeks to reduce a company's impact on the environment. With the threat of climate change, natural resource depletion, and pollution threatening the world, companies are being increasingly called upon to adopt practices that will ensure environmental stewardship. Firms have been challenged to cut down on carbon emissions, enhance waste reduction, save water, and adopt renewable sources of energy. Implementing sustainable practices not only minimizes the environmental footprint but may also lead to cost reductions and operational efficiencies. Organizations that have good track records on the environment are likely to attract green-conscious customers and investors who value environmentally friendly products and services. In addition, government policies and subsidies are focusing more on environmental performance, compelling firms further to incorporate sustainable practices. Adding ESG to business models has a tangible, quantifiable effect on the environment, allowing firms to align with the worldwide trend towards sustainability. By integrating environmental initiatives, there is innovation as firms engage in cleaner technologies, green products, and clean energy solutions.

The social aspect of ESG focuses on a firm's duty towards its workers, customers, and wider societies. Firms are required to put emphasis on ethical labor practices, diversity and inclusion, and positive contribution to the community. Social responsibility involves issues like safe labor, equitable wages, ethical supply chain management, and making products and services available and safe. It also involves corporate giving and community engagement to bring about positive social change. For example, companies may donate to local charities, sponsor educational initiatives, or invest in healthcare programs. A solid social responsibility record boosts the company's brand reputation, fostering trust among consumers and generating a loyal customer base. In the corporate environment, companies focused on social issues have more satisfied employees, less turnover, and improved productivity. They also attract best-in-class talent, particularly from younger generations who care about ethical workplaces and a firm's social contribution. Social responsibility can also reduce risks associated with mistreating workers or adverse media coverage from unethical behavior.

Good governance is at the heart of a company's success and longevity. It refers to the practices, policies, and institutions that inform decision-making and provide accountability to stakeholders. Ethical leadership, accountability, and transparency are what governance is all about. Organizations with good governance systems are less likely to practice corruption, fraud, or unethical behavior. Investors give high value to companies with good governance since such firms are likely to be well-managed, efficient, and less susceptible to scandals. Good governance has the effect of ensuring that the leadership of a company acts in the shareholders', the employees', and the public's best interest. It entails boards that are diverse and independent, transparent executive compensation guidelines, and sound risk management policies. A well-governed company also complies with regulation, legislation, and industry codes, thereby lowering the chances of legal or reputational harm. ESG and ethical business practice are linked together—there can be no good governance without ethical decision-making.

The incorporation of ESG into company strategy can have a major impact on a company's financial performance. It seems that firms with good ESG practice tend to perform well in the long term. Companies that prioritize sustainability can attract investment from ESG investors who favor ethical and responsible practices. In addition, adoption of ESG tends to result in operational efficiencies and cost savings, such as lower energy usage, waste management, or better supply chain practices. Companies that incorporate social and governance factors in their operations enjoy superior employee morale, reduced turnover, and increased customer loyalty, resulting in superior financial performance. ESG-oriented companies also reduce risks related to environmental catastrophes, regulatory fines, and public outcry, which harm profitability. In contrast, firms that disregard ESG criteria may face financial penalties, legal liabilities, and reputational damage that can harm their bottom line. Therefore, adopting ESG not only helps businesses align with ethical principles but also strengthens their financial position.

Investors are increasingly considering ESG factors when making investment decisions. ESG investing, commonly known as sustainable or socially responsible investing, has experienced tremendous growth with investors looking for firms that reflect their ethical standards. Firms that adopt ESG practices tend to enjoy greater access to capital from investors who think that long-term sustainable development is associated with sound environmental, social, and governance policies. In addition, ESG-oriented companies attract impact investors who value companies that create positive social and environmental effects. The investors are also aware that companies with good ESG practices have fewer chances of being hit by regulatory fines, lawsuits, or reputation crises. Good ESG performance results in increased investor confidence, better stock performance, and an improved risk profile. Also, proactive companies that address ESG opportunities and risks stand a better chance of being valued more highly by investors looking for long-term growth potential. Therefore, incorporating ESG into business strategy can appeal to institutional and retail investors.

As awareness among consumers increases about environmental and social concerns, there has been an increased demand for sustainable products and services. Consumers are now more inclined to make purchasing choices on the basis of a company's ESG performance. This is especially noticeable among younger generations, including Millennials and Gen Z, who prefer brands that share their values. For instance, a number of consumers currently want businesses to utilize ethically sourced materials, minimize plastic usage, and show a dedication to fair labor practices. Through integrating ESG methods, companies can address these consumer expectations, thereby encouraging sales and brand loyalty. Moreover, sustainable and socially responsible products tend to have a premium price, which generates higher profitability. Businesses that fail to heed consumers' choice in terms of ESG risk losing market share to socially responsible peers. Thus, incorporating ESG not only helps the environment and society but also makes a business more competitive in a saturated market. This transition towards sustainability is a big opportunity for companies to align product portfolios with expanding consumer needs for accountability and transparency.

ESG practices are important risk management elements that assist companies in identifying and confronting potential risks associated with environmental, social, and governance matters. Global warming, natural disasters, and scarcity of resources pose serious risks that can affect supply chains, operations, and profitability. By managing these environmental issues ahead of time, businesses can reduce the risk of possible disruptions and ensure resilience in the long run. Social risks, for example, employee discontent, unsafe working conditions, or unfavorable public attitudes, could also be controlled through effective ESG programs. In addition, good governance practices prevent businesses from legal and regulatory risks, i.e., environmental or labor law non-compliance. By incorporating ESG into business activities, companies are better able to manage emerging risks and navigate an ever-growing web of global complexities. This strategic move is what makes the company more sustainable in a dynamic world while protecting its reputation and financial health. A solid ESG framework is essentially an essential element of long-term resilience.

With governments across the globe enforcing more rigorous environmental, social, and governance regulations, companies are in greater need than ever to keep pace with these standards. ESG disclosure requirements are increasingly mandatory for listed companies in most parts of the world. Not meeting the requirements can result in legal penalties, fines, and reputational damage. Being an early adopter of ESG best practices is a way for businesses to get ahead of regulatory shifts and escape compliance risks. Furthermore, firms that go beyond regulatory compliance in their ESG initiatives are likely to receive tax breaks, grants, or special treatment from governments. In this regard, ESG integration is both an active business initiative and a compliance measure to ensure that firms meet both domestic and international regulations. By being transparent and committing to sustainable practices, companies can earn the trust of investors, regulators, and the public. Compliance with regulations is one of the most important drivers motivating companies to put ESG principles ahead of others.

With growing ESG considerations, companies putting these principles first will be at a competitive advantage in an ever-changing global marketplace. Sustainability and ethical responsibility are no longer add-ons to business models; they have become a necessity for success in the long term. Business firms that adopt ESG are poised to meet the challenges of the future, reduce risks, and unlock new opportunities. The increasing interest in ESG is transforming industries, changing consumer behavior, and shifting investment patterns. As more businesses realize the value of sustainability, ethical leadership, and good corporate governance, ESG will remain a driving force in determining business success. Over the next few years, organizations able to harmoniously embed ESG into their practices will take center stage in creating a sustainable, inclusive, and responsible global economy. Therefore, ESG is not so much a trend—it is a revolution in the way that business is being done in the 21st century.

Goyal and Rahman (2013) study is limited in its scope to corporate sustainability performance and firm performance, which is mainly based on secondary data sources. The use of archival data could lead to biases since it neglects the dynamic organization of companies' changing sustainability practices. The literature review also falls short in industry-specific information, which could restrict its usage in specific industries. The lack of extensive empirical research on the cause-and-effect nature of the sustainability-firm performance relationship is another limitation since the paper is based to a large extent on correlational data and does not include causality analysis in depth (Goyal & Rahman, 2013).

Lokuwaduge and Heenetigala (2016) include ESG disclosure for sustainable development but have the limitation of drawing data from a single national setting, Australia. The findings might not be extrapolated to other areas with varying regulatory systems and market conditions. The study further fails to consider the entire range of ESG drivers, emphasizing disclosures and omitting the underlying operational and strategic processes influencing sustainability. The cross-sectional nature of the study further restricts it to observing long-term trends in ESG performance over time (Lokuwaduge&Heenetigala, 2016).

Manita et al. (2018) analyze board gender diversity and ESG disclosure, but the sample of the study is restricted to U.S. firms, and this may lead to a geographical bias. Focusing on gender diversity as the only independent variable might also simplify too much the intricate relationships between ESG disclosures and other variables, for instance, firm size or industry. Additionally, the research draws primarily on publicly available data, which, in turn, might not reflect the full magnitude of efforts not disclosed under ESG. Utilization of a static dataset further limits examination of long-term impacts (Manita et al., 2018).

Eccles et al. (2011) consider market interest in non-financial information but are constrained by their use of voluntary ESG disclosures, which tend to be uncomplete or uneven. The research does not consider the effects of mandatory ESG reporting, which would reflect a more complete picture of market reactions. The research also mainly considers large listed companies, ignoring potential variations in ESG effects for small and medium-sized firms (Eccles et al., 2011).

Ong et al. (2014) examine the effect of environmental gains on bottom line but are constrained by their emphasis on a geographically small area, Malaysia. The geographical constraint makes the generalizability of the research to other areas with dissimilar environmental policies or economic contexts weak. Additionally, the study is founded on a comparatively short period, which may be too brief to reflect the long-term return from environmental upgrades. The research also fails to adequately address extrinsic factors like government policies or market fluctuations that may affect the connection between environmental actions and finance performance (Ong et al., 2014).

Lee et al. (2016) examine the connection between environmental responsibility and firm performance in an ESG model. Nonetheless, the research has its limitation in that it is based on self-reported data, hence prone to biases particularly when companies exaggerate their sustainability initiatives. The concentration on one model could be too simplistic to appreciate the intricacies of ESG factors, and neither does the research adequately investigate the impact of governance and social factors in isolation. Moreover, the sample size could be too small to make strong inferences across various industries (Lee et al., 2016).

Barnett and Salomon (2012) consider social and financial performance but are limited in using a wide generalization of the relationship. The research does not include industry-specific analysis, which would be essential to consider the different effects of social performance in different industries. Additionally, the cross-sectional nature of the research does not allow it to measure long-term effects or cause-and-effect relationships between social and financial performance (Barnett & Salomon, 2012).

Al-Janadi et al. (2016) analyze the impact of government ownership on corporate governance and disclosure. The focus of the study, however, on government-owned enterprises in a particular region might restrict its scope to privately-owned or multinational companies. The research fails to take into account the possible role of other governance mechanisms, for example, independent directors or audit committees, which can also influence corporate governance practices. Further, the research methodology fails to treat the potential endogeneity between governance practices and government ownership (Al-Janadi et al., 2016).

Zuraida et al. (2016) investigate the value relevance of ESG disclosure, although the research is constrained by its exploration of one component of ESG—disclosure—without investigating the underlying actions influencing these disclosures. The research also does not have a longitudinal focus, which would have enabled an understanding of how the applicability of ESG disclosure changes over time. Moreover, the research is mostly theoretical in nature and has no empirical data to support its arguments (Zuraida et al., 2016).

Tarmuji et al. (2016) examine the effect of ESG on economic performance but are constrained by the small sample size of their sample, which could fail to reflect the larger market broadly. Second, the study mostly depends on ESG scores, which are subjective and can change with the rating agency used. The examination does not take into account the possible interactions between ESG factors and other fundamental performance indicators such as innovation or market share, which might give a better picture of the influence of ESG on economic performance (Tarmuji et al., 2016).

Theory by Jensen and Meckling is largely centered on agency costs and ownership structure but does not address the dynamic reality of corporate governance in the contemporary business world. Furthermore, the assumptions of the theory regarding the firm and its stakeholders may not hold across all industries since the agency problem is sector-dependent (Jensen and Meckling, 1976).

Although Freeman and Dmytriyev provide useful discussions of the interconnection between corporate social responsibility and stakeholder theory, their contribution is not explicitly concerned with the challenges of implementation by firms in seeking to incorporate CSR into their strategy. In addition, contextual concentration on stakeholder theory can possibly fail to appreciate fully the money aspect of concerns for firms, especially in developing markets (Freeman and Dmytriyev, 2017).

Freeman's strategic management approach focuses on stakeholder theory but neglects the complexity of reconciling stakeholder interests in globalized business environments. The model supposes that stakeholders' interests are congruent, which does not always hold true, particularly in multinational companies where heterogeneous stakeholder interests could clash (Freeman, 1984).

Jensen's value maximization strategy proposes that companies should maximize value at the expense of stakeholder interest but does not adequately respond to the long-term viability and ethical considerations of such a strategy. The emphasis on financial performance may restrict the scope for the incorporation of social and environmental considerations that are gaining prominence in contemporary corporate governance (Jensen, 2001).

Guthrie and Parker's criticism of legitimacy theory of corporate social reporting is insightful but fails to consider the impact of pressures from outside, like government rules and public opinion, on corporate social responsibility activities. Additionally, the generalizability of their results could be geographically specific because standards for corporate social reporting vary across the world (Guthrie and Parker, 1989).

The study by Brammer and Pavelin into environmental disclosure quality is informative but disadvantaged by only considering data from one country. This geographic limitation limits the external validity of the results to companies operating in other regulatory and cultural settings (Brammer and Pavelin, 2008).

Hahn and Kuhnen's synopsis of trends in sustainability reporting provides a broad theoretical framework but no empirical data directly connecting sustainability reporting to enhanced corporate performance. The theoretical orientation of the paper might keep practitioners short of practical guidance (Hahn and Kuhnen, 2013).

Healy and Palepu's literature review on corporate disclosure gives a basic understanding of information asymmetry but misses the increasing prominence of non-financial disclosures, including environmental, social, and governance (ESG) reporting, that have taken on considerable prominence over the past few years (Healy and Palepu, 2001).

Although Lys et al. offer an examination of signaling through corporate accountability reporting, their research targets financial consequences at the expense of illumination of general social and environmental effects of such disclosures. This specificity might give their results a constrained relevance in relation to integrated corporate responsibility (Lys et al., 2015).

The conceptual framework developed by An et al. for voluntary disclosure of intellectual capital is useful but does not respond to the real practical issues faced by firms in terms of measuring and disclosing intangible assets. The complexity of the framework can prove challenging to apply in less-resourced firms or firms that lack experience with intellectual capital (An et al., 2011).

Whereas the research work conducted by Simnett et al. establishes an international comparison of assurance on sustainability reports, it fails to conduct a thorough assessment of the influence of such assurance on stakeholders' perceptions and company performance. The findings in the study may also be affected by variations in the adoption of the practice of sustainability reporting across regions (Simnett et al., 2009).

Brooks and Oikonomou's review of literature on ESG disclosure and firm value provides useful observations but fails to adequately explain the highly multifaceted and complex characteristics of ESG performance. The review also fails to recognize the long-term effects of ESG disclosures on reputation and customer trust, which can influence firm value over periods longer than the short term (Brooks and Oikonomou, 2018).

Dalal and Thaker's research on ESG and Indian corporate financial performance provides significant insights but is handicapped by its use of the context of one country only. The findings cannot be generalized to companies listed on advanced market economies where ESG practices and regulatory regimes are stronger (Dalal and Thaker, 2019).

Li et al.'s research on the CEO power role in ESG disclosure offers a rich insight but is constrained by the use of cross-sectional data. The analysis does not control for variations in CEO power through time or its long-run impact on corporate sustainability practices (Li et al., 2018).

Doh et al.'s study of the market reaction to endorsements of social responsibility stresses the institutions and legitimacy but fails to consider the possible difficulties that companies might encounter in acquiring stakeholder trust while endorsing social responsibility, particularly in weak institutional environments (Doh et al., 2010).

Bajic and Yurtogluanalyze the aspects of CSR that identify firm market value but do not capture the contribution of external variables like government policy and society's opinions appropriately. Measuring CSR effectiveness using market value as the core indicator can disregard the overall social and environmental consequences of a company's CSR activities (Bajic and Yurtoglu, 2018).

Manrique and Marti-Ballester's study on corporate environmental performance and financial performance in developed and developing nations is informative but constrained by its use of aggregate data. The results might not capture the full complexity of corporate environmental performance between industries or even regions (Manrique and Marti-Ballester, 2017).

Al-Tuwaijri et al.'s study of corporate environmental disclosure based on a T-equations model provides useful insights but suffers from its theoretical background, which might not adequately capture the dynamic nature of current environmental reporting practice. The model could also fail to capture the changing stakeholder expectations within an increasingly globalized economy (Al-Tuwaijri et al., 2004).

The Li et al. research on corporate disclosure of environmental liability information gives an introductory insight into environmental reporting but does not examine fully the consequences of such disclosures on stakeholder actions, especially regarding consumer confidence and corporate reputation (Li et al., 1997).

Friedman's opinion that the social duty of business is to maximize profits gives a limited view that ignores the increasing significance of corporate social responsibility in the modern business world. His argument does not consider the long-term advantage of sustainable practices like enhanced reputation, customer retention, and risk management (Friedman, 2007).

Whereas Porter and Linde advocate a new vision of the environment-competitiveness link, their emphasis on the economic gains of environmental upgrading might be too optimistic. The pragmatic realities of making environmental upgrading work, particularly in highly polluting industries, are not adequately discussed (Porter and Linde, 1995).

Gupta and Sharma (1996) offer early basis knowledge for environmental operations management but are restricted due to their early publishing year, which might be out of date in terms of technological improvements or modern sustainability strategies (Gupta & Sharma, 1996).

International corporate environmental disclosures are explored by Aerts et al. (2008), but the results might not be applicable in fast-changing media environments and under new regulatory pressures (Aerts et al., 2008).

Klassen and Whybark (1999) connect environmental technologies with manufacturing performance, but the research is potentially not reflective of the move towards service-based economies or newer performance measures (Klassen & Whybark, 1999).

Brockett and Rezaee (2012) provide a rich framework for synthesizing performance and reporting; however, the prescriptive nature of their method might not be able to fit firm-specific complexities or changing ESG metrics (Brockett & Rezaee, 2012).

Brammer and Millington (2008) examine financial and corporate social performance but risk missing sectoral dynamics and the time lag between CSR expenditure and financial performance (Brammer & Millington, 2008).

Sila and Ceka (2017) present Australian evidence of ESG effects but are hampered by low generalizability to account for regional economic systems and regulatory frameworks (Sila & Ceka, 2017).

Barringer and Harrison (2000) examine interorganizational relationships, but the contextual emphasis on value creation potentially minimizes environmental or social constraints of such alliances (Barringer & Harrison, 2000).

Bosse et al. (2009) address stakeholder reciprocity, but their theoretical context perhaps does not capture power disparities or practical difficulties in stakeholder participation (Bosse et al., 2009).

Vitaliano (2010) connects CSR with labor turnover, though causality might prove hard to discern considering the many variables affecting staff retention (Vitaliano, 2010).

Hussainey and Salama (2010) highlight environmental reputation for investors but perhaps underestimates the way investor priorities change in times of market volatility or short-run profit incentives (Hussainey& Salama, 2010).

Roberts and Dowling (2002) link reputation with accounting performance, but the research can be insufficient to consider the impact of intangible resources and online presence on contemporary reputation management (Roberts & Dowling, 2002).

Jitmaneeroj (2016) focuses on reforming across ESG factors but can be limited to application across countries because of institutional and cultural heterogeneity (Jitmaneeroj, 2016).

Escrig-Olmedo et al. (2017) utilize a fuzzy multicriteria approach to ESG preferences but the sophisticated methodology might be challenging to implement in practice by average investors (Dhaliwal et al., 2017).

Dhaliwal et al. (2011) connect CSR disclosure to cost of equity capital, but their emphasis on voluntary disclosure may require ignoring mandatory frameworks that have come into prominence since then (Dhaliwal et al., 2011).

Ferrero-Ferrero et al. (2013) highlight board diversity as critical to sustainability integration, albeit potentially overlooking deeper cognitive or experiential considerations in their focus on surface-level diversity metrics (Ferrero-Ferrero et al., 2013).

Casey and Grenier (2015) analyze CSR assurance within the U.S., but a U.S.-focused perspective may restrict applicability in other global environments where assurance standards and stakeholder expectations are very different (Casey & Grenier, 2015).

Abeyrathna and Priyadarshaa (2019) evaluate the effect of firm size on profitability in Sri Lanka, but limiting the scope to manufacturing companies limits generalizability across industries (Abeyrathna&Priyadarshaa, 2019).

Hummel and Schlick (2016) integrate disclosure and legitimacy theory, but their method of analysis might not entirely reflect the strategic use of sustainability information by firms (Hummel & Schlick, 2016).

Li (2016) canvases CEO power endogeneity, but experimental setting could minimize actual boardroom dynamic and agency complexity (Li, 2016).

Kiron et al. (2015) promote cooperative sustainability leadership, although the inspirational language may not speak to structural resistance or the price of alignment by a wide range of actors (Kiron et al., 2015).

Jensen (1989) is critical of public corporations over private ownership structures, though the dated context means the applicability to current stakeholder-focused governance trends is restricted (Jensen, 1989).

Herbohn et al. (2017) examine carbon risk within bank lending choices, though their evidence is still restricted by the availability of standardized carbon disclosure data across industries (Herbohn et al., 2017).

Li (2018) offers an overarching description of CSR and corporate governance, although the absence of empirical testing in this survey reduces its utility for pragmatic policy suggestions (Li, 2018).

Jolin et al. (2025) suggested a fingerprint and MAC address verification-based two-factor authentication system but has limitations when implemented within dynamic networks where MAC addresses could be spoofed or updated with regularity, which could compromise its security effectiveness. Kathirvel et al. (2021) developed an Improved IDR Response System for sensor networks, but the centralization of the system hinders its scalability in large-scale deployments. Subramaniam et al. (2021) employed a semantic information retrieval technique based on a Firefly algorithm adapted and fuzzy clustering, while the method has excessive computational burden because of the sophistication of the optimization and cluster techniques involved. Sundar and Kathirvel (2020a) utilized a simulated annealing algorithm for MANET route optimization, while its performance declines with higher node mobility and network density. They pursued their subsequent research (Sundar & Kathirvel, 2020b) on path routing in a stable context with an artificial bee colony algorithm, which is less efficient in the case of high node failure because of static cluster assumptions.

Additionally, Sundar and Kathirvel (2019) made a channel-aware routing algorithm but were delayed by the complexity of real-time estimation of channel conditions. Hamela and Kathirvel (2019a) introduced an energy-efficient OLSR routing model; however, its advantages are lost in highly mobile networks. In another paper, they proposed a multi-objective ALO-based OLSR protocol that enhances routing security at the cost of increased network overhead due to its optimization layers (Hamela & Kathirvel, 2019b). Josh Kumar and Kathirvel (2019) proposed MANET routing enhancements, but without traffic prioritization, its use in multimedia applications is inappropriate. Sangeetha and Kathirvel (2019) proposed a CNN-based model for adipose tissue measurement, although it is not yet very generalizable because of the low diversity of training sets.

Josh Kumar and Kathirvel (2018) proposed power management in MANETs, although the technique falters under uncertain mobility conditions. Black hole attack prevention mechanism through game theory suggested by Hamela and Kathirvel (2017) largely depends on the correct prediction of behavior, which cannot be sustained in unstable networks. Sundar and Kathirvel (2015) presented a trust-based delegation scheme but subjective trust calculation can be misleading for routing decisions. Josh Kumar and Kathirvel (2015) also proposed a mechanism for detecting selfish nodes, though it could generate high false positive rates as it involves strict thresholding.

Geetha et al. (2015) also suggested SCTP redundant transmission, which enhances reliability but has a high bandwidth overhead. Suresh et al. (2015) designed a TDMA-based slot assignment scheme, though it is inefficient under session variations. Kirubakaran and Kathirvel (2014) discussed enhancing MANET security but failed to test their approach by implementation or simulation, reducing useful practice insights. Kathirvel and Rajabushanam (2011) suggested implementing a security system based on umpire nodes, which generates inordinate communication overhead. Similarly, their burglar detection approach (Kathirvel et al., 2011) is susceptible to false alarms during dynamic network environments.

Kathirvel and Srinivasan's (2011a, 2011b) Enhanced Triple Umpiring System (ETUS) enhances security at the cost of complexity and synchronization requirements, and fails to scale with network size. A previous version of ETUS (Kathirvel & Srinivasan, 2010) also exacerbated latency through extra authentication layers. In computer vision, Kathirvel et al. (2023) improved number plate recognition with YOLOv5, although accuracy drops under occlusion or low light. Kathirvel and Shobitha (2023) discussed AI-based asset estimation, but the model is not accurate for highly volatile assets. Kathirvel and Ale (2023) suggested machine learning models for 5G network data analytics, which need to be retrained regularly to change according to emerging data patterns.

The conceptualized model transcends the shortcomings of current models by offering a holistic and dynamic method of environmental, social, and governance (ESG) assessment, which current studies tend to approach in singular isolation or with exclusive focus. In contrast to previous research like Gupta and Sharma (1996), which focuses on operations without integrating changing sustainability measures, the model in question integrates real-time environmental information and dynamic strategies to conform to contemporary standards. It overcomes the problem of generalizability of region-based research like Sila and Ceka (2017) and Abeyrathna and Priyadarshaa (2019) by employing heterogeneous, cross-sectoral datasets, thus increasing global applicability. Moreover, the model overcomes the limitations in previous disclosure-based studies (e.g., Aerts et al., 2008; Dhaliwal et al., 2011) by using a hybrid approach that integrates voluntary and obligatory ESG indicators for promoting transparency and comparability.

Moreover, the model uses sophisticated stakeholder mapping and feedback mechanisms to overcome engagement imbalances identified in Bosse et al. (2009) and Barringer and Harrison (2000), thus enhancing stakeholder inclusivity and reciprocity. It also goes beyond level-one diversity measures recognized in Ferrero-Ferrero et al. (2013) through the use of deep-learning methods to assess board member backgrounds for cognitive diversity. In contrast to fixed frameworks such as those shown by Jitmaneeroj (2016), the model is iterative and responsive, with the capacity to adapt to policy shifts and investor behavior on a real-time basis. Finally, by integrating intelligent decision-support systems, the model addresses the methodological complexity identified in Escrig-Olmedo et al. (2017) and is more friendly to users for firms' and investors' practical application.

MATERIAL AND METHODS

The approach to incorporating ESG factors into business analysis with Bi-Stacked LSTM entails some major steps. To begin, ESG information is gathered from diverse sources such as company reports, news items, and financial statements and preprocessed for relevance and consistency. The Bi-LSTM model is then trained on sequential data to extract past and future trends in ESG performance. The model's two-layer structure enables bidirectional analysis and enhances the ability to forecast ESG effects over time. The model is then tested and validated for accuracy upon completion of training with suitable metrics. Lastly, the findings obtained from the model are employed to make strategic decisions that promote sustainability and ethical business practices.

MATERIAL

The data gathered extensive picture of different industries in the industrial sector, and the industrial sector was the most prominent one, making up 23.17% of the overall sample. The high percentage of this sector in the dataset reflects its leading position in the dataset, which can probably be attributed to its wide and versatile presence in economic activities. Consumer discretionary and consumer staples were the other two significant sectors with contribution levels of 21.12% and 7.84% to the dataset, respectively. These industries emphasize consumer-oriented sectors, the former being concerned with non-essential commodities and services and the latter concerning essential items which consumers need on a day-to-day basis. Real estate is also prominent, making up 7.73% of the sample, suggesting its importance in the context of the data, perhaps highlighting the increasing importance of property markets. On the other hand, industries like health care, energy, and telecom and utilities are each under 5% of the dataset. Although these industries cannot be disputed in their significance, their comparatively smaller percentage could imply either a more intense concentration in other sectors or a suggested area for deeper examination in the dataset, especially given the increasing relevance of sustainability and health care innovations in today's economies.

PREPROCESSING

Preprocessing of the gathered dataset entails various important steps to make the data clean, standardized, and ready for analysis. Missing values or null entries are first located and treated accordingly. For industries with low representation, including energy, healthcare, and telecommunications, missing data might have to be imputed or, if unavoidable, excluded in order not to bias results. Second, categorical variables such as sector names are converted to numerical values through methods like one-hot encoding or label encoding in order to allow for quantitative analysis. This is important for machine learning algorithms that can only process numerical data. The outliers in the dataset, especially in more represented sectors such as industrial and consumer discretionary, are checked to ensure they do not overly skew the analysis. Any outliers are adjusted or dropped depending on their effect on the integrity of the dataset.

The data is then normalized or standardized, particularly when industries have varying scales of influence or monetary values so that no feature overpowers the rest based on its magnitude. This process is mostly necessary when performing comparative analysis between industries such as industrial, consumer discretionary, and real estate, which could have different financial values. Data transformation methods are used to maintain the dataset in accordance with the assumptions of the analytical models to be applied. For example, in case the dataset has skewed distributions, logarithmic transformations could be used to gain normality. Furthermore, any irrelevant and redundant features are removed to minimize dimensionality and improve the performance of the model. The last preprocessing phase includes dividing the dataset into train and test sets so that the data is properly distributed across sectors to allow for a balanced and fair process of model training. This guarantees that the dataset is ready for any additional exploratory analysis, modeling, or prediction work.

FEATURE SELECTION

Feature selection with Ant Colony Optimization (ACO) is a powerful method of determining the most salient and influential features within a data set, particularly helpful when working with big and complicated data. ACO, taking cue from the natural process of ants foraging for food, replicates the process of discovering the best path along a problem space through mimicry of the pheromone trail-depositing behavior of ants. In the context of feature selection, ACO is utilized by considering every feature to be a possible "node" and employing an artificial swarm of ants that crawl over various feature combinations. Every ant appraises a set of features according to a user-defined fitness function, which may be such measures as information gain or accuracy of classification.

When the ants move in the feature space, they deposit pheromone trails signaling the quality of chosen subsets of features. Subsets that receive higher performance scores over time (i.e., improved classification performance or prediction accuracy) are reinforced with more intense pheromone concentrations so that other ants have more chances to choose similar features. This repeated process assists the algorithm to move towards a solution for the set of features that optimizes the predictive model's performance. ACO provides a balance between search for new subsets of features (exploration) and exploration of the best-performing sets (exploitation), enabling a robust and efficient feature selection process.

One of the important strengths of feature selection using ACO is its capability to deal with high-dimensional data, which characterizes industries like industrial or consumer discretionary, by efficiently reducing the feature space while keeping the most important information. It is especially efficient in cases where conventional feature selection approaches, such as filter or wrapper techniques, would be computationally costly or not efficient enough in discovering the best subset. ACO can also be beneficial in preventing overfitting by only choosing the most significant features, thus enabling the improvement of the generalization capability of machine learning models. In summary, ACO offers a dynamic and adaptive solution to feature selection, which improves model performance and lowers computational cost.

BISTACKED LSTM

Embedding Environmental, Social, and Governance (ESG) into business strategies plays a significant role in developing long-term sustainability and ethical responsibility. A Bi-Stacked Long Short-Term Memory (Bi-LSTM) model provides a sophisticated method for modeling ESG data, particularly when considering temporal dependencies and trends that are innate in business performance on these criteria. ESG factors change with time, and knowledge of these changes can give great insight into how much a company values sustainability and responsible practices. A Bi-LSTM, in that it processes data in both forward and backward directions, can extract both past and future trends, and hence is very effective in forecasting the effect of ESG factors on a company's performance and public image.

The Bi-LSTM model is particularly effective for processing sequential data, and that's often well-suited for seeing how ESG activities progress over time. Environmental policy, for instance, social responsibility actions, and governance shifts within a company can come with lagged effects, and therefore, examining both historical data and possible trends going forward helps get the complete picture. By employing a Bi-LSTM model, where two LSTM layers (one for the past data and the other for the future data) are used, companies can better estimate the long-run effects of their ESG initiatives. This approach allows companies to capture patterns and relationships that may go undetected with conventional models that look at data in one direction only.

In business decision-making, the Bi-LSTM model assists executives and stakeholders in assessing the performance of ESG initiatives on a real-time basis to make informed decisions for ongoing improvement. The model also assists in forecasting possible environmental regulation risks, social issues, and governance practices that may arise, allowing companies to address these ahead of time. In addition, the integration of Bi-LSTM with ESG information can improve transparency by presenting a better indication of how ESG actions are driving important business performance. The integration ultimately enables firms to be more aligned with the increasing consumer pull for sustainability, draw ethically conscious investors, and build a better image for ethical corporate management, thus building long-term success and resistance in a fast-changing business world.

EXPERIMENTAL RESULTS

The experimental findings illustrate the efficacy of the suggested method for analyzing and predicting the influence of Environmental, Social, and Governance (ESG) factors on business performance. Through a Bi-Stacked LSTM model, the analysis is able to successfully capture the temporal relationships contained in ESG data and gain insightful knowledge about how historical and future trends affect corporate choices and sustainability performance. The model was tested on a diverse data set covering multiple industries with disparate ESG performance measures and assessed based on common performance measures including accuracy, precision, recall, and F1 score. These outcomes identify the power of the model in forecasting the long-term implications of ESG approaches, providing enterprises with actionable insights to optimize their corporate governance models and enhance their sustainability efforts.

Table 1 displays a ranking of the contrast of the ESG scores in different industries by their total ESG score. The industry sector scored 74, ranked position one, followed by consumer discretionary 73 and consumer staples 70. The lowest is in the energy sector, with a score of 50, which reflects the underperformance in ESG factors. Other sectors like health care and financials also have impressive ESG performance with more than 70 scores. Tech and industrial firms also display good environmental and governance metrics. The table demonstrates diversified ESG performance by industry profiles and strategic goals.

Table 1. ESG Performance Across Different Sectors

Sector	Environmental Score	Social Score	Governance Score	Overall ESG Score	ESG Rank
Industrial	75	68	80	74	1
Consumer Discretionary	70	85	65	73	2
Consumer Staples	65	75	70	70	3
Real Estate	80	60	70	73	4
Energy	60	50	40	50	5
Health Care	70	85	50	68	6
Telecommunications	60	65	55	60	7
Utilities	65	55	60	60	8
Financials	75	70	80	75	9
Technology	80	75	85	80	10

Table 2 disaggregates ESG performance by sectors across different industries, reflecting environment, social, and governance influence percentages. The industrial sector leads with a high environmental impact score, followed by consumer discretionary and consumer staples with high social impact. Energy is the worst-performing sector in terms of ESG scores, meaning it is the least environmentally sustainable. Real estate, health care, and technology sectors have good performance, especially in compliance with governance. This table illustrates industry-based initiatives and success in ESG strategy implementation in detail.

Table 2. Sector-Specific ESG Performance Metrics

Sector	Environmental Impact (%)	Social Impact (%)	Governance Compliance (%)	ESG Implementation	Average ESG Score	ESG Improvement Rate (%)
Industrial	78	60	85	High	74	5
Consumer Discretionary	70	82	68	Moderate	73	4
Consumer Staples	65	72	74	Moderate	70	3
Real Estate	82	55	72	High	73	6
Energy	60	50	42	Low	50	2
Health Care	72	80	53	High	68	7

continued on following page

Table 2. Continued

Sector	Environmental Impact (%)	Social Impact (%)	Governance Compliance (%)	ESG Implementation	Average ESG Score	ESG Improvement Rate (%)
Telecommunications	62	64	57	Low	60	1
Utilities	66	54	60	Low	60	3
Financials	78	67	83	High	75	6
Technology	82	75	87	High	80	8

Table 3 illustrates the monetary investment in ESG strategies, which is the investment in environmental, social, and governance initiatives by industries.Technology, financials, and health care industries are heavily invested in, resulting in high ESG returns. The energy industry, with less investment in ESG strategies, has less effect on stock returns. Real estate and industrial sectors have moderate returns, which show the impact of ESG investments on stock price movement. This table shows how levels of ESG investment correspond to performance in different industries.

Table 3. ESG Investment Impact

Sector	ESG Investment Amount ($M)	ESG Return (%)	Environmental Investment ($M)	Social Investment ($M)	Governance Investment ($M)
Industrial	150	10	60	40	50
Consumer Discretionary	120	8	50	40	30
Consumer Staples	100	6	40	30	30
Real Estate	130	9	60	30	40
Energy	80	3	30	20	30
Health Care	110	12	50	40	20
Telecommunications	90	4	30	30	30
Utilities	95	5	35	25	35
Financials	160	11	70	50	40
Technology	180	15	80	60	40

Table 4 analyzes ESG-related risks in different sectors, such as environmental, social, and governance risks. Energy and telecommunication sectors are highlighted with the highest risks, especially in environmental and social issues.Conversely, sectors of financials, technology, and industrials have lower percentages of total risk, indicating more compliance and management of risk. The table identifies the need to handle ESG-based risks to avoid negative effects on sector performance, and high-risk sectors require urgent concern and improved implementation of strategy.

Table 4. ESG Risk Assessment by Sector

Sector	Environmental Risk (%)	Social Risk (%)	Governance Risk (%)	Overall Risk (%)	ESG Risk Rating
Industrial	22	28	15	22	Low
Consumer Discretionary	30	12	20	21	Moderate
Consumer Staples	32	25	18	25	Moderate
Real Estate	18	30	20	22	Low
Energy	45	40	60	50	High
Health Care	28	10	25	21	Low
Telecommunications	35	22	30	29	Moderate
Utilities	33	27	28	29	Moderate
Financials	23	18	12	18	Low
Technology	20	15	10	15	Low

Table 5 shows the model performance and data quality of ESG strategies by industry, measuring the precision, recall, and F1 score criteria. Technology and health care sectors have the best model performance with maximum accuracy and precision rates. Energy and telecommunication sectors have lower performance rates, indicating a difficulty in achieving stable ESG model outcomes.Training time: The models' training time is also presented in the table, indicating that more complex industries take more time for training so that they can perform well on ESG strategy predictions. These findings confirm the need for adjusting the models to the appropriate ESG strategy analysis.

Table 5. ESG Data Accuracy and Model Performance

Sector	Data Accuracy (%)	Model Precision (%)	Model Recall (%)	F1 Score (%)	Model Training Time (hrs)
Industrial	95	90	88	89	8
Consumer Discretionary	92	85	87	86	7
Consumer Staples	93	83	85	84	6
Real Estate	94	88	86	87	7
Energy	89	75	78	76	9
Health Care	96	91	90	90.5	6
Telecommunications	91	82	80	81	8
Utilities	90	80	82	81	7
Financials	97	92	94	93	6
Technology	98	95	94	94.5	5

Table 6 cross-tabulates between sector and stock price performance and ESG scores. It indicates that industries that possess better ESG scores, like financials and technology, have favorable stock price performance. On the contrary, the influence of the ESG performance on the energy industry is low, which indicates toward the lower composite ESG scores of the industry. The table further indicates that successful ESG strategies contribute toward long-term growth, especially among those industries having good social and governance practices.This reflects the financial advantages of making ESG initiatives a priority when developing business strategy.

Table 6. ESG Impact on Stock Performance

Sector	Stock Price Change (%)	ESG Score Change (%)	ESG Influence on Stock Price (%)	ESG Strategy Impact (%)	Long-Term Growth (%)
Industrial	8	6	4	3	12
Consumer Discretionary	7	5	3	2	10
Consumer Staples	6	4	2	1	9
Real Estate	9	7	5	4	15
Energy	2	1	0.5	0.2	3

continued on following page

Table 6. Continued

Sector	Stock Price Change (%)	ESG Score Change (%)	ESG Influence on Stock Price (%)	ESG Strategy Impact (%)	Long-Term Growth (%)
Health Care	10	8	6	5	14
Telecommunications	5	3	2	1	6
Utilities	4	3	2	1.5	7
Financials	11	9	7	6	18
Technology	12	10	8	7	20

Table 7 indicates strategy implementation in ESG by industry, with the industrials and financials sectors possessing the highest levels of strategy implementation. Energy ranks lowest on the basis of ESG scores since execution levels decline. Real estate and technology are high on implementation and governance as well as environment priorities. From the table, it can be seen that effective implementation leads to a good aggregate sector performance on ESG, where consistent implementation yields improved aggregate ESG scores as well as positive risk management.

Table 7. Sector-wise ESG Strategy Implementation

Sector	Environmental Strategies (%)	Social Strategies (%)	Governance Strategies (%)	Overall Strategy (%)	ESG Rating
Industrial	80	75	85	80	High
Consumer Discretionary	75	80	70	75	Moderate
Consumer Staples	70	75	65	70	Moderate
Real Estate	85	65	72	74	High
Energy	60	50	40	50	Low
Health Care	78	85	60	74	High
Telecommunications	65	70	55	63	Moderate
Utilities	70	60	62	64	Moderate
Financials	80	70	85	78	High
Technology	85	80	90	85	High

Table 8 investigates the impact of ESG activities on customer satisfaction, with a special focus on sectors such as health care and real estate, which witness considerable improvements in customer loyalty and satisfaction.

These industries also attain high net promoter scores, revealing strong consumer sentiment towards their ESG efforts. Telecommunications and energy industries derive limited benefits to customer satisfaction corresponding to their weaker ESG standing. The table highlights the power of ESG practices on the customer attitude and how the role of ethical and sustainable business gains importance in holding on to as well as in acquiring customers.

Table 8. ESG Impact on Customer Satisfaction

Sector	Customer Satisfaction (%)	ESG Initiatives Influence (%)	Net Promoter Score (NPS)	Customer Loyalty (%)	ESG-Driven Satisfaction Change (%)
Industrial	78	80	65	72	7
Consumer Discretionary	82	85	72	75	10
Consumer Staples	75	70	68	71	5
Real Estate	85	80	80	85	12
Energy	60	50	45	50	3
Health Care	90	92	85	90	15
Telecommunications	70	68	60	65	6
Utilities	65	60	55	60	4
Financials	88	90	85	89	11
Technology	90	92	88	90	13

Table 9 compares sectors' environmental, social, and governance compliance for ESG policy, where compliance in the environmental aspect is most dominant among industries such as industrials and financials. Compliance remains low among the energy sector, particularly on environmental and governance aspects.Strong compliance on governance is found in sectors like technology and health care and ranks highly as among the best performing overall ESG sectors. Compliance with policy is recognized as a leading indicator in this table and the direct correlation between compliance and sector-level ESG performance and reputation.

Table 9. ESG Policy Compliance by Sector

Sector	Environmental Compliance (%)	Social Compliance (%)	Governance Compliance (%)	Total Compliance (%)	Compliance Rank
Industrial	85	75	90	83	1
Consumer Discretionary	78	80	70	76	2
Consumer Staples	74	70	72	72	3
Real Estate	88	70	80	79	4
Energy	65	50	40	52	5
Health Care	80	85	60	75	6
Telecommunications	70	65	60	65	7
Utilities	72	60	65	66	8
Financials	90	85	92	89	9
Technology	95	90	95	93	10

Table 10 compares rates of execution, improvement in performance, and gains in efficiency in an attempt to measure the effectiveness of ESG strategies. Health care and tech sectors are highly effective, with widespread improvements in performance and efficiency through effective ESG strategies. The energy industry, however, has low gains levels, which indicate its failure to implement successful ESG programs.This table indicates the need to link business strategies with ESG objectives and gives insights into the real benefits of well-implemented ESG programs, such as growth and efficiency gains.

Table 10. ESG Strategy Effectiveness

Sector	ESG Strategy Execution (%)	Performance Improvement (%)	Efficiency Gain (%)	ESG Goals Achieved (%)	Strategy Effectiveness (%)
Industrial	80	70	15	85	High
Consumer Discretionary	75	65	10	80	Moderate
Consumer Staples	70	60	8	72	Moderate
Real Estate	85	80	18	90	High
Energy	60	40	3	50	Low
Health Care	88	90	22	95	High

continued on following page

Table 10. Continued

Sector	ESG Strategy Execution (%)	Performance Improvement (%)	Efficiency Gain (%)	ESG Goals Achieved (%)	Strategy Effectiveness (%)
Telecommunications	65	55	7	60	Moderate
Utilities	70	60	5	64	Moderate
Financials	90	85	20	95	High
Technology	92	88	25	98	High

CONCLUSION

In general, the incorporation of ESG factors into business strategy is necessary for long-term sustainability and ethical accountability. Bi-Stacked LSTM models provide an effective way of ESG analysis, extracting temporal patterns that may not be detected by other means. Bi-LSTM, with past and future information, enables companies to make well-informed decisions regarding their sustainability initiatives and predict future challenges. This not only becomes more accountable and transparent but also gives actionable intelligence whereby organizations can respond to evolving market conditions and stakeholder expectations. Finally, embedding ESG considerations into business operations not only enhances societal performance but also creates a competitive edge, as firms position themselves for long-term growth and success in a sustainable and ethical way.

REFERENCES

Abeyrathna, S. P. G. M., & Priyadarshana, A. J. M. (2019). Impact of firm size on profitability (special reference to listed manufacturing companies in Sri Lanka). *International Journal of Scientific and Research Publications*, *9*(9), 561–564. DOI: 10.29322/IJSRP.9.09.2019.p9356

Aerts, W., Cormier, D., & Magnan, M. (2008). Corporate environmental disclosure, financial markets and the media: An international perspective. *Ecological Economics*, *64*(3), 643–659. DOI: 10.1016/j.ecolecon.2007.04.012

Al-Janadi, Y., Rahman, R. A., & Alazzani, A. (2016). Does government ownership affect corporate governance and corporate disclosure? *Managerial Auditing Journal*, *31*(8/9), 871–890. DOI: 10.1108/MAJ-11-2015-1270

Al-Tuwaijri, S. A., Christensen, T. E., & Hughes, K. E.II. (2004). The relations among environmental disclosure, environmental performance, and economic performance: A simultaneous equations approach. *Accounting, Organizations and Society*, *29*(5–6), 447–471. DOI: 10.1016/S0361-3682(03)00032-1

An, Y., Davey, H., & Eggleton, I. R. C. (2011). Towards a comprehensive theoretical framework for voluntary IC disclosure. *Journal of Intellectual Capital*, *12*(4), 571–585. DOI: 10.1108/14691931111181733

Atan, R., Alam, M. M., Said, J., & Zamri, M. (2018). The impacts of environmental, social, and governance factors on firm performance: Panel study of Malaysian companies. *Management of Environmental Quality*, *29*(2), 182–194. DOI: 10.1108/MEQ-06-2017-0051

Bajic, S., & Yurtoglu, B. B. (2018). Which aspects of CSR predict firm market value? *Journal of Capital Markets Studies*, *2*(1), 50–69. DOI: 10.1108/JCMS-10-2017-0002

Barnett, M. L., & Salomon, R. M. (2012). Does it pay to be really good? Addressing the shape of the relationship between social and financial performance. *Strategic Management Journal*, *33*(11), 1304–1320. DOI: 10.1002/smj.1980

Barringer, B. R., & Harrison, J. S. (2000). Walking a tightrope: Creating value through interorganizational relationships. *Journal of Management, 26*(3), 367–403. DOI: 10.1177/014920630002600302

Bassen, A., & Kovács, A. M. (2008). Environmental, social and governance key performance indicators from a capital market perspective. *Zeitschrift für Wirtschafts- und Unternehmensethik, 9*(2), 182–192.

Bosse, D. A., Phillips, R. A., & Harrison, J. S. (2009). Stakeholders, reciprocity, and firm performance. *Strategic Management Journal, 30*(4), 447–456. DOI: 10.1002/smj.743

Brammer, S., & Millington, A. (2008). Does it pay to be different? An analysis of the relationship between corporate social and financial performance. *Strategic Management Journal, 29*(12), 1325–1343. DOI: 10.1002/smj.714

Brammer, S., & Pavelin, S. (2008). Factors influencing the quality of corporate environmental disclosure. *Business Strategy and the Environment, 17*(2), 120–136. DOI: 10.1002/bse.506

Brockett, A., & Rezaee, Z. (2012). *Corporate sustainability: Integrating performance and reporting*. John Wiley & Sons.

Brooks, C., & Oikonomou, I. (2018). The effects of environmental, social and governance disclosures and performance on firm value: A review of the literature in accounting and finance. *The British Accounting Review, 50*(1), 1–15. DOI: 10.1016/j.bar.2017.11.005

Casey, R. J., & Grenier, J. H. (2015). Understanding and contributing to the enigma of corporate social responsibility (CSR) assurance in the United States. *Auditing, 34*(1), 97–130. DOI: 10.2308/ajpt-50826

Dalal, K. K., & Thaker, N. (2019). ESG and corporate financial performance: A panel study of Indian companies. *IUP Journal of Corporate Governance, 18*(1), 44–59.

Dhaliwal, D. S., Li, O. Z., Tsang, A., & Yang, Y. G. (2011). Voluntary nonfinancial disclosure and the cost of equity capital: The initiation of corporate social responsibility reporting. *The Accounting Review, 86*(1), 59–100. DOI: 10.2308/accr.00000005

Doh, J. P., Howton, S. D., Howton, S. W., & Siegel, D. S. (2010). Does the market respond to an endorsement of social responsibility? The role of institutions, information, and legitimacy. *Journal of Management*, *36*(6), 1461–1485. DOI: 10.1177/0149206309337892

Eccles, R. G., Serafeim, G., & Krzus, M. P. (2011). Market interest in nonfinancial information. *Journal of Applied Corporate Finance*, *23*(4), 113–127. DOI: 10.1111/j.1745-6622.2011.00359.x

Elkington, J. (1998). *Cannibals with forks: The triple bottom line of 21st century business*. New Society Publishers.

Escrig-Olmedo, E., Rivera-Lirio, J. M., Muñoz-Torres, M. J., & Fernández-Izquierdo, M. Á. (2017). Integrating multiple ESG investors' preferences into sustainable investment: A fuzzy multicriteria methodological approach. *Journal of Cleaner Production*, *162*, 1334–1345. DOI: 10.1016/j.jclepro.2017.06.143

Ferrero-Ferrero, I., Fernández-Izquierdo, M. Á., & Muñoz-Torres, M. J. (2015). Integrating sustainability into corporate governance: An empirical study on board diversity. *Corporate Social Responsibility and Environmental Management*, *22*(4), 193–207. DOI: 10.1002/csr.1334

Freeman, R. E. (1984). *Strategic management: A stakeholder approach*. Pitman.

Freeman, R. E., & Dmytriyev, S. (2017). Corporate social responsibility and stakeholder theory: Learning from each other. Symposium: Emerging Issues in Management, (2), 7–15. https://doi.org/DOI: 10.4468/2017.2.02

Friedman, M. (2007). The social responsibility of business is to increase its profits. In Zimmerli, W. C., Holzinger, M., & Richter, K. (Eds.), *Corporate ethics and corporate governance* (pp. 173–178). Springer. (Original work published 1970)

Geetha, D. M., Muthusundar, S. K., Subramaniam, M., & Kathirvel, A. (2015). Temporary redundant transmission mechanism for SCTP multi-homed hosts. *TheScientificWorldJournal*, *2015*, 158697. Advance online publication. DOI: 10.1155/2015/158697

Global Sustainable Investment Alliance. (2018). Global sustainable investment review 2018. http://www.gsi-alliance.org/wp-content/uploads/2019/03/GSIR_Review2018.3.28.pdf

Goyal, P., Rahman, Z., & Kazmi, A. A. (2013). Corporate sustainability performance and firm performance research: Literature review and future research agenda. *Management Decision*, *51*(2), 361–379. DOI: 10.1108/00251741311301867

Gupta, M., & Sharma, K. (1996). Environmental operations management: An opportunity for improvement. *Production and Inventory Management Journal*, *37*(3), 40–46.

Guthrie, J., & Parker, L. D. (1989). Corporate social reporting: A rebuttal of legitimacy theory. *Accounting and Business Research*, *19*(76), 343–352. DOI: 10.1080/00014788.1989.9728863

Hahn, R., & Kühnen, M. (2013). Determinants of sustainability reporting: A review of results, trends, theory, and opportunities in an expanding field of research. *Journal of Cleaner Production*, *59*, 5–21. DOI: 10.1016/j.jclepro.2013.07.005

Hamela, K., & Kathirvel, A. (2017). Alleviating black hole attack in OLSR protocol adopting an evolutionary game theory approach for MANET. Journal of Advanced Research in Dynamical and Control Systems, 9(Sp. Iss. 14), 666–678.

Hamela, K., & Kathirvel, A. (2019a). EIMO-ESOLSR: Energy efficient and security based model for OLSR routing protocol in mobile ad-hoc network. *IET Communications*, *13*(5), 553–559. DOI: 10.1049/iet-com.2018.5564

Hamela, K., & Kathirvel, A. (2019b). Multi objective ALO based energy efficient and secure routing OLSR protocol in MANET. *International Journal of Intelligent Engineering and Systems*, *12*(1), 74–83. DOI: 10.22266/ijies2019.0228.08

Healy, P. M., & Palepu, K. G. (2001). Information asymmetry, corporate disclosure, and the capital markets: A review of the empirical disclosure literature. *Journal of Accounting and Economics*, *31*(1–3), 405–440. DOI: 10.1016/S0165-4101(01)00018-0

Herbohn, K., Gao, R., & Clarkson, P. (2019). Evidence on whether banks consider carbon risk in their lending decisions. *Journal of Business Ethics, 158*(1), 155–175. DOI: 10.1007/s10551-017-3713-7

Hummel, K., & Schlick, C. (2016). The relationship between sustainability performance and sustainability disclosure—Reconciling voluntary disclosure theory and legitimacy theory. *Journal of Accounting and Public Policy, 35*(5), 455–476. DOI: 10.1016/j.jaccpubpol.2016.06.001

Hussainey, K., & Salama, A. (2010). The importance of corporate environmental reputation to investors. *Journal of Applied Accounting Research, 11*(3), 229–241. DOI: 10.1108/09675421011088122

Ioannou, I., & Serafeim, G. (2017). The consequences of mandatory corporate sustainability reporting (Harvard Business School Research Working Paper No. 11-100). Harvard Business School.

Jain, P. K., Jain, A., & Rezaee, Z. (2016). Value-relevance of corporate social performance: Evidence from short selling. *Journal of Management Accounting Research, 28*(2), 29–52. DOI: 10.2308/jmar-51350

Jensen, M. C. (1989). Eclipse of the public corporation. *Harvard Business Review, 67*(5), 61–74.

Jensen, M. C. (2001). Value maximization, stakeholder theory, and the corporate objective function. *Journal of Applied Corporate Finance, 14*(3), 8–21. DOI: 10.1111/j.1745-6622.2001.tb00434.x

Jensen, M. C., & Meckling, W. H. (1976). Theory of the firm: Managerial behavior, agency costs and ownership structure. *Journal of Financial Economics, 3*(4), 305–360. DOI: 10.1016/0304-405X(76)90026-Xscholar.google.com

Jitmaneeroj, B. (2016). Reform priorities for corporate sustainability: Environmental, social, governance, or economic performance? *Management Decision, 54*(6), 1497–1521. DOI: 10.1108/MD-11-2015-0505

Jolin, J. S., Theophilus, A., & Kathirvel, A. (2025). Two factor mutual authentication with fingerprint and MAC address validation. *International Journal of Communication Networks and Information Security, 16*(6), 56–68. DOI: 10.5815/ijcnis.2024.06.05

Josh Kumar, J. P., & Kathirvel, A. (2015). A unified approach for detecting and eliminating selfish nodes in MANETs using TBUT. *EURASIP Journal on Wireless Communications and Networking, 2015*(1), 143. Advance online publication. DOI: 10.1186/s13638-015-0375-1

Josh Kumar, J. P., & Kathirvel, A. (2018). Optimum power management in mobile ad hoc networks. *Journal of Engineering Science and Technology, 13*(6), 1805–1815.

Josh Kumar, J. P., & Kathirvel, A. (2019). Analysis and ideas for improved routing in MANET. *International Journal of Interactive Mobile Technologies, 13*(4), 164–177. DOI: 10.3991/ijim.v13i04.10344

Kathirvel, A., Danny, B. J., Shalem, P., Hinn, J. T. O., Kennedy, R. C., & Immanuel, A. J. (2023). Systematic number plate detection using improved YOLOv5 detector. In 2023 2nd IEEE International Conference on Vision Towards Emerging Trends in Communication and Networking Technologies (ViTECoN) (pp. 1–6). IEEE. https://doi.org/ (ISBN 979-8-3503-4798-2) DOI: 10.1109/ViTECoN58111.2023.10156845

Kathirvel, A., & Mavuri, S. (2023). Digital assets fair estimation using artificial intelligence. In 2023 2nd IEEE International Conference on Vision Towards Emerging Trends in Communication and Networking Technologies (ViTECoN) (pp. 1–6). IEEE. https://doi.org/DOI: 10.1109/ViTECoN58111.2023.10156912

Kathirvel, A., & Rajabushanam, C. (2011). System of one to three umpire security system for wireless mobile ad hoc networks. *Journal of Computational Science, 7*(12), 1854–1858. DOI: 10.3844/jcssp.2011.1854.1858

Kathirvel, A., & Srinivasan, R. (2010). Enhanced triple umpiring system for security and performance improvement in wireless MANETs. *International Journal of Communication Networks and Information Security, 2*(2), 77–84.

Kathirvel, A., & Srinivasan, R. (2011a). ETUS: An enhanced triple umpiring system for security and performance improvement of mobile ad hoc networks. *International Journal of Network Management, 21*(5), 341–359. DOI: 10.1002/nem.770

Kathirvel, A., & Srinivasan, R. (2011b). ETUS: An enhanced triple umpiring system for security and robustness of mobile ad hoc networks. *International Journal of Communication Networks and Distributed Systems*, *7*(1/2), 153–187. DOI: 10.1504/IJCNDS.2011.040978

Kathirvel, A., Subramaniam, M., Navaneethan, S., & Sabarinath, C. (2021). Improved IDR response system for sensor network. *Journal of Web Engineering*, *20*(1), 53–88. DOI: 10.13052/jwe1540-9589.201003

Kathirvel, A., Subramaniam, M., & Rajabushanam, C. (2011). Burglar detecting system for wireless mobile ad hoc network. *European Journal of Scientific Research*, *62*(1), 14–23.

Khan, M., Serafeim, G., & Yoon, A. (2016). Corporate sustainability: First evidence on materiality. *The Accounting Review*, *91*(6), 1697–1724. DOI: 10.2308/accr-51383

Kim, Y., Park, M. S., & Wier, B. (2012). Is earnings quality associated with corporate social responsibility? *The Accounting Review*, *87*(3), 761–796. DOI: 10.2308/accr-10209

Kiron, D., Kruschwitz, N., Haanaes, K., Reeves, M., Fuisz-Kehrbach, S.-K., & Kell, G. (2015). Joining forces: Collaboration and leadership for sustainability [MIT Sloan Management Review Research Report]. *MIT Sloan Management Review*.

Kirubakaran, N., & Kathirvel, A. (2014). Performance improvement of security attacks in wireless mobile ad hoc networks. *Asian Journal of Information Technology*, *13*(2), 68–76. DOI: 10.3923/ajit.2014.68.76

Klassen, R. D., & Whybark, D. C. (1999). The impact of environmental technologies on manufacturing performance. *Academy of Management Journal*, *42*(6), 599–615. DOI: 10.5465/256982

Lee, K.-H., Cin, B. C., & Lee, E. Y. (2016). Environmental responsibility and firm performance: The application of an environmental, social and governance model. *Business Strategy and the Environment*, *25*(1), 40–53. DOI: 10.1002/bse.1851

Li, F. (2016). Endogeneity in CEO power: A survey and experiment. *The Investment Analysts Journal*, *45*(3), 149–162. DOI: 10.1080/10293523.2016.1196382

Li, F. (2018). A survey of corporate social responsibility and corporate governance. In S. Boubaker, D. Cumming, & D. K. Nguyen (Eds.), Research handbook of finance and sustainability (pp. 272–290). Edward Elgar Publishing.

Li, Y., Gong, M., Zhang, X.-Y., & Koh, L. (2018). The impact of environmental, social, and governance disclosure on firm value: The role of CEO power. *The British Accounting Review*, *50*(1), 60–75. DOI: 10.1016/j.bar.2017.09.007

Li, Y., Richardson, G. D., & Thornton, D. B. (1997). Corporate disclosure of environmental liability information: Theory and evidence. *Contemporary Accounting Research*, *14*(3), 435–474. DOI: 10.1111/j.1911-3846.1997.tb00535.x

Lokuwaduge, C. S. D. S., & Heenetigala, K. (2017). Integrating environmental, social and governance (ESG) disclosure for a sustainable development: An Australian study. *Business Strategy and the Environment*, *26*(4), 438–450. DOI: 10.1002/bse.1927

Lys, T., Naughton, J. P., & Wang, C. (2015). Signaling through corporate accountability reporting. *Journal of Accounting and Economics*, *60*(1), 56–72. DOI: 10.1016/j.jacceco.2015.03.001

Manita, R., Bruna, M. G., Dang, R., & Houanti, L. (2018). Board gender diversity and ESG disclosure: Evidence from the USA. *Journal of Applied Accounting Research*, *19*(2), 206–224. DOI: 10.1108/JAAR-01-2017-0008

Manrique, S., & Martí-Ballester, C.-P. (2017). Analyzing the effect of corporate environmental performance on corporate financial performance in developed and developing countries. *Sustainability*, *9*(10), 1957. Advance online publication. DOI: 10.3390/su9101957

Nicolaescu, E., Alpopi, C., & Zaharia, C. (2015). Measuring corporate sustainability performance. *Sustainability*, *7*(1), 851–865. DOI: 10.3390/su7010851

Ong, T. S., Teh, B. H., & Ang, Y. W. (2014). The impact of environmental improvements on the financial performance of leading companies listed in Bursa Malaysia. International Journal of Trade. *Economics and Finance*, *5*(5), 386–391. DOI: 10.7763/IJTEF.2014.V5.401

Porter, M. E., & van der Linde, C. (1995). Toward a new conception of the environment-competitiveness relationship. *The Journal of Economic Perspectives*, *9*(4), 97–118. DOI: 10.1257/jep.9.4.97

Rezaee, Z. (2016). Business sustainability research: A theoretical and integrated perspective. *Journal of Accounting Literature*, *36*(1), 48–64. DOI: 10.1016/j.acclit.2016.05.003

Roberts, P. W., & Dowling, G. R. (2002). Corporate reputation and sustained superior financial performance. *Strategic Management Journal*, *23*(12), 1077–1093. DOI: 10.1002/smj.274

Sangeetha, N., & Kathirvel, A. (2019). Quantification of epicardial and thoracic adipose tissue using WOA optimized CNN. International Journal of Innovative Technology and Exploring Engineering, 8(9S2), 720–724. https://doi.org/DOI: 10.35940/ijitee.I1135.0789S219

Sila, I., & Cek, K. (2017). The impact of environmental, social and governance dimensions of corporate social responsibility on economic performance: Australian evidence. Procedia Computer Science, 120, 797–804. https://doi.org/ (From Proceedings of the 9th International Conference on Theory and Application of Soft Computing, Computing with Words and Perception, ICSCCW 2017)DOI: 10.1016/j.procs.2017.11.312

Simnett, R., Vanstraelen, A., & Chua, W. F. (2009). Assurance on sustainability reports: An international comparison. *The Accounting Review*, *84*(3), 937–967. DOI: 10.2308/accr.2009.84.3.937

Social Investment Forum. (2012). *Report on sustainable and responsible investing trends in the United States*. US SIF Foundation.

Subramaniam, M., Kathirvel, A., Sabitha, E., & Anwar Basha, H. (2021). Modified firefly algorithm and fuzzy C-mean clustering based semantic information retrieval. *Journal of Web Engineering*, *20*(1), 33–52. DOI: 10.13052/jwe1540-9589.201002

Sundar, R., & Kathirvel, A. (2015). Enhanced trust based delegation for load balancing in MANETs. *International Journal of Applied Engineering Research: IJAER, 10*(92), 41–46.

Sundar, R., & Kathirvel, A. (2019). Efficient prior path failure recovery algorithm using channel aware routing in MANET. *International Journal of Innovative Technology and Exploring Engineering, 8*(5), 97–103.

Sundar, R., & Kathirvel, A. (2020a). Aggressively delivered mechanism over variable length density using a simulated annealing algorithm in mobile ad hoc network. *Transactions on Emerging Telecommunications Technologies, 31*(7), e3863. Advance online publication. DOI: 10.1002/ett.3863

Sundar, R., & Kathirvel, A. (2020b). Enhanced cluster based stable path for load balancing and reducing overhead using artificial bee colony in MANETs. *International Journal of Vehicle Information and Communication Systems, 5*(1), 41–54. DOI: 10.1504/IJVICS.2020.107087

Suresh, K. C., Prakash, S., Priya, A. E., & Kathirvel, A. (2015). Primary path reservation using enhanced slot assignment in TDMA for session admission. *TheScientificWorldJournal, 2015*, 405371. Advance online publication. DOI: 10.1155/2015/405371

Tarmuji, I., Maelah, R., & Tarmuji, N. H. (2016). The impact of environmental, social and governance practices (ESG) on economic performance: Evidence from ESG scores. International Journal of Trade. *Economics and Finance, 7*(2), 67–74. DOI: 10.18178/IJTEF.2016.7.2.499

Vitaliano, D. F. (2010). Corporate social responsibility and labor turnover. *Corporate Governance (Bradford), 10*(5), 563–573. DOI: 10.1108/14720701011085544

Zuraida, Z., Houqe, M. N., & van Zijl, T. (2016). Value relevance of environmental, social and governance disclosure. In S. Boubaker, D. Cumming, & D. K. Nguyen (Eds.), Handbook of finance and sustainability (pp. 401–417). Edward Elgar Publishing.

Compilation of References

Abbott, M. L., & Fisher, M. T. (2017). *Scalability rules: 50 principles for scaling web sites*. Addison-Wesley Professional.

Abdallah, A. B., & Al-Ghwayeen, W. S. (2020). Green supply chain management and business performance: The mediating roles of environmental and operational performances. *Business Process Management Journal*, *26*(2), 489–512. DOI: 10.1108/BPMJ-03-2018-0091

Abdulahi, E. W., & Fan, L. (2021). Exploring and Validating Container Operational Risk Scale in Container Shipping: The Case of Ethiopian Shipping and Logistics Service Enterprise. *Sustainability*, *13*, 9248.

Abeyrathna, S. P. G. M., & Priyadarshana, A. J. M. (2019). Impact of firm size on profitability (special reference to listed manufacturing companies in Sri Lanka). *International Journal of Scientific and Research Publications*, *9*(9), 561–564. DOI: 10.29322/IJSRP.9.09.2019.p9356

Accenture. (2020, June). Elevate every decision with intelligent supply chain operations. https://www.accenture.com/content/dam/accenture/final/a-com-migration/r3-3/pdf/pdf-157/accenture-supply-chain-operations-pov-june-2020.pdf

Acerbi, F., Forterre, D. A., & Taisch, M. (2021). Role of artificial intelligence in circular manufacturing: A systematic literature review. *IFAC-PapersOnLine*, *54*(1), 367–372.

Aerts, W., Cormier, D., & Magnan, M. (2008). Corporate environmental disclosure, financial markets and the media: An international perspective. *Ecological Economics*, *64*(3), 643–659. DOI: 10.1016/j.ecolecon.2007.04.012

Agrawal, R., Majumdar, A., Kumar, A., & Luthra, S. (2023). Integration of artificial intelligence in sustainable manufacturing: Current status and future opportunities. *Operations Management Research*, *16*(4), 1720–1741. DOI: 10.1007/s12063-023-00383-y

Aguirre, S., & Rodriguez, A. (2017). *Automation of a business process using robotic process automation (RPA): A case study*. In J. C. Figueroa-Garcia, E. R. Lopez-Santana, R. Ferro-Escobar, & J. L. Villa-Ramirez (Eds.), Applied Computer Sciences in Engineering - 4th Workshop on Engineering Applications, WEA 2017, Proceedings (pp. 65-71). (Communications in Computer and Information Science; Vol. 742). Springer Verlag. https://doi.org/DOI: 10.1007/978-3-319-66963-2_7

AIMultiple Research. (2025, May 7). Low/No Code RPA Software ['25]: Benefits & Best Practices. https://research.aimultiple.com/no-code-rpa/

Albu, D. (2021). The sustainable development goals report 2021. Drepturile Omului, 115.

Alfalla-Luque, R., Medina-Lopez, C., & Dey, P. K. (2013). Supply chain integration framework using literature review. *Production Planning and Control*, *24*(8–9), 800–817. DOI: 10.1080/09537287.2012.666870

Al-Janadi, Y., Rahman, R. A., & Alazzani, A. (2016). Does government ownership affect corporate governance and corporate disclosure? *Managerial Auditing Journal*, *31*(8/9), 871–890. DOI: 10.1108/MAJ-11-2015-1270

Al-Tuwaijri, S. A., Christensen, T. E., & Hughes, K. E.II. (2004). The relations among environmental disclosure, environmental performance, and economic performance: A simultaneous equations approach. *Accounting, Organizations and Society*, *29*(5–6), 447–471. DOI: 10.1016/S0361-3682(03)00032-1

Alverhed, E., Hellgren, S., Isaksson, H., Olsson, L., Palmqvist, H., & Flodén, J. (2024). Autonomous last-mile delivery robots: A literature review. *European Transport Research Review*, *16*(1), 4.

Amaya, J., Encarnación, T., & Cantillo, V. (2025). Sustainable last mile delivery alternatives: Influencing factors and willingness to use. *Transportation Research Part D, Transport and Environment*, *139*, 104574.

Ambra, T., Caris, A., Macharis, C., & Should, I. (2019). Stay or Should I Go? Assessing Intermodal and Synchromodal Resilience from a Decentralized Perspective. *Sustainability*, *11*, 1765.

Amine, H., & Mesnaoui, A. (2018). *Electronic Data Interchange (EDI) in the supply chain: Impact on customer satisfaction*. IJRDO -. *Journal of Business and Management*, *4*(6), 15–22. DOI: 10.53555/bm.v4i6.2072

Amosu, O. R., Kumar, P., Ogunsuji, Y. M., Oni, S., & Faworaja, O. (2024). AI-driven demand forecasting: Enhancing inventory management and customer satisfaction. *World Journal of Advanced Research and Reviews*, *23*(2), 708–719. DOI: 10.30574/wjarr.2024.23.2.2394

Anagnoste, S. (2018). *Robotic Automation Process – The Operating System for the Digital Enterprise. Proceedings of the International Conference on Business Excellence*, vol. 12, no. 1, The Bucharest University of Economic Studies, pp. 54-69. https://doi.org/DOI: 10.2478/picbe-2018-0007

An, Y., Davey, H., & Eggleton, I. R. C. (2011). Towards a comprehensive theoretical framework for voluntary IC disclosure. *Journal of Intellectual Capital*, *12*(4), 571–585. DOI: 10.1108/14691931111181733

Asatiani, A., & Penttinen, E. (2016). *Turning robotic process automation into commercial success – Case OpusCapita*. Journal of Information Technology Teaching Cases. https://doi.org/DOI: 10.1057/jittc.2016.5

Atan, R., Alam, M. M., Said, J., & Zamri, M. (2018). The impacts of environmental, social, and governance factors on firm performance: Panel study of Malaysian companies. *Management of Environmental Quality*, *29*(2), 182–194. DOI: 10.1108/MEQ-06-2017-0051

Ataseven, C., & Nair, A. (2017). Assessment of supply chain integration and performance relationships: A meta-analytic investigation of the literature. *International Journal of Production Economics*, *185*, 252–265. DOI: 10.1016/j.ijpe.2017.01.007

Automotive Industry Action Group (AIAG). (March 2011). *CQI-18: Guidelines to Effective Error-Proofing*. AIAG Store. https://www.aiag.org/store/publications/details?ProductCode=CQI-18

Autor, D. H. (2015). Why are there still so many jobs? The history and future of workplace automation. *The Journal of Economic Perspectives*, *29*(3), 3–30. DOI: 10.1257/jep.29.3.3

Babić, D., Kalić, M., Janić, M., Dožić, S., & Kukić, K. (2022). Integrated Door-to-Door Transport Services for Air Passengers: From Intermodality to Multimodality. *Sustainability*, *14*, 6503.

Bag, S., Gupta, S., & Kumar, S. (2021). Industry 4.0 adoption and 10R advance manufacturing capabilities for sustainable development. *International Journal of Production Economics*, *231*, 107844. DOI: 10.1016/j.ijpe.2020.107844

Bag, S., Pretorius, J.-H. C., & Gupta, S. (2021). Role of institutional pressures and resources in the adoption of big data analytics–powered artificial intelligence, sustainable manufacturing practices and circular economy capabilities. *Technological Forecasting and Social Change*, *163*, 120420.

Bag, S., Pretorius, J.-H. C., Gupta, S., & Dwivedi, Y. K. (2021a). Role of institutional pressures and resources in the adoption of big data analytics powered artificial intelligence, sustainable manufacturing practices and circular economy capabilities. *Technological Forecasting and Social Change*, *163*, 120420. DOI: 10.1016/j.techfore.2020.120420

Bai, C., Dallasega, P., Orzes, G., & Sarkis, J. (2020). Industry 4.0 technologies assessment: A sustainability perspective. *International Journal of Production Economics*, *229*, 107776. DOI: 10.1016/j.ijpe.2020.107776

Baird, A., & Raghu, T. (2015). Associating consumer perceived value with business models for digital services. *European Journal of Information Systems*, *24*(1), 4–22. DOI: 10.1057/ejis.2013.12

Bajic, S., & Yurtoglu, B. B. (2018). Which aspects of CSR predict firm market value? *Journal of Capital Markets Studies*, *2*(1), 50–69. DOI: 10.1108/JCMS-10-2017-0002

Barnett, M. L., & Salomon, R. M. (2012). Does it pay to be really good? Addressing the shape of the relationship between social and financial performance. *Strategic Management Journal*, *33*(11), 1304–1320. DOI: 10.1002/smj.1980

Barot, S. (2025, March 5). AI in Warehouse Management - Transitioning to Intelligent Automation. Aglowid IT Solutions. https://aglowiditsolutions.com/blog/ai-warehouse-automation/

Barreto, L., Amaral, A., & Pereira, T. (2017). Industry 4.0 implications in logistics: An overview. *Procedia Manufacturing*, *13*, 1245–1252. DOI: 10.1016/j.promfg.2017.09.045

Barringer, B. R., & Harrison, J. S. (2000). Walking a tightrope: Creating value through interorganizational relationships. *Journal of Management*, *26*(3), 367–403. DOI: 10.1177/014920630002600302

Bartholdi, J. J., III, & Hackman, S. T. (2019). *Warehouse & Distribution Science*. Release 0.98.1. https://www.warehouse-science.com/book/editions/wh-sci-0.98.1.pdf

Barua, A., Konana, P., Whinston, A. B., & Yin, F. (2004). An empirical investigation of net-enabled business value. *Management Information Systems Quarterly*, *28*(4), 585–620. DOI: 10.2307/25148656

Bassen, A., & Kovács, A. M. (2008). Environmental, social and governance key performance indicators from a capital market perspective. *Zeitschrift für Wirtschafts- und Unternehmensethik*, *9*(2), 182–192.

Batini, C., & Scannapieco, M. (2016). *Data and information quality: Dimensions, principles and techniques*. Springer., DOI: 10.1007/978-3-319-24106-7

Beysenbaev, R., & Dus, Y. (2020). Proposals for improving the Logistics Performance Index. *Asian J. Shipp. Logist.*, *36*, 34–42.

Björkdahl, J. (2020). Strategies for digitalization in manufacturing firms. *California Management Review*, *62*(4), 17–36. DOI: 10.1177/0008125620920349

Blue Prism. (2025). The Future of RPA: Trends & Predictions 2025. https://www.blueprism.com/resources/blog/future-of-rpa-trends-predictions/

Bocken, N. M. P., de Pauw, I., Bakker, C., & van der Grinten, B. (2016). Product design and business model strategies for a circular economy. *Journal of Industrial and Production Engineering*, *33*(5), 308–320. DOI: 10.1080/21681015.2016.1172124

Bogataj, D., Bogataj, M., & Hudoklin, D. (2017). Mitigating risks of perishable products in the cyber-physical systems based on the extended MRP model. *International Journal of Production Economics*, *193*, 51–62.

Bosse, D. A., Phillips, R. A., & Harrison, J. S. (2009). Stakeholders, reciprocity, and firm performance. *Strategic Management Journal*, *30*(4), 447–456. DOI: 10.1002/smj.743

Boysen, N., Briskorn, D., & Emde, S. (2016). Just-in-time vehicle scheduling with capacity constraints. *IIE Transactions*, *48*, 134–145. DOI: 10.1080/0740817X.2015.1056390

Brammer, S., & Millington, A. (2008). Does it pay to be different? An analysis of the relationship between corporate social and financial performance. *Strategic Management Journal*, *29*(12), 1325–1343. DOI: 10.1002/smj.714

Brammer, S., & Pavelin, S. (2008). Factors influencing the quality of corporate environmental disclosure. *Business Strategy and the Environment*, *17*(2), 120–136. DOI: 10.1002/bse.506

Brockett, A., & Rezaee, Z. (2012). *Corporate sustainability: Integrating performance and reporting*. John Wiley & Sons.

Brooks, C., & Oikonomou, I. (2018). The effects of environmental, social and governance disclosures and performance on firm value: A review of the literature in accounting and finance. *The British Accounting Review, 50*(1), 1–15. DOI: 10.1016/j.bar.2017.11.005

Brynjolfsson, E., & McAfee, A. (2014). *The second machine age: Work, progress, and prosperity in a time of brilliant technologies.* W. W. Norton & Company. https://psycnet.apa.org/record/2014-07087-000

Büyüközkan, G., & Göçer, F. (2018). Digital supply chain: Literature review and a proposed framework for future research. *Computers in Industry*, *97*, 157–177. DOI: 10.1016/j.compind.2018.02.010

Cao, J., Zhang, J., Liu, M., Yin, S., & An, Y. (2022). Green Logistics of Vehicle Dispatch under Smart IoT. *Sensors and Materials*, *34*, 3317–3338.

Carter, C. R., & Ellram, L. M. (1998). Reverse logistics: A review of the literature and framework for future investigation. *Journal of Business Logistics*, *19*(1), 85–102.

Casey, R. J., & Grenier, J. H. (2015). Understanding and contributing to the enigma of corporate social responsibility (CSR) assurance in the United States. *Auditing*, *34*(1), 97–130. DOI: 10.2308/ajpt-50826

Centobelli, P., Cerchione, R., & Esposito, E. (2020). Pursuing supply chain sustainable development goals through the adoption of green practices and enabling technologies: A cross-country analysis of LSPs. *Technological Forecasting and Social Change*, *153*, 119920. DOI: 10.1016/j.techfore.2020.119920

Chang, W., Ellinger, A. E., & Kim, K. (Kate), & Franke, G. R. (2016). Supply chain integration and firm financial performance: A meta-analysis of positional advantage mediation and moderating factors. *European Management Journal*, *34*(3), 282–295. DOI: 10.1016/j.emj.2015.11.008

Chaudhuri, A., Boer, H., & Taran, Y. (2018). Supply chain integration, risk management and manufacturing flexibility. *International Journal of Operations & Production Management*, *38*(3), 690–712. DOI: 10.1108/IJOPM-08-2015-0508

Chejarla, K. C., Vaidya, O. S., & Kumar, S. (2022). MCDM applications in logistics performance evaluation: A literature review. *Journal of Multi-Criteria Decision Analysis*, *29*, 274–297.

Chen, M., Mao, S., & Liu, Y. (2012). Big Data: A Survey. *Mobile Networks and Applications*, *19*(2), 171–209.

Choi, T. M., Wallace, S. W., & Wang, Y. (2017). Big Data Analytics in operations management. *Production and Operations Management*, *27*(10), 1868–1883. DOI: 10.1111/poms.12838 PMID: 26766385

Choi, T.-M., & Sun, X. (2025). Prescriptive analytics for sustainable supply chain operations: The PASO framework for Industry 5.0. *Transportation Research Part E, Logistics and Transportation Review*, *183*, 104206. DOI: 10.1016/j.tre.2025.104206

Chopra, S., & Meindl, P. (2016). *Supply chain management: Strategy, planning, and operation* (6th ed.). Pearson. ISBN: 978-0133800203.

Chow, G., & Heaver, T. D. (1994). Henriks son, L.E. Logistics Performance: Definition and Measurement. *International Journal of Physical Distribution & Logistics Management*, *24*, 17–28.

Christopher, M. (2016). Logistics & supply chain management (5th ed.). Pearson. ISBN: 978-1292083797.

Christopher, M., & Holweg, M. (2011). "Supply Chain 2.0": Managing Supply Chains in the Era of Turbulence. *International Journal of Physical Distribution & Logistics Management*, *41*, 63–82. DOI: 10.1108/09600031111101439

Cicek, D., Kantarci, B., & Schillo, S. (2025). A Comparative Review of User Acceptance Factors for Drones and Sidewalk Robots in Autonomous Last Mile Delivery. *Green Energy and Intelligent Transportation*, 100310.

Cohen, M. A., Agrawal, N., & Agrawal, V. (2006). Winning in the aftermarket. *Harvard Business Review*, *84*(5), 129–138. https://hbr.org/2006/05/winning-in-the-aftermarket

Crosby, M., Pattanayak, P., Verma, S., & Kalyanaraman, V. (2016). Blockchain technology: Beyond Bitcoin. *Applied Innovation Review*, *2*, 6–10.

Dalal, K. K., & Thaker, N. (2019). ESG and corporate financial performance: A panel study of Indian companies. *IUP Journal of Corporate Governance*, *18*(1), 44–59.

Dave, S. (2023, June). *The Job Openings & Labor Turnover Survey (JOLTS) and the Tightest Labor Markets in the US*. Minnesota Department of Employment and Economic Development. https://mn.gov/deed/newscenter/publications/trends/june-2023/jolts.jsp

De Maio, A., Ghiani, G., Laganà, D., & Manni, E. (2024). Sustainable last-mile distribution with autonomous delivery robots and public transportation. *Transportation Research Part C, Emerging Technologies*, *163*, 104615.

Deepu, T. S., & Ravi, V. (2021). Supply chain digitalization: An integrated MCDM approach for inter-organizational information systems selection in an electronic supply chain. *International Journal of Information Management Data Insights*, *1*(2), 100038. DOI: 10.1016/j.jjimei.2021.100038

Delbart, T., Molenbruch, Y., Braekers, K., & Caris, A. (2021). Uncertainty in Intermodal and Synchromodal Transport: Review and Future Research Directions. *Sustainability*, *13*, 3980.

Delle Donne, D., Santini, A., & Archetti, C. (2025). Integrating public transport in sustainable last-mile delivery: Column generation approaches. *European Journal of Operational Research*.

Deloitte AG. (2015). *Industry 4.0: Challenges and solutions for the digital transformation*.

Deloitte. (2018). *2018 global automotive consumer study: Asia-Pacific highlights.* https://www2.deloitte.com/content/dam/Deloitte/global/Documents/Consumer-Business/2018-global-automotive-consumer-study-asia-pacific-highlights.pdf

Deloitte. (2019). *The robots are ready. Are you? Untapped opportunity in robotic process automation.* Deloitte Insights. https://www2.deloitte.com/content/dam/Deloitte/global/Documents/Technology/gx-consulting-robots-are-ready.pdf

Dhaliwal, D. S., Li, O. Z., Tsang, A., & Yang, Y. G. (2011). Voluntary nonfinancial disclosure and the cost of equity capital: The initiation of corporate social responsibility reporting. *The Accounting Review*, *86*(1), 59–100. DOI: 10.2308/accr.00000005

Dhl-green-logistics-toolkit. (2024, May 16). https://www.dhl.com/discover/en-in/logistics-advice/sustainability-and-green-logistics/dhl-green-logistics-toolkit

Digital Workforce. (2021, June 21). Empowering agile customer service with RPA - Case Toyota Material Handling. https://digitalworkforce.com/rpa-news/empowering-agile-customer-service-with-rpa-case-toyota-material-handling/

DigitalDefynd. (2025). Top 5 AI use in automotive industry case studies [2025]. https://digitaldefynd.com/IQ/ai-in-automotive-industry-case-studies/

Dilmegani, C. (2025, May 7). Low/No Code RPA Software ['25]: Benefits & Best Practices. AIMultiple Research. https://research.aimultiple.com/no-code-rpa/

Doh, J. P., Howton, S. D., Howton, S. W., & Siegel, D. S. (2010). Does the market respond to an endorsement of social responsibility? The role of institutions, information, and legitimacy. *Journal of Management*, *36*(6), 1461–1485. DOI: 10.1177/0149206309337892

Dubey, R., Gunasekaran, A., Childe, S. J., Bryde, D. J., Giannakis, M., Foropon, C., Roubaud, D., & Hazen, B. T. (2019). Big data analytics and artificial intelligence pathway to operational performance under the effects of entrepreneurial orientation and environmental dynamism: A study of manufacturing organisations. *International Journal of Production Economics, 226*, 107599. DOI: 10.1016/j.ijpe.2019.107599

Dubey, R., Gunasekaran, A., Childe, S. J., Papadopoulos, T., Luo, Z., Wamba, S. F., & Roubaud, D. (2019). Can big data and predictive analytics improve social and environmental sustainability? *Technological Forecasting and Social Change, 144*, 534–545. DOI: 10.1016/j.techfore.2017.06.020

Dwivedi, Y. K., Hughes, L., Ismagilova, E., Aarts, G., Coombs, C., Crick, T., Duan, Y., Dwivedi, R., Edwards, J., Eirug, A., Galanos, V., Ilavarasan, P. V., Janssen, M., Jones, P., Kar, A. K., Kizgin, H., Kronemann, B., Lal, B., Lucini, B., & Williams, M. D. (2019). Artificial Intelligence (AI): Multidisciplinary perspectives on emerging challenges, opportunities, and agenda for research, practice and policy. *International Journal of Information Management, 57*, 101994. DOI: 10.1016/j.ijinfomgt.2019.08.002

Eccles, R. G., Ioannou, I., & Serafeim, G. (2014). The impact of corporate sustainability on organizational processes and performance. *Management Science, 60*(11), 2835–2857. DOI: 10.1287/mnsc.2014.1984

Eccles, R. G., Serafeim, G., & Krzus, M. P. (2011). Market interest in nonfinancial information. *Journal of Applied Corporate Finance, 23*(4), 113–127. DOI: 10.1111/j.1745-6622.2011.00359.x

El Ghazali, M., & Boutgayout, B. (2020). Fintech: la gestion de la performance à l'ère du digital. *Revue du Contrôle, de la Comptabilité et de l'Audit*, 4(1), 713–733.

Elkington, J. (1998). *Cannibals with forks: The triple bottom line of 21st century business.* New Society Publishers.

Escrig-Olmedo, E., Rivera-Lirio, J. M., Muñoz-Torres, M. J., & Fernández-Izquierdo, M. Á. (2017). Integrating multiple ESG investors' preferences into sustainable investment: A fuzzy multicriteria methodological approach. *Journal of Cleaner Production, 162*, 1334–1345. DOI: 10.1016/j.jclepro.2017.06.143

Ezmigna, I., Alghizzawi, M., Alqsass, M., Abu-AlSondos, I. A., Abualfalayeh, G., & Aldulaimi, S. H. (2024, December). The Impact of AI Tools on Last-Mile Delivery in the E-Commerce Sector in Saudi Arabia. In *2024 International Conference on Decision Aid Sciences and Applications (DASA)* (pp. 1-6). IEEE.

Ferrero-Ferrero, I., Fernández-Izquierdo, M. Á., & Muñoz-Torres, M. J. (2015). Integrating sustainability into corporate governance: An empirical study on board diversity. *Corporate Social Responsibility and Environmental Management*, *22*(4), 193–207. DOI: 10.1002/csr.1334

Flynn, B. B., Huo, B., & Zhao, X. (2010). The impact of supply chain integration on performance: A contingency and configuration approach. *Journal of Operations Management*, *28*(1), 58–71. DOI: 10.1016/j.jom.2009.06.001

Fosso Wamba, S., Gunasekaran, A., & Akter, S. (2020). Blockchain technology for enhancing supply chain transparency: An empirical study. *International Journal of Production Economics*, *220*, 107475.

Freeman, R. E., & Dmytriyev, S. (2017). Corporate social responsibility and stakeholder theory: Learning from each other. Symposium: Emerging Issues in Management, (2), 7–15. https://doi.org/DOI: 10.4468/2017.2.02

Freeman, R. E. (1984). *Strategic management: A stakeholder approach.* Pitman.

Friedman, M. (2007). The social responsibility of business is to increase its profits. In Zimmerli, W. C., Holzinger, M., & Richter, K. (Eds.), *Corporate ethics and corporate governance* (pp. 173–178). Springer. (Original work published 1970)

Gagliordi, N. (2025, April 8). *AI in Warehouse Management: Impacts and Use Cases*. Oracle. https://www.oracle.com/scm/ai-warehouse-management/

Garikapati, D., & Shetiya, S. S. (2024). Autonomous vehicles: Evolution of artificial intelligence and the current industry landscape. *Big Data and Cognitive Computing*, *8*(4), 42.

Gartner. (2018). *Robotic process automation*. Gartner IT Glossary. https://www.gartner.com/en/information-technology/glossary/robotic-process-automation-rpa

Garus, A., Christidis, P., Mourtzouchou, A., Duboz, L., & Ciuffo, B. (2024). Unravelling the last-mile conundrum: A comparative study of autonomous delivery robots, delivery bicycles, and light commercial vehicles in 14 varied European landscapes. *Sustainable Cities and Society*, *108*, 105490.

Gaudenzi, B., Confente, I., & Russo, I. (2021). Logistics service quality and customer satisfaction in B2B relationships: A qualitative comparative analysis approach. *The TQM Journal*, *33*, 125–140.

Gautr, R. (2020). Digitization in supply chain: Digital technologies in chemical industries. *Chemical Industry Digest*. https://doi.org/DOI: 10.4018/JGIM.311450

Geetha, D. M., Muthusundar, S. K., Subramaniam, M., & Kathirvel, A. (2015). Temporary redundant transmission mechanism for SCTP multi-homed hosts. *TheScientificWorldJournal*, *2015*, 158697. Advance online publication. DOI: 10.1155/2015/158697

Geissdoerfer, M., Savaget, P., Bocken, N. M. P., & Hultink, E. J. (2016). The Circular Economy–A new sustainability paradigm? *Journal of Cleaner Production*, *143*, 757–768. DOI: 10.1016/j.jclepro.2016.12.048

Germain, R., & Iyer, K. N. S. (2006). The interaction of internal and downstream integration and its association with performance. *Journal of Business Logistics*, *27*(2), 29–52. DOI: 10.1002/j.2158-1592.2006.tb00216.x

Ghobakhloo, M., Tang, S. H., Sabouri, M. S., & Zulkifli, N. (2014). The impact of information system-enabled supply chain process integration on business performance: A resource-based analysis. *International Journal of Information Technology & Decision Making*, *13*(5), 1075–1113. DOI: 10.1142/S0219622014500163

Ghosh, S. K., & Sar, A. K. (2022). Impact of effective supply chain management and supply chain risk management capabilities on construction project performance. *Indian Journal of Science and Technology*, *15*(12), 505–517.

Giusti, R., Manerba, D., Bruno, G., & Tadei, R. (2019). Synchromodal logistics: An overview of critical success factors, enabling technologies, and open research issues. Transp. Res. Part E Logist. *Transport Reviews*, *129*, 92–110.

Global Sustainable Investment Alliance. (2018). Global sustainable investment review 2018. http://www.gsi-alliance.org/wp-content/uploads/2019/03/GSIR_Review2018.3.28.pdf

Gong, Z., & Liu, N. (2020). Mitigative and adaptive investments for natural disasters and labor strikes in a seaport–dry port inland logistics network. *Maritime Policy & Management*, *47*, 92–108.

Goyal, P., Rahman, Z., & Kazmi, A. A. (2013). Corporate sustainability performance and firm performance research: Literature review and future research agenda. *Management Decision*, *51*(2), 361–379. DOI: 10.1108/00251741311301867

Guide, V. D. R.Jr, & Van Wassenhove, L. N. (2002). The reverse supply chain. *Harvard Business Review*, *80*(2), 25–26. https://hbr.org/2002/02/the-reverse-supply-chain

Gunasekaran, A., Yusuf, Y. Y., Adeleye, E. O., Papadopoulos, T., Kovvuri, D., & Geyi, D. G. (2019). Agile manufacturing: An evolutionary review of practices. *International Journal of Production Research*, *57*(15-16), 5154–5174.

Gupta, S., Rani, S., & Dixit, A. (2019). *Recent Trends in Automation - A Study of RPA Development Tools*. 2019 3rd International Conference on Recent Developments in Control, Automation & Power Engineering (RDCAPE), Noida, India, pp. 159-163, doi: DOI: 10.1109/RDCAPE47089.2019.8979084

Gupta, M., & Sharma, K. (1996). Environmental operations management: An opportunity for improvement. *Production and Inventory Management Journal*, *37*(3), 40–46.

Guthrie, J., & Parker, L. D. (1989). Corporate social reporting: A rebuttal of legitimacy theory. *Accounting and Business Research*, *19*(76), 343–352. DOI: 10.1080/00014788.1989.9728863

Hahn, R., & Kühnen, M. (2013). Determinants of sustainability reporting: A review of results, trends, theory, and opportunities in an expanding field of research. *Journal of Cleaner Production*, *59*, 5–21. DOI: 10.1016/j.jclepro.2013.07.005

Hamela, K., & Kathirvel, A. (2017). Alleviating black hole attack in OLSR protocol adopting an evolutionary game theory approach for MANET. Journal of Advanced Research in Dynamical and Control Systems, 9(Sp. Iss. 14), 666–678.

Hamela, K., & Kathirvel, A. (2019a). EIMO-ESOLSR: Energy efficient and security based model for OLSR routing protocol in mobile ad-hoc network. *IET Communications*, *13*(5), 553–559. DOI: 10.1049/iet-com.2018.5564

Hamela, K., & Kathirvel, A. (2019b). Multi objective ALO based energy efficient and secure routing OLSR protocol in MANET. *International Journal of Intelligent Engineering and Systems*, *12*(1), 74–83. DOI: 10.22266/ijies2019.0228.08

Haris, M., & Khan, R. Z. (2018). A systematic review on cloud computing. *International Journal on Computer Science and Engineering*, *6*(12).

Healy, P. M., & Palepu, K. G. (2001). Information asymmetry, corporate disclosure, and the capital markets: A review of the empirical disclosure literature. *Journal of Accounting and Economics, 31*(1–3), 405–440. DOI: 10.1016/S0165-4101(01)00018-0

Herbohn, K., Gao, R., & Clarkson, P. (2019). Evidence on whether banks consider carbon risk in their lending decisions. *Journal of Business Ethics, 158*(1), 155–175. DOI: 10.1007/s10551-017-3713-7

Herm, L. V., Janiesch, C., & Helm, A.. (2023). A framework for implementing robotic process automation projects. *Information Systems and e-Business Management, 21*, 1–35. DOI: 10.1007/s10257-022-00553-8

Hofmann, E., & Rüsch, M. (2017). Industry 4.0 and the current status as well as future prospects on logistics. *Computers in Industry, 89*, 23–34. DOI: 10.1016/j.compind.2017.04.002

Hopkins, J., & Hawking, P. (2018). Big Data Analytics and IoT in logistics: A case study. *International Journal of Logistics Management, 29*, 575–591.

Hopp, W. J., & Spearman, M. L. (2011). Factory physics (3rd ed.). McGraw-Hill/Irwin. ISBN: 978-1577667391.

Huang, Y., Ding, Z., & Lee, W. J. (2022). Charging Cost Aware Fleet Management for Shared on-Demand Green Logistic System. *IEEE Internet of Things Journal, 10*, 7505–7516.

Hummel, K., & Schlick, C. (2016). The relationship between sustainability performance and sustainability disclosure—Reconciling voluntary disclosure theory and legitimacy theory. *Journal of Accounting and Public Policy, 35*(5), 455–476. DOI: 10.1016/j.jaccpubpol.2016.06.001

Hussainey, K., & Salama, A. (2010). The importance of corporate environmental reputation to investors. *Journal of Applied Accounting Research, 11*(3), 229–241. DOI: 10.1108/09675421011088122

IBM. (2022). *IBM Food Trust: Building apps overview*. https://www.ibm.com/support/pages/ibm-food-trust-building-apps-overview

Iddris, F. (2018). Digital supply chain: Survey of the literature. *International Journal of Business Research and Management*, *9*(1), 47.

Ieva, S., Bilenchi, I., Gramegna, F., Pinto, A., Scioscia, F., Ruta, M., & Loseto, G. (2025). Enhancing Last-Mile Logistics: AI-Driven Fleet Optimization, Mixed Reality, and Large Language Model Assistants for Warehouse Operations. *Sensors (Basel)*, *25*(9), 2696. PMID: 40363135

Ioannou, I., & Serafeim, G. (2017). The consequences of mandatory corporate sustainability reporting (Harvard Business School Research Working Paper No. 11-100). Harvard Business School.

Islam, M. S., Suad, S. F. R., & Rahman, A. (2024). Leveraging AI to Overcome Key Challenges in Last-Mile Delivery: Enhancing Customer Experience and Operational Efficiency in E-commerce. *Supply Chain Insider| ISSN: 2617-7420 (Print), 2617-7420 (Online)*, *14*(1).

Ivančić, L., Suša Vugec, D., & Bosilj Vukšić, V. (2019). Robotic Process Automation: Systematic Literature Review. In *Di Ciccio, C., et al. Business Process Management: Blockchain and Central and Eastern Europe Forum. BPM 2019. Lecture Notes in Business Information Processing* (Vol. 361). Springer., DOI: 10.1007/978-3-030-30429-4_19

Ivanov, D., & Dolgui, A. (2020). A digital supply chain twin for managing the disruption risks and resilience. *International Journal of Production Research*, *58*(12), 3860–3875.

Ivanov, D., Dolgui, A., & Sokolov, B. (2018). The impact of digital technology and Industry 4.0 on the ripple effect and supply chain risk analytics. *International Journal of Production Research*, *57*(3), 829–846. DOI: 10.1080/00207543.2018.1488086

Jain, P. K., Jain, A., & Rezaee, Z. (2016). Value-relevance of corporate social performance: Evidence from short selling. *Journal of Management Accounting Research*, *28*(2), 29–52. DOI: 10.2308/jmar-51350

Janinhoff, L., Klein, R., Sailer, D., & Schoppa, J. M. (2024). Out-of-home delivery in last-mile logistics: A review. *Computers & Operations Research*, •••, 106686.

Jayaram, J., & Xu, K. (2013). The relative influence of external versus internal integration on plant performance in China. *International Journal of Production Economics, 146*(1), 59–69. DOI: 10.1016/j.ijpe.2013.03.024

Jensen, M. C. (1989). Eclipse of the public corporation. *Harvard Business Review, 67*(5), 61–74.

Jensen, M. C. (2001). Value maximization, stakeholder theory, and the corporate objective function. *Journal of Applied Corporate Finance, 14*(3), 8–21. DOI: 10.1111/j.1745-6622.2001.tb00434.x

Jensen, M. C., & Meckling, W. H. (1976). Theory of the firm: Managerial behavior, agency costs and ownership structure. *Journal of Financial Economics, 3*(4), 305–360. DOI: 10.1016/0304-405X(76)90026-Xscholar.google.com

Jitmaneeroj, B. (2016). Reform priorities for corporate sustainability: Environmental, social, governance, or economic performance? *Management Decision, 54*(6), 1497–1521. DOI: 10.1108/MD-11-2015-0505

Jolin, J. S., Theophilus, A., & Kathirvel, A. (2025). Two factor mutual authentication with fingerprint and MAC address validation. *International Journal of Communication Networks and Information Security, 16*(6), 56–68. DOI: 10.5815/ijcnis.2024.06.05

Josh Kumar, J. P., & Kathirvel, A. (2015). A unified approach for detecting and eliminating selfish nodes in MANETs using TBUT. *EURASIP Journal on Wireless Communications and Networking, 2015*(1), 143. Advance online publication. DOI: 10.1186/s13638-015-0375-1

Josh Kumar, J. P., & Kathirvel, A. (2018). Optimum power management in mobile ad hoc networks. *Journal of Engineering Science and Technology, 13*(6), 1805–1815.

Josh Kumar, J. P., & Kathirvel, A. (2019). Analysis and ideas for improved routing in MANET. *International Journal of Interactive Mobile Technologies, 13*(4), 164–177. DOI: 10.3991/ijim.v13i04.10344

Judijanto, L., Asniar, N., Kushariyadi, K., Utami, E. Y., & Telaumbanua, E. (2024). Application of integrated logistics networks in improving the efficiency of distribution and delivery of goods in indonesia a literature review. *Sciences du Nord Economics and Business, 1*(01), 01-10.

Kache, F., & Seuring, S. (2017). Challenges and opportunities of digital information at the intersection of big data analytics and supply chain management. *International Journal of Operations & Production Management*, *37*(1), 10–36.

Kamala, V., Yamini, S., Gajanand, M. S., & Jagadeeswaran, K. R. (2025). Investigating the physical ergonomic risks associated with last-mile delivery personnel riding motorcycles. *International Journal of Productivity and Performance Management.*

Kamble, S., Gunasekaran, A., & Dhone, N. C. (2019). Industry 4.0 and lean manufacturing practices for sustainable organisational performance in Indian manufacturing companies. *International Journal of Production Research*, *58*(5), 1319–1337. DOI: 10.1080/00207543.2019.1630772

Kathirvel, A., & Mavuri, S. (2023). Digital assets fair estimation using artificial intelligence. In 2023 2nd IEEE International Conference on Vision Towards Emerging Trends in Communication and Networking Technologies (ViTECoN) (pp. 1–6). IEEE. https://doi.org/DOI: 10.1109/ViTECoN58111.2023.10156912

Kathirvel, A., Danny, B. J., Shalem, P., Hinn, J. T. O., Kennedy, R. C., & Immanuel, A. J. (2023). Systematic number plate detection using improved YOLOv5 detector. In 2023 2nd IEEE International Conference on Vision Towards Emerging Trends in Communication and Networking Technologies (ViTECoN) (pp. 1–6). IEEE. https://doi.org/ (ISBN 979-8-3503-4798-2) DOI: 10.1109/ViTECoN58111.2023.10156845

Kathirvel, A., & Rajabushanam, C. (2011). System of one to three umpire security system for wireless mobile ad hoc networks. *Journal of Computational Science*, *7*(12), 1854–1858. DOI: 10.3844/jcssp.2011.1854.1858

Kathirvel, A., & Srinivasan, R. (2010). Enhanced triple umpiring system for security and performance improvement in wireless MANETs. *International Journal of Communication Networks and Information Security, 2*(2), 77–84.

Kathirvel, A., & Srinivasan, R. (2011a). ETUS: An enhanced triple umpiring system for security and performance improvement of mobile ad hoc networks. *International Journal of Network Management, 21*(5), 341–359. DOI: 10.1002/nem.770

Kathirvel, A., & Srinivasan, R. (2011b). ETUS: An enhanced triple umpiring system for security and robustness of mobile ad hoc networks. *International Journal of Communication Networks and Distributed Systems, 7*(1/2), 153–187. DOI: 10.1504/IJCNDS.2011.040978

Kathirvel, A., Subramaniam, M., Navaneethan, S., & Sabarinath, C. (2021). Improved IDR response system for sensor network. *Journal of Web Engineering, 20*(1), 53–88. DOI: 10.13052/jwe1540-9589.201003

Kathirvel, A., Subramaniam, M., & Rajabushanam, C. (2011). Burglar detecting system for wireless mobile ad hoc network. *European Journal of Scientific Research, 62*(1), 14–23.

Kayikci, Y. (2018). Sustainability impact of digitization in logistics. *Procedia Manufacturing, 21*, 782–789. DOI: 10.1016/j.promfg.2018.02.184

Khajavi, S. H., & Holmström, J. (2015). Manufacturing digitalization and its effects on production planning and control practices. In *IFIP International Conference on Advances in Production Management Systems* (pp. 179–185). https://doi.org/DOI: 10.1007/978-3-319-22756-6_22

Khan, M., Serafeim, G., & Yoon, A. (2016). Corporate sustainability: First evidence on materiality. *The Accounting Review, 91*(6), 1697–1724. DOI: 10.2308/accr-51383

Kim, Y., Park, M. S., & Wier, B. (2012). Is earnings quality associated with corporate social responsibility? *The Accounting Review, 87*(3), 761–796. DOI: 10.2308/accr-10209

Kiron, D., Kruschwitz, N., Haanaes, K., Reeves, M., Fuisz-Kehrbach, S.-K., & Kell, G. (2015). Joining forces: Collaboration and leadership for sustainability [MIT Sloan Management Review Research Report]. *MIT Sloan Management Review*.

Kirubakaran, N., & Kathirvel, A. (2014). Performance improvement of security attacks in wireless mobile ad hoc networks. *Asian Journal of Information Technology*, *13*(2), 68–76. DOI: 10.3923/ajit.2014.68.76

Klassen, R. D., & Whybark, D. C. (1999). The impact of environmental technologies on manufacturing performance. *Academy of Management Journal*, *42*(6), 599–615. DOI: 10.5465/256982

Kotter, J. (2012). *Leading Change*. Harvard Business Review Press.

Kreuzwieser, S., Kimmig, A., & Ovtcharova, J. (2021). Robotic Process Automation: A case study in quality management at Mercedes-Benz AG. *American Journal of Intelligent Systems*, *11*(1), 8–13. http://article.sapub.org/10.5923.j.ajis.20211101.02.html

Lai, P. L., Jang, H., Fang, M., & Peng, K. (2022). Determinants of customer satisfaction with parcel locker services in last-mile logistics. *Asian J. Shipp. Logist.*, *38*, 25–30.

Lal, P., & Bharadwaj, S. (2020). Understanding the drivers of cloud-based service adoption and their impact on the organizational performance: An Indian perspective. *Journal of Global Information Management*, *28*(1), 56–85. DOI: 10.4018/JGIM.2020010104

Lambert, D. M. (2014). *Supply chain management: Processes, partnerships, performance* (4th ed.). Supply Chain Management Institute., DOI: 10.1007/978-3-8349-6515-8_29

Lambert, D. M., & Cooper, M. C. (2000). Issues in Supply Chain Management. *Industrial Marketing Management*, *29*(1), 65–83. DOI: 10.1016/S0019-8501(99)00113-3

Lee, H. L., & Billington, C. (1992). Managing supply chain inventory: Pitfalls and opportunities. *Sloan Management Review, 33*(3), 65–73. https://sloanreview.mit.edu/article/managing-supply-chain-inventory-pitfalls-and-opportunities/

Lee, K.-H., Cin, B. C., & Lee, E. Y. (2016). Environmental responsibility and firm performance: The application of an environmental, social and governance model. *Business Strategy and the Environment, 25*(1), 40–53. DOI: 10.1002/bse.1851

LeewayHertz. (2023). *AI in logistics and supply chain: Use cases, applications, solution and implementation.* https://www.leewayhertz.com/ai-in-logistics-and-supply-chain/

Leuschner, R., Rogers, D. S., & Charvet, F. F. (2013). A meta-analysis of supply chain integration and firm performance. *The Journal of Supply Chain Management, 49*(2), 34–57. DOI: 10.1111/jscm.12013

Li, F. (2018). A survey of corporate social responsibility and corporate governance. In S. Boubaker, D. Cumming, & D. K. Nguyen (Eds.), Research handbook of finance and sustainability (pp. 272–290). Edward Elgar Publishing.

Li, F. (2016). Endogeneity in CEO power: A survey and experiment. *The Investment Analysts Journal, 45*(3), 149–162. DOI: 10.1080/10293523.2016.1196382

Li, H., Hao, Y., Xie, C., Han, Y., & Wang, Z. R. (2023). Emerging technologies and policies for carbon–neutral transportation. *Int. J. Transp. Sci. Technol., 12*, 329–334.

Li, Y., Gong, M., Zhang, X.-Y., & Koh, L. (2018). The impact of environmental, social, and governance disclosure on firm value: The role of CEO power. *The British Accounting Review, 50*(1), 60–75. DOI: 10.1016/j.bar.2017.09.007

Li, Y., Richardson, G. D., & Thornton, D. B. (1997). Corporate disclosure of environmental liability information: Theory and evidence. *Contemporary Accounting Research, 14*(3), 435–474. DOI: 10.1111/j.1911-3846.1997.tb00535.x

Lokuwaduge, C. S. D. S., & Heenetigala, K. (2017). Integrating environmental, social and governance (ESG) disclosure for a sustainable development: An Australian study. *Business Strategy and the Environment, 26*(4), 438–450. DOI: 10.1002/bse.1927

Lys, T., Naughton, J. P., & Wang, C. (2015). Signaling through corporate accountability reporting. *Journal of Accounting and Economics, 60*(1), 56–72. DOI: 10.1016/j.jacceco.2015.03.001

Manavalan, E., & Jayakrishna, K. (2019). A review of Internet of Things (IoT) embedded sustainable supply chain for industry 4.0 requirements. *Computers & Industrial Engineering, 127*(C), 925–953. DOI: 10.1016/j.cie.2018.11.030

Manita, R., Bruna, M. G., Dang, R., & Houanti, L. (2018). Board gender diversity and ESG disclosure: Evidence from the USA. *Journal of Applied Accounting Research, 19*(2), 206–224. DOI: 10.1108/JAAR-01-2017-0008

Manrique, S., & Martí-Ballester, C.-P. (2017). Analyzing the effect of corporate environmental performance on corporate financial performance in developed and developing countries. *Sustainability, 9*(10), 1957. Advance online publication. DOI: 10.3390/su9101957

Masorgo, N., Dobrzykowski, D. D., & Fugate, B. S. (2024). Last-mile delivery: A process view, framework, and research agenda. *Journal of Business Logistics, 45*(4), e12397.

McKinsey & Company. (2020, March 30). *Beyond coronavirus: The road ahead for the automotive aftermarket*. https://www.mckinsey.com/industries/automotive-and-assembly/our-insights/beyond-coronavirus-the-road-ahead-for-the-automotive-aftermarket

McKinsey & Company. (2021). *Succeeding in the AI supply-chain revolution.* https://www.mckinsey.com/industries/metals-and-mining/our-insights/succeeding-in-the-ai-supply-chain-revolution

McKinsey. (2016). *Supply Chain 4.0: The next-generation digital supply chain*. McKinsey Insights.

McLennan, M. (2022). The global risks report 2022 17th edition. Cologny, Switzerland: World Economic Forum.

Mejjaouli, S. (2022). Internet of Things based Decision Support System for Green Logistics. *Sustainability*, *14*, 4756.

Mentzer, J. T., DeWitt, W., Keebler, J. S., Min, S., Nix, N. W., Smith, C. D., & Zacharia, Z. G. (2001). Defining Supply Chain Management. *Journal of Business Logistics*, *22*(2), 1–25. DOI: 10.1002/j.2158-1592.2001.tb00001.x

Mofokeng, T. M., & Chinomona, R. (2019). Supply chain partnership, supply chain collaboration and supply chain integration as the antecedents of supply chain performance. *South African Journal of Business Management*, *50*(1). Advance online publication. DOI: 10.4102/sajbm.v50i1.193

Mohsen, B. M. (2024). Ai-driven optimization of urban logistics in smart cities: Integrating autonomous vehicles and iot for efficient delivery systems. *Sustainability*, *16*(24), 11265.

Moktadir, M. A., Ali, S. M., Paul, S. K., & Shukla, N. (2019). Barriers to big data analytics in manufacturing supply chains: A case study from Bangladesh. *Computers & Industrial Engineering*, *128*, 1063–1075.

Moloi, T., & Marwala, T. (2021). Robotic Process Automation in Strategy and Strategy Implementation. In *Artificial Intelligence and the Changing Nature of Corporations. Future of Business and Finance*. Springer., DOI: 10.1007/978-3-030-76313-8_7

Montero-Vega, M., Estrada, M., & Thigulla, D. T. (2025). Understanding the impact of socio-demographic differences on acceptance of last-mile delivery technologies: A comparative analysis. *Journal of Transport Geography*, *126*, 104244.

Montreuil, B. (2011). Toward a Physical Internet: Meeting the global logistics sustainability grand challenge. *Logistics Research*, *3*, 71–87.

Moschovou, T., Vlahogianni, E., & Rentziou, A. (2019). Challenges for data sharing in freight transport. *Adv. Transp. Stud.*, *48*, 141–152.

Mounaim, H., & Boutaqbout, Z. (2020). Gestion digitale de la chaîne logistique: Une vue d'ensemble. *Revue Internationale des Sciences de Gestion*, *3*(2), 628–652. DOI: 10.5281/zenodo.3778891

Mukhopadhyay, T., & Kekre, S. (2002). Strategic and operational benefits of electronic integration in B2B procurement processes. *Management Science*, *48*(10), 1301–1313. DOI: 10.1287/mnsc.48.10.1301.273

Mu, Q. L., & Ming, C. W. (2023). The integration of supply chain and digitalization: The influence on SME's business performance in Chengdu, Sichuan Province, China. *Journal of Digitainability* [DREAM]. *Realism & Mastery*, *2*(9). Advance online publication. DOI: 10.56982/dream.v2i09.154

Narasimhan, R., & Kim, S. W. (2002). Effect of supply chain integration on the relationship between diversification and performance: Evidence from Japanese and Korean firms. *Journal of Operations Management*, *20*(3), 303–323. DOI: 10.1016/S0272-6963(02)00008-6

Nicolaescu, E., Alpopi, C., & Zaharia, C. (2015). Measuring corporate sustainability performance. *Sustainability*, *7*(1), 851–865. DOI: 10.3390/su7010851

Nourmohammadi, Z., Hu, B., Rey, D., & Saberi, M. (2025). A data-driven preference learning approach for multi-objective vehicle routing problems in last-mile delivery. *Transportation Research Part C, Emerging Technologies*, *174*, 105101.

Ojha, R., & Agarwal, A. (2025). Examining environmental sustainability in last-mile delivery: A quality function deployment analysis. *The TQM Journal.*

Okyere, S., Osei, A., Akuh, R., & Addo, L. (2023). The effect of supply chain digitalization on internal supply chain integration of cement manufacturing and distribution firms in Ghana. *African Journal of Applied Research*, *9*(1), 232–256. DOI: 10.26437/ajar.v9i1.532

Olsen, T. L., & Tomlin, B. (2019). *Industry 4.0: Opportunities and challenges for operations management.* Tuck School of Business Working Paper No. 3365733, The University of Auckland Business School Research Paper, Available at *SSRN*: https://ssrn.com/abstract=3365733 or http://dx.doi.org/DOI: 10.2139/ssrn.3365733

Ong, T. S., Teh, B. H., & Ang, Y. W. (2014). The impact of environmental improvements on the financial performance of leading companies listed in Bursa Malaysia. International Journal of Trade. *Economics and Finance*, *5*(5), 386–391. DOI: 10.7763/IJTEF.2014.V5.401

Opresnik, D., & Taisch, M. (2015). The value of big data in servitization. *International Journal of Production Economics*, *165*, 174–184. DOI: 10.1016/j.ijpe.2014.12.036

Oracle. (2025, April 8). *AI in Warehouse Management: Impacts and Use Cases*. https://www.oracle.com/scm/ai-warehouse-management/

Park, K. H., Pan, X., & Dresner, M. E. (2025). Targeting online sales through last-mile delivery platform integration. *Journal of Operations Management*, *71*(2), 195–219.

Parviainen, P., Tihinen, M., Kääriäinen, J., & Teppola, S. (2017). Tackling the digitalization challenge: How to benefit from digitalization in practice. *International Journal of Information Systems and Project Management*, *5*(1), 63–77. DOI: 10.12821/ijispm050104

Porter, M. E., & van der Linde, C. (1995). Toward a new conception of the environment-competitiveness relationship. *The Journal of Economic Perspectives*, *9*(4), 97–118. DOI: 10.1257/jep.9.4.97

Power, D. J. (2002). *Decision support systems: Concepts and resources for managers*. Praeger. ISBN: 978-1567204971.

Prabhu, T. (2016). Modern rapid 3D printer – A design review. *International Journal of Mechanical Engineering and Technology*, *7*(3), 29–37.

Rai, A., Patnayakuni, R., & Seth, N. (2006). Firm performance impacts of digitally enabled supply chain integration capabilities. *Management Information Systems Quarterly*, *30*(2), 225–246.

Ramírez, J. G. C. & mafiqul Islam, M. (2024). Application of Artificial Intelligence in Practical Scenarios. *Journal of Artificial Intelligence General science (JAIGS) ISSN: 3006-4023,* 2(1), 14-19.

Rejeb, A., Simske, S., Rejeb, K., Treiblmaier, H., & Zailani, S. (2020). Internet of Things research in supply chain management and logistics: A bibliometric analysis. *Internet of Things : Engineering Cyber Physical Human Systems*, *12*, 100318.

Rezaee, Z. (2016). Business sustainability research: A theoretical and integrated perspective. *Journal of Accounting Literature*, *36*(1), 48–64. DOI: 10.1016/j.acclit.2016.05.003

Roberts, P. W., & Dowling, G. R. (2002). Corporate reputation and sustained superior financial performance. *Strategic Management Journal*, *23*(12), 1077–1093. DOI: 10.1002/smj.274

Rogers, D. S., & Tibben-Lembke, R. S. (1999). *Going backwards: Reverse logistics trends and practices*. Reverse Logistics Executive Council.

Rohit, G., Krishnan, R., & Kumar, P. R. (2025). A Systematic Review and Morphological Analysis of the Literature on Last Mile Delivery Using Drones: Quo Vadis?. *IIM Kozhikode Society & Management Review*, 22779752251329395.

Ross, J. W., Beath, C. M., & Sebastian, I. M. (2017). Digitized ≠ Digital. *MIT CISR Research Briefings*, *18*(10), 1–3.

Rushton, A., Croucher, P., & Baker, P. (2017). *The handbook of logistics and distribution management* (6th ed.). Kogan Page. ISBN.

Saberi, S., Kouhizadeh, M., Sarkis, J., & Shen, L. (2019). Blockchain technology and its relationships to sustainable supply chain management. *International Journal of Production Research, 57*(7), 2117–2135.

Sabir, R., & Irfan, M. (2014). Levels & barriers to supply chain integration: A conceptual model of supply chain performance. *International Journal of Management Science and Business Administration, 1*(1), 52–59. DOI: 10.18775/IJMSBA.1849-5664-5419.2014.11.1005

Sabri, Y., Harchi, S., & El Kamoun, N. (2022). Managing health supply chain using blockchain technology: State of the art, challenges, and solution. [IJRES]. *International Journal of Reconfigurable and Embedded Systems, 11*(1), 49–57. DOI: 10.11591/ijres.v11.i3.pp258-264

Salonitis, K., Fadiji, T., Trollman, H., Garcia-Garcia, G., Bader, F., & Jagtap, S. (2021). Food Logistics 4.0: Opportunities and challenges. *Logistics (Basel), 5*(1), 1–19.

Sangeetha, N., & Kathirvel, A. (2019). Quantification of epicardial and thoracic adipose tissue using WOA optimized CNN. International Journal of Innovative Technology and Exploring Engineering, 8(9S2), 720–724. https://doi.org/DOI: 10.35940/ijitee.I1135.0789S219

Sarkis, J., Zhu, Q., & Lai, K. (2010). An organizational theoretic review of green supply chain management literature. *International Journal of Production Economics, 130*(1), 1–15. DOI: 10.1016/j.ijpe.2010.11.010

Sethi, S. P., Yan, H., & Zhang, H. (2005). *Inventory and supply chain management with forecast updates*. Springer US., DOI: 10.1007/0-387-25663-6_6

Shafique, M. N., Rashid, A., Bajwa, I. S., Kazmi, R., Khurshid, M. M., & Tahir, W. A. (2018). Effect of IoT capabilities and energy consumption behavior on green supply chain integration. *Applied Sciences (Basel, Switzerland), 8*, 2481.

Shuaibu, A. S., Mahmoud, A. S., & Sheltami, T. R. (2025). A Review of Last-Mile Delivery Optimization: Strategies, Technologies, Drone Integration, and Future Trends. *Drones (Basel), 9*(3), 158.

Siemens. (2023). *Blockchain and IoT in digital supply chains*. Siemens Digital Industries. https://xcelerator.siemens.com/global/en/industries/food-beverage/exclusive-area/blockchain-iot.html

Sila, I., & Cek, K. (2017). The impact of environmental, social and governance dimensions of corporate social responsibility on economic performance: Australian evidence. Procedia Computer Science, 120, 797–804. https://doi.org/ (From Proceedings of the 9th International Conference on Theory and Application of Soft Computing, Computing with Words and Perception, ICSCCW 2017)DOI: 10.1016/j.procs.2017.11.312

Simchi-Levi, D., Kaminsky, P., & Simchi-Levi, E. (2009). *Designing and managing the supply chain: Concepts, strategies, and case studies* (3rd ed.). McGraw-Hill/Irwin. ISBN: 978-0071270977.

Simnett, R., Vanstraelen, A., & Chua, W. F. (2009). Assurance on sustainability reports: An international comparison. *The Accounting Review, 84*(3), 937–967. DOI: 10.2308/accr.2009.84.3.937

Singh, K. (2025, May 12). The Future of Robotic Process Automation (RPA) in 2025: Trends and Innovations. AquSag Technologies. https://www.aqusag.com/blog/aqusag-technologies-blog-5/the-future-of-robotic-process-automation-rpa-in-2025-trends-and-innovations-57

Social Investment Forum. (2012). *Report on sustainable and responsible investing trends in the United States*. US SIF Foundation.

Som, J. O., Cobblah, C., & Anyigba, H. (2019). The effect of supply chain integration on supply chain performance. *IUP Journal of Supply Chain Management, 16*(4), 7–38.

Soysal, M., & Bloemhof-Ruwaard, J. M. (2017). Toward Sustainable Logistics. In *Springer Optimization and Its Applications* (Vol. 129, pp. 1–17). Springer.

Spekman, R. E., & Davis, E. W. (2004). Risky business: Expanding the discussion on risk and the extended enterprise. *International Journal of Physical Distribution & Logistics Management, 34*(5), 414–433. DOI: 10.1108/09600030410545454

Srikanteswara, R., Kalshetty, J. N., Molakatala, N., Chandra, S., & Manoj, A. (2025). Enhancing Electric Vehicle Performance Through 5G and Cloud Computing Integration. In *Integrating Artificial Intelligence Into the Energy Sector* (pp. 211-236). IGI Global Scientific Publishing.

Srinivasan, K., Kekre, S., & Mukhopadhyay, T. (1994). Impact of electronic data interchange technology on JIT shipments. *Management Science, 40*(10), 1291–1304. DOI: 10.1287/mnsc.40.10.1291

Stank, T., Esper, T., Goldsby, T. J., Zinn, W., & Autry, C. (2019). Toward a digitally dominant paradigm for twenty-first century supply chain scholarship. *International Journal of Physical Distribution & Logistics Management, 49*(10), 956–971. DOI: 10.1108/IJPDLM-03-2019-0076

Steadieseifi, M., Dellaert, N. P., Nuijten, W., Van Woensel, T., & Raoufi, R. (2014). Multimodal freight transportation planning: A literature review. *European Journal of Operational Research, 233*, 1–15.

Subramaniam, M., Kathirvel, A., Sabitha, E., & Anwar Basha, H. (2021). Modified firefly algorithm and fuzzy C-mean clustering based semantic information retrieval. *Journal of Web Engineering, 20*(1), 33–52. DOI: 10.13052/jwe1540-9589.201002

Sultana, S., Akter, S., Kyriazis, E., & Wamba, S. (2021). Architecting and developing big data-driven innovation (DDI) in the digital economy. *Journal of Global Information Management, 29*(3), 165–187. DOI: 10.4018/JGIM.2021050107

Sundar, R., & Kathirvel, A. (2015). Enhanced trust based delegation for load balancing in MANETs. *International Journal of Applied Engineering Research: IJAER, 10*(92), 41–46.

Sundar, R., & Kathirvel, A. (2019). Efficient prior path failure recovery algorithm using channel aware routing in MANET. *International Journal of Innovative Technology and Exploring Engineering, 8*(5), 97–103.

Sundar, R., & Kathirvel, A. (2020a). Aggressively delivered mechanism over variable length density using a simulated annealing algorithm in mobile ad hoc network. *Transactions on Emerging Telecommunications Technologies*, *31*(7), e3863. Advance online publication. DOI: 10.1002/ett.3863

Sundar, R., & Kathirvel, A. (2020b). Enhanced cluster based stable path for load balancing and reducing overhead using artificial bee colony in MANETs. *International Journal of Vehicle Information and Communication Systems*, *5*(1), 41–54. DOI: 10.1504/IJVICS.2020.107087

SupplyChainDigest. (2016). *SCDigest supply chain digitization benchmark survey.*

Suresh, K. C., Prakash, S., Priya, A. E., & Kathirvel, A. (2015). Primary path reservation using enhanced slot assignment in TDMA for session admission. *TheScientificWorldJournal*, *2015*, 405371. Advance online publication. DOI: 10.1155/2015/405371

Sustainability at Maersk. (n.d.). https://maersk.com/sustainability

Swamy, S.N.; Kota, S.R. (2020). An empirical study on system level aspects of Internet of Things (IoT). IEEE Access 2020, 8, 188082–188134.

Tanimu, J. A., & Abada, W. (2025). Addressing cybersecurity challenges in robotics: A comprehensive overview. *Cyber Security and Applications*, *3*, 100074. DOI: 10.1016/j.csa.2024.100074

Tarmuji, I., Maelah, R., & Tarmuji, N. H. (2016). The impact of environmental, social and governance practices (ESG) on economic performance: Evidence from ESG scores. International Journal of Trade. *Economics and Finance*, 7(2), 67–74. DOI: 10.18178/IJTEF.2016.7.2.499

Tavasszy, L., Behdani, B., & Konings, R. (2017). Intermodality and Synchromodality. In *Ports and Networks—Strategies, Operations and Perspectives* (1st ed., pp. 251–266). Routledge.

Taylor, A. (2025, March 9). How Auto Parts Wholesalers Like AutoZone and NAPA Optimize Distribution with AI. Cleverence. https://www.cleverence.com/articles/business-blogs/how-auto-parts-wholesalers-like-autozone-and-napa-optimize-distribution-with-ai/

Techment. (2023). *7 ways of leveraging AI in supply chain.* Techment Technology. https://www.techment.com/7-ways-of-leveraging-ai-in-supply-chain/

The climate pledge. (n.d.). https://www.aboutamazon.com/planet/climate-pledge

Tran-Dang, H., Krommenacker, N., Charpentier, P., & Kim, D. S. (2020). Toward the internet of things for physical internet: Perspectives and challenges. *IEEE Internet of Things Journal*, *7*, 4711–4736.

Tsang, Y. P., Choy, K. L., Wu, C. H., Ho, G. T., Lam, H. Y., & Koo, P. S. (2017). An IoT-based cargo monitoring system for enhancing operational effectiveness under a cold chain environment. *International Journal of Engineering Business Management*, *9*, 1847979017749063.

Tsolaki, K., Vafeiadis, T., Nizamis, A., Ioannidis, D., & Tzovaras, D. (2022). (in press). Utilizing machine learning on freight transportation and logistics applications: A review. *ICT Express*.

UiPath. (2024a). RPA improves warehouse efficiency at SF Supply Chain. https://www.uipath.com/resources/automation-case-studies/rpa-improves-warehouse-efficiency-at-sf-supply-chain

UiPath. (2024b). RPA use case in automotive - Constellation. https://www.uipath.com/resources/automation-case-studies/rpa-at-constellation-automotive

Unilever. (2024). We're tackling plastic pollution through reduction, circulation and collaboration https://www.unilever.com/sustainability/plastics/

Uniyal, S., Mangla, S., Sarma, P., Tseng, M., & Patil, P. (2021). ICT as "knowledge management" for assessing sustainable consumption and production in supply chains. *Journal of Global Information Management, 29*(1), 164–198. DOI: 10.4018/JGIM.2021010109

Uvet, H. (2020). Importance of Logistics Service Quality in Customer Satisfaction: An Empirical Study. *Oper. Supply Chain Manag. Int. J., 13*, 1–10.

van der Aalst, W. M. P., Bichler, M., & Heinzl, A. (2018). Robotic Process Automation. *Business & Information Systems Engineering, 60*, 269–272. DOI: 10.1007/s12599-018-0542-4

Vitaliano, D. F. (2010). Corporate social responsibility and labor turnover. *Corporate Governance (Bradford), 10*(5), 563–573. DOI: 10.1108/14720701011085544

Wamba, F S., & Akter, S. (2019). Understanding supply chain analytics capabilities and agility for data-rich environments. International Journal of Operations & Production Management, 39(6/7/8), 887-912.

Wamba, S. F., Gunasekaran, A., Akter, S., Ren, S. J.-F., Dubey, R., & Childe, S. J. (2017). Big data analytics and firm performance: Effects of dynamic capabilities. *Journal of Business Research, 70*, 356–365. DOI: 10.1016/j.jbusres.2016.08.009

Wang, X., Yu, L., & Li, Q. (2018). The role of IoT in enhancing supply chain management and logistics: A review and future research agenda. *International Journal of Production Economics, 205*, 3–16.

Westerman, G., Bonnet, D., & McAfee, A. (2014). *Leading digital: Turning technology into business transformation*. Harvard Business Review Press.

Wewerka, J., & Reichert, M. (2021). *Robotic Process Automation in the automotive industry - Lessons learned from an exploratory case study*. Institute of Databases and Information Systems, Ulm University., https://dbis.eprints.uni-ulm.de/2015/1/RoboticProcessAutomationintheAutomotiveIndustry-LessonsLearnedformanExploratoryCaseStudy.pdf

Willcocks, L., Lacity, M., & Criag, A. (2016, March). Robotic Process Automation: Strategic Transformation Lever for Global Business Services? *Journal of Information Technology Teaching Cases*, *7*(1), 1–12. DOI: 10.1057/s41266-016-0016-9

Wu, L., Zhang, Z., & Huang, J., Su, I-Hsuan, & Tian, S. (2025). Digital Technologies and Supply Chain Resilience: A Resource-Action-Performance Perspective. *Information Systems Frontiers*.

Xue, L. (2014). Governance–knowledge fit and strategic risk taking in supply chain digitization. *Decision Support Systems*, *62*, 54–65. DOI: 10.1016/j.dss.2014.03.003

Yadav, A., Garg, R. K., & Sachdeva, A. (2024). Artificial intelligence applications for information management in sustainable supply chain management: A systematic review and future research agenda. *International Journal of Information Management Data Insights*, *4*(2), 100292.

Yavari, A., Bagha, H., Korala, H., Mirza, I., Dia, H., Scifleet, P., Sargent, J., & Shafiei, M. (2022). ParcEMon: IoT Platform for Real-Time Parcel Level Last-Mile Delivery Greenhouse Gas Emissions Reporting and Management. *Sensors (Basel)*, *22*, 7380.

Zahoor, N., & Lew, Y. K. (2021). The drivers of the post-entry internationalisation commitment of small and medium-sized enterprises. *International Small Business Journal Researching Entrepreneurship*, *40*(4), 477–506. DOI: 10.1177/02662426211042775

Zhang, C., & Li, S. (2024). Involving purchasing and supply chain management in open ecological innovation: The moderating role of digital technologies. *International Journal of Logistics: Research and Applications*, *27*(7), 1047–1070. DOI: 10.1080/1375567.2024.2316647

Zhou, B., & Peng, T. (2019). Scheduling just-in-time part replenishment of the automobile assembly line with unrelated parallel machines. Proceedings of the Institution of Mechanical Engineers, Part C: Journal of Mechanical Engineering Science. https://doi.org/DOI: 10.1177/0954406219839083

Zuraida, Z., Houqe, M. N., & van Zijl, T. (2016). Value relevance of environmental, social and governance disclosure. In S. Boubaker, D. Cumming, & D. K. Nguyen (Eds.), Handbook of finance and sustainability (pp. 401–417). Edward Elgar Publishing.

About the Contributors

Omar Ali is an Associate Professor in Management Information Systems (MIS) at Abdullah Al Salem University (AASU), Kuwait. He is also acting head of Digital Marketing, Entrepreneurship and Innovation Department. In addition, he is the assistant of Vice President for Development and Intuitional Excellence at AASU. He received his PhD in MIS from the University of Southern Queensland (USQ), Australia. Also, he holds two master's degrees, the first one in Information and Communication Technology, and the second one in Information Systems and Technology by research, both from the University of Wollongong, Australia. His research interests include RFID; cloud computing; blockchain; artificial intelligence; security; and system analysis and design. He is the reviewer of many leading journals such as International Journal of Information Management, Government Information Quarterly, Information Systems Management, Technological Forecasting and Social Change, and Behavior and Information Technology. Also, he has published in top international leading journals such as International Journal of Information Management, Technological Forecasting and Social Change, Journal of Innovation and Knowledge, Government Information Quarterly, Information Technology and People, and Behavior and Information Technology.

Wael Farag earned his Ph.D. from the University of Waterloo, Canada in 1998; M.Sc. from the University of Saskatchewan, Canada in 1994; and B.Sc. from Cairo University, Egypt in 1990. His research, teaching, and industrial experience focus on machine learning, embedded systems, robotics, renewable energy, and control systems. He has combined 17 years of industrial and senior management experience in Automotive (Valeo), Oil & Gas (Schneider) and Construction Machines (CNH) positioned in several countries including Canada, USA & Egypt. Moreover, he has 15 Years of academic experience at Wilfrid Laurier University, Cairo University, American University of the Middle East, and Abdullah Al-Salem University. Spanning several topics of electrical and computer engineering. He is the holder of 2 US patents; ISO9000 Lead Auditor Certified, Senior IEEE member, and Scrum Master Certified. He is ranked among the top 2% scientists on Elsevier/Stanford list for 4 consecutive years from 2021 to 2024, as well as among the top 2% career-long scientists in year 2024.

Ashraf Jaradat currently is an Associate Professor in the department of Management Information Systems at American University of the Middle East, Kuwait. He received his PhD in Information System from National University of Malaysia. After obtaining his Doctoral degree, he was an Assistant Professor in the department of Management Information Systems at Yarmouk University. He also worked in Spring Hill group as advisor business development. His research interest includes effects of data integration, uncertainty management, data fusion, information system modelling, E-learning, Fog computing and blockchain. He has published in IEEE Access, Journal of Network and Computer Applications, Business Process Management Journal, Journal of Science and Technology Policy Management, and International Journal of Intelligent Information and Database Systems.

Mostafa Abdrabou, holds two master's degrees: one in marketing and finance from Cardiff Metropolitan University (UK) and another in mechanical engineering from Alexandria University (Egypt). They are currently serving as a senior instructor at Abdullah Al Salem University (Kuwait), where they combine their technical expertise and business knowledge to contribute to both academic development and professional training.

Ida Evangeline is presently working as an Assistant Professor in the Department of Electrical and Electronics Engineering at the Government

College of Engineering, Tirunelveli, Tamilnadu, India. She obtained her Bachelor's in Electrical and Electronics Engineering from Manonmaniam Sundaranar University in 2003, and Master's in Power Systems Engineering from Anna University, Chennai, Tamilnadu, India in 2005. She completed her PhD degree in 2023 at Anna University, Chennai, Tamilnadu, India. She has published six research papers in international journals. Her current research interests include optimal power flow, renewable energy, soft computing, machine learning, and deep learning.

Purushothaman R is a dedicated researcher and academician, currently serving as a Research Assistant at the Srinivasa Ramanujan Center, SASTRA University, Kumbakonam. His research interests span across multiple disciplines, including circular economy, supply chain management, operations management, general management, and human resource management. With a passion for advancing knowledge in these fields, he actively contributes to academia through research and scholarly pursuits.

M Sudha has a Doctorate in Digital Image processing

Index

A

B

C

D

E

F

I

L

M

P

S

W

www.ingramcontent.com/pod-product-compliance
Lightning Source LLC
LaVergne TN
LVHW080855300926
849162LV00003B/430
* 9 7 9 8 3 3 7 3 2 8 4 3 0 *